Creating the Artful Home

Creating the Artful Home

The Aesthetic Movement

Karen Zukowski

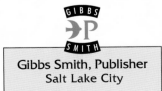

Gibbs Smith, Publisher
Salt Lake City

TO THE ARTFUL HOMEMAKERS OF THE
PAST, AND TO DAVID DIAMOND, MY
PARTNER IN ARTFUL HOMEMAKING

First Edition
10 09 08 07 06   5 4 3 2 1

Published by
Gibbs Smith, Publisher
PO Box 667
Layton, Utah 84041

Orders: 1.800.835.4993
www.gibbs-smith.com

Designed by m:GraphicDesign / Maralee Oleson
Printed and bound in Hong Kong

Library of Congress Cataloging-in-Publication Data
Zukowski, Karen.
Creating the artful home : the aesthetic movement / Karen Zukowski.
—1st ed. p. cm.
ISBN 1-58685-766-5
1. Aesthetic movement (Art)—United States. 2. Interior decoration—United States. I. Title.

N6512.5.A37Z85 2006
747.0973—dc22

2006010859

Front jacket:
MacConnel/Lowe house, 2005, photo © Undine Pröhl (see page 10)

Back jacket, clockwise from upper left:
Tile, Mintons, Ltd., Stoke-on-Trent, ca late 1870s, photo © author, (see page 91)

Detail of a design for window curtains, published in *Peterson's Magazine,* 1878 (see page 120)

Wallpaper, Robert Graves Company, ca 1880, photo © Thies Wulf and Egon Zippel (see page 145)

Detail, door in the Samuel Tilton house, McKim, Mead and White architects, 1882, photo © Jonathan Wallen (see page 97)

Back jacket, interior flap:
Much in Little Space, from Clarence Cook, *The House Beautiful,* 1881 (see page 48)

Background to title pages of each chapter:
Wallpaper, William Morris, Morris & Co., 1875 (see page 14)

Background to sidebars:
Wallpaper, Wook Kim Wallcoverings, 2004 (see page 89)

Contents

Acknowledgments

TO AIMEE STODDARD AND JENNIFER GRILLONE, my editors at Gibbs Smith, Publisher, and to all the others there who transformed my e-mails, disks and printouts into a book.

For making contacts and getting me going: Shawn Brennan, Mimi Findlay, Cheryl Robertson and Bill Turner.

To Hannah Sigur and Brian Coleman, fellow writers, for moral support.

For legal and strategic advice: Emily Barr, Tom Clareson, Charles Danziger, Elaine English, Carol Haefner, Cynthia Chapman Kaufmann, Virginia Rutledge and Charles Salzberg.

For valuable reactions to my ideas: Steve Bauer at Bradbury & Bradbury, John Cooper, Anita Ellis, Donna Ghelerter, Arthur and Esther Goldberg, Nina Gray, Paul Stirton, Robert Tuggle and Paul Jeromack, and the audience for "Aesthetic Evangelists" at the Salve Regina conference "Domesticity and Design in the Gilded Age." A special thanks to Tara Tappert, who read the entire manuscript and helped me think about the whole ball of wax.

For sharing their views on specific objects and topics: Fred Baker, Anna Tobin D'Ambrosio, Elizabeth De Rosa, Anita Ellis, Barbara Gallati, Marin Hanson, Carrie T. Hayter, Susan Hobbs, Paul Miller and Yamiko Yamamori. And, a special thank-you to the curators and librarians at the Cooper-Hewitt National Design Museum for two days spent examining objects in the collections: Susan Brown, Elizabeth Bowman, Flora Mae Cates, Greg Herringshaw, Jordan Kim and Stephen Van Dyk.

To my image assistants: Helena Winston, for her photo wrangling, and to Egon Zippel and Thies Wulf, who photographed many of the items in the book. And, to Ted Diamond and Parker Nelson for technical support.

The superb images in this book came from many sources. The photo credits acknowledge many, but others can only be credited here. Many artists supplied images of their works and some waived copyright fees. Art dealers, manufacturers, retailers and other businesses were generous with their time and their files. Collectors lent me works to photograph, and some even allowed me to invade their homes with my camera! I am grateful to them all.

Erin Johnson of ABC Carpet & Home; Jennifer Peifer and Andrea Leiser at Aid to Artisans; David Parker and Barbara Lloyd at Associated Artists, LLC; Ralph Bacerra and Masha Portiansky at Garth Clark Gallery; Jennifer Bahssin; Lester Barnett; Michael Snyder and Daniel Basiletti at Moss for the image of Tord Boontje's chair; John Burrows of J. R. Burrows & Company; Harlan Butt; Christopher Cantwell; Dave Cheadle for trade cards; Anita Ellis and Scott Hisey at the Cincinnati Art Museum; Martin Cohen and José Arias; Bruce Cummings of Southampton Antiques; Kurt Dolnier; Sarah Eigen; Cory Grace at the Arthur M. Sackler Gallery and the Freer Gallery of Art; Sue Grinols at the Fine Arts Museums of San Francisco; Fred Hill and Bruce Weber of Berry-Hill Galleries; Susan and Jon Huberman; Wook Kim; Robert Kushner, Terrie Hancock Mangat, Kim MacConnel and Jean Lowe; Marianne McEvoy; Kenneth Andrew Mroczek; Evelyn Trebilcock and Valerie Balint at Olana; Amelie Rennolds; Richard Reutlinger; Kait Rhodes; John Robshaw; Elaine and Paul Rocheleau; Laurie Simmons; Missy Stevens; Dana Supernowicz; William Vareika; James L. Yarnall; Tanja Yokum at Mryiad Restaurant Group.

To all the authors who have written on the topic of the Aesthetic movement and artful homes. My brief bibliography cannot list all of the publications that have formed the backbone of this book. If I have written persuasively, it is because I have synthesized so much excellent scholarship.

Introduction

 DURING THE AESTHETIC MOVEMENT, Americans realized that if they made their homes artful, they would make their lives better. An artful home was not only beautiful, it could sustain the soul. The artful home was a product of the Aesthetic movement, a late-nineteenth-century approach to design in which the power of art was cultivated. This was no small matter. The beauty of art gives pleasure to the beholder and refines all around it. Beauty should be sought out, nourished and instilled, everywhere, in everyday life. If the beauty of art could be interwoven in domestic life, if the artistic could become the warp and weft of the home, all who lived there would be ennobled. Creating an artful home, a daily activity, made life joyful. Today, Americans are rediscovering this joy.

The rallying cry of aesthetes succinctly describes the philosophy: *l'art pour l'art,* or art for art's sake. Art need not tell a story or teach a moral; it should exist on its own to celebrate the beauty of pure line, form, color, shape and texture. The Aesthetic movement germinated in Britain among artists who exploited opulent color, decorative patterning and lavish materials for their aesthetic effects in both the fine arts and in the decorative arts. Tastemakers like Oscar Wilde and Louis Comfort Tiffany urged Americans to create artful homes. Their words were heard by a growing middle class populated by women who stayed at home and who had expanded purchasing power. Ordinary people—most of them housewives—embraced the Aesthetic movement and brought it into their homes.

The impulses that moved Americans to make their homes artful are alive today. The purchasing power of the

top: My Lady's Chamber, by Walter Crane, the frontispiece for Clarence Cook's *The House Beautiful,* 1881 ed., by Charles Scribner's Sons. Cook's best-selling household art manual began with this illustration showing a lady in the artful home she presumably crafted.

bottom: Amelie Rennolds in her living room, Pawling, NY. Rennolds, an architect, designed her own house. (Photo by the author.)

American middle class is a strong, global force. In the post-9/11 world, Americans are reexamining home life. Of course we want to make the home a safe haven. But more than that, we recognize that the home sustains the psyche. There is an instinctual understanding that the physical composition of the home enables a fulfilling life. What should a home look like? What should it feel like? Americans are bored with the discipline of minimalism and mistrust strong allegiances to any one style. Eclecticism reigns. To catch our attention, designers, manufacturers and retailers deploy the stylistic markers of the Aesthetic movement: rich color, layers of patterns and textures, mixtures of historic motifs. The homemaker must discriminate among many choices, from the handcrafted to machine styled, in all styles and at all price points. She (and also increasingly he) shops everywhere, from department stores to the Web. Americans still make their own art, but now they use digital cameras as often as embroidery needles. Then as now, it is homemakers who bring it all together, shaping artful homes to satisfy their artistic selves.

During the Aesthetic movement, homemakers learned the basics of beauty by looking and doing. They examined art and took courses in drawing, painting and modeling. They painted on canvas, glass and china; they carved and burned wood. They mastered an encyclopedia of stitches; they plied embroidery, crochet and knitting needles. They also shopped. They scoured department stores, specialty art-goods stores, shops full of Oriental novelties and furniture warehouses. They hunted antiques in attics and at country auctions.

Objects and rooms in the new artful style had certain qualities: careful craftsmanship, graceful form, luxurious materials, luminous color, abstract but poetic effects. The artful home would have connecting rooms hung with complementary patterns of wallpaper. The rooms could be divided by folding screens and hanging portieres. Mantels and cabir.ets displayed the best: a silver vase, a Japanese fan, a peacock feather. A harmony was achieved through asymmetrical balance and through a palette of subtle, grayed, saturated colors, with glints of brass, silver or iridescence. The discriminating eye composed the artful home from these elements.

The star designers of the Aesthetic movement are still recognized, and bits and pieces of the Aesthetic movement have been given familiar stylistic labels. In architecture, the Aesthetic movement produced Queen Anne town houses with their cheerful red brick, white window trim and stained-glass transoms. Out in the new suburbs, the Stick Style joined the Queen Anne. The rambling wooden houses with their gingerbread, now lovingly restored, still enrich the streetscapes of thousands of American towns. The walls of

this page: The dining room at Kingscote, Newport, RI, the home of David and Ella King. In 1881, the Kings commissioned McKim, Mead and White to add this dining room to their house. (John Corbett photo courtesy of the Preservation Society of Newport County.)

facing: The Court Hall at Olana, near Hudson, NY, the home of Frederic and Isabel Church. The architect of the house was Calvert Vaux; Frederic Church designed many of the architectural details, including the stenciling. This photograph shows the re-creation of the late 1880s appearance of the room. (Photo by Kurt A. Dolnier; courtesy of Olana State Historic Site.)

these houses were hung with William Morris wallpapers and textiles featuring abstracted botanical motifs. Two sorts of medievalizing Eastlake furniture might be found, either sturdy plain oak, with mortise and tenon proudly showing, or the more elegant ebonized variety, with its black limbs and incised gilt lines. The Aesthetic movement drew heavily from Japan. This borrowing was either outright, with fans, parasols, and blue-and-white plates becoming commonplace decor, or indirect, with the rendering of the abstracted naturalism of Japonisme in American-made products, especially china, silver and textiles. The wealthiest homeowners might commission Louis Comfort Tiffany or the Herter Brothers as interior decorators. And a host of firms made iconic Aesthetic movement goods that appeared in middle class houses: the ceramics of Rookwood or Royal Worcester; Louis Prang's greeting cards; the glassware of Louis Comfort Tiffany; the wallpapers of Warren, Fuller and Company; and silver by Gorham Manufacturing Company or Tiffany and Company. These are the names that are now connected to the Aesthetic movement.

Happily, whole rooms from the historic Aesthetic movement still survive. Standing in them, one experiences timeless visual effects. In 1881, David and Ella King commissioned the newly formed architectural firm of McKim, Mead and White to add an addition to Kingscote, the family's

1840s Carpenter Gothic cottage, in Newport, Rhode Island. The addition included a large dining room that could also function as a ballroom. Stanford White acted as the principal designer, and he orchestrated an extraordinary range of styles and materials for the room. Newport's colonial past was referenced in the built-in Queen Anne–style sideboard and spindled screen; Louis Comfort Tiffany provided dahlia-motif stained-glass windows and opalescent glass bricks and tiles; the upper walls and ceiling were covered in cork tiles, laid in a herringbone design; and the furnishings ranged from Italian ebony-and-ivory hall chairs to a King family spinning wheel. Although the objects and motifs are drawn from history and nature, the effect evokes no one time or place. Instead, it is original, existing as visual and tactile stimuli.

Around 1886, the artist Frederic Edwin Church and his wife, Isabel, reorganized their living hall at Olana, their country home high above the Hudson. The couple built the Persian-style villa in the 1870s, but the furnishing of the home became an ongoing process. Under its stenciled arches, the Court Hall eventually contained ceramics from Mexico, Japan and Persia; Middle Eastern carpets laid over wall-to-wall patterned carpeting; and numerous images of innocent girls and idealized women hung on the walls. The backdrop to the room is a Moresque patterned window; the effect was achieved by sandwiching cut black paper between panes of yellow glass. The aged, exotic, handcrafted furnishings stand in contrast to the view of the Churches' picturesque estate, sloping down to the Hudson River Valley, that is framed by the arch-shaped window. The two spaces summarize Frederic Church's artwork: his early work as a painter of primeval new-world landscapes, and his later work as a painter of ancient, old-world landscapes. The effect is artfully complex and only unfolds over time as the space is experienced. Both the dining room at Kingscote and the Court Hall at Olana depend upon visual effects and the ideas they evoke; artistic effects are paramount. They are icons of the Aesthetic movement.

The Aesthetic movement was eclipsed when Americans, especially women and their children, began to move away from their private, separate lives in the home and into more public spheres, including philanthropic work, public education and even the workplace. With the acquisition of the Philippines, Puerto Rico and Guam in 1898 at the end of the Spanish American War and the annexation of Hawaii that same year, the United States became an empire. The American Renaissance, a cultural movement that sought to forge ties to Europe and its Greco-Roman heritage, became manifest in classicist motifs in architecture, painting and the decorative arts. "The White City," a collection of modern Roman temples that was the centerpiece of the World's Columbian Exposition in Chicago in 1893, was a harbinger of the many classicist public buildings erected during the American Renaissance. By the time the simple Craftsman bungalow mushroomed across America in the 1910s, the "artful" home was an anachronism.

A new aestheticism is now on the ascendancy and it relates to the historic Aesthetic movement. The outlook has acquired several labels. It is predicated on strong visual effects, carried out through basic design principles: color, shape, texture, line and form. The new aestheticism draws on a rich vocabulary of historical styles and a wide range of geographical sources. When the decor veers towards curves and playful "Louis anything"–style furniture, we call it "modern baroque." When the decor uses riotous patterns and color, we christen it "maximalism." When the decor mixes and matches styles and periods we commend "the new eccentrics." The new aestheticism has its stars, too. Michael Czysz of Architropolis created a posh pad for rock star Lenny Kravitz; it has luminous glass walls in the entry, convex bubble mirrors framing a reflecting pool, stainless

steel walls with inset flashing lights, and a very red living room featuring a red vinyl dance floor. The public buildings by Frank Ghery, with their sinuous silver surfaces, are a part of our era's extreme aesthetic. These places push the envelope, celebrating the redness of red, startling contrasts of textures, the reflectiveness of glass, mirror and metal. The rooms play out all possible visual effects, pursuing the artful for its own sake.

It is too soon to name the iconic works of the new aestheticism, but we can begin to describe what qualities they will have. New artful homes will be glamorous, exotic and full of personal, eclectic collections. They will reject the conformism of the contractor. Startling parallels with the historic Aesthetic movement are already apparent: interconnecting rooms, a high density of furnishings, mix-and-match patterning, inventive use of rich materials, an embrace of rich color. The point of the artful home then and now is to sustain life with beauty. Homemakers find the art in the everyday, and they bring it home to enrich the soul.

This book explores the ideas and the objects of the Aesthetic movement in America, and its parallels in modern-day design. We begin with the background, "The Soil and the Seeds," a look at the intellectual underpinnings and the evolution of the design hallmarks of the Aesthetic movement. Next, we meet the tastemakers. The Aesthetic movement was spread by way of a few people of great

significance, such as Oscar Wilde and many others of more diffuse influence, like the authors of dozens of household art manuals. The next chapter, "Selling the Style," tells the story of how the Aesthetic movement was marketed to Americans. The new idea of the "artistic" became the buzz of the day—flaunted in the pages of magazines, in all sorts of stores, in restaurants and bars. "Artistic" ads sold everything. The Aesthetic movement held sway over most household furnishings produced in the 1880s; the next chapter examines the range of these goods, from the deluxe to the mass marketed. Although the Aesthetic movement was about design, it had its influence over everyday activities. The next chapter, "Living in the Artful Home," describes those activities, such as dress reform, making artistic objects at home, dining artfully, child rearing and artistic entertainments. The book culminates with "Creating the Artful Home," which explains how average homemakers assembled their homes, from choosing an architectural style to orchestrating transient effects of light and shadow.

Throughout the book historical events and objects are contrasted with modern parallels. The pitch card for potential subscribers to the *Art Amateur,* a home craft and decorating magazine of the 1880s, reads much like the bulk-rate letter sent to select zip codes by *Dwell* magazine. The visual similarities between a Gorham mixed-metal pitcher and an enamel incense burner by Harlan Butt are astonishing. Today's great rooms are the descendants of the Aesthetic movement's living halls. Images of modern objects and rooms that exemplify the new aestheticism appear alongside their historic counterparts.

The ideas as well as the objects from the Aesthetic movement have enduring appeal. In museums, we admire Tiffany lamps, Morris carpets and Herter furniture. We visit Aesthetic movement homes that are now museums. We collect busy patterned plates and Eastlake-style doorknobs. A few bold families restore Aesthetic movement houses to their original appearance and live by gaslight. We are drawn to modern objects that are modified by the same adjectives used for Aesthetic movement objects: asymmetrical, inventive, richly colored. At base, we operate under some of the same forces that were at work upon American homemakers at the end of the nineteenth century. We, too, live in a consumerist society. We value art. We use the timeless criteria of beauty to sort through the profusion of household goods on the market. We want to find our taste. We want to build our homes using the reserve of our artistic talents, and we want to continue to drink from that source, sustaining ourselves at home. In the end, the Aesthetic movement informs us as we continue to create the artful home.

facing: The living room of Kim MacConnel and Jean Lowe, ca 2003, Encinitas, CA, architect Ted Smith. MacConnel and Lowe, both artists, created this not-quite-conventional artful room. Lowe painted the faux tapestry on the wall, and MacConnel painted the furniture and designed the sconces, which are composed of beach flotsam. The cupboard is a "highboy" made from shipping crates with thrift store "print paintings" as doors. The rug is made from thrift store hooked-rug pieces. And the lamp at the rear is made around an African sculpture. (Photo: © Undine Pröhl.)

above: An incense burner (left) by Harlan Butt, 2002, and a pitcher (right) by Gorham Manufacturing Company, 1883. The two objects, made over one hundred years apart, share the same qualities of elegance, rich colors and intricate craftsmanship. (Photo: Thies Wulf and Egon Zippel.)

NOTES ON SOURCES
Full citations can be found in the bibliography.

The "bible" of the Aesthetic movement in the United States is *In Pursuit of Beauty: Americans and the Aesthetic Movement,* an exhibition catalog published in 1986 by the Metropolitan Museum of Art. Each of the eleven chapters covers a different media and is written by a different specialist, and there is an extensive biographical dictionary. Hundreds of pictures of the masterworks of the Aesthetic movement provide an excellent visual testimony of the style. Both Olana and Kingscote are discussed. A more recent cultural study is Lambourne's *The Aesthetic Movement.* This book deals mostly with Britain.

For the new aestheticism see the following: Rohrlich, "More Shows Less the Door"; Castillo, *MXM: Maximalist Interiors;* and Goodman, "The New Eccentrics."

The Soil and
the Seeds

 ## DESIGN REFORM

All things considered, the Crystal Palace Exhibition of 1851 was unsettling for Queen Victoria and her husband, Prince Albert. True, the United Kingdom had made an impressive showing at the fair, making up 6,861 of the total 13,937 exhibitors. England outshone every other country, even given its natural advantage as the host. The structure for the fair was a miraculous achievement: a vast glass-and-iron, many-armed greenhouse designed by Joseph Paxton, ornamented with a coherent color scheme by Owen Jones. Such expanses of light-filled halls had never been built. The visitor wandered among raw materials like minerals and foodstuffs, among historical artifacts and zoological specimens, and among the multifarious products of the modern world, from armaments to writing inks. A great many of the exhibits were everyday products that the viewer might buy: fabrics, furniture and small domestic goods, from coal scuttles to cutlery. The developing power of industry was impressive. But, the homemaker in search of simple but attractive furnishings was confounded.

At the fair, manufacturers felt compelled to rise to the occasion by producing ornate exhibition pieces—and that was the problem. In booth after booth, visitors gazed upon lamps that resembled miniature statues, chairs bowed under the weight of "Louis style" carving and carpets whose patterns could hypnotize. All sorts of new technologies and materials were on display in home furnishings: bentwood, gutta-percha, papier-mâché, cast iron, electroplating. History was mined for motifs, so furnishings might be termed Renaissance or Rococo, Egyptian or simply English. It was all ingenious and impressive but confusing.

Prince Albert and Henry Cole, two of the organizers of the exhibition, recognized the issues at work. Clearly, the Great Exhibition of the Works of the Industry of All Nations had lived up to its formal title; the world had witnessed the possibilities of the industrial age. Tens of thousands of entries had been categorized, prizes awarded (by juries composed half of British and half of foreign experts) and analytical essays written on the prospects for the development of the each of the categories of objects on display. British exhibitors won 78 of the 170 medals, but the more success in a category depended upon good design, the less likely the winner was British. Advances in technology had not translated into advances in design. Manufacturers were straining too hard to achieve effect. Owen Jones noted "a fruitless struggle after novelty, irrespective of fitness," and enjoined European nations as a whole to look to traditional designs, for "construction should be decorated; decoration should never be purposefully constructed."[1] The *Journal of Design and Manufactures*, published by Henry Cole, criticized the objects: wallpapers should give "a proper impression of flatness," "ironwork should be treated in harmony with the material and its manufacture," and "ornament is not . . . principal . . . it must be secondary to the thing decorated."[2] As the jury for "Class XXVI: Furniture, Upholstery, Paper Hangings, Papier Mache and Japanned Goods" blandly summarized in their report, "Articles of furniture are too often crowded with

-- --

[1] Briggs, *Victorian Things*, 62.
[2] Ibid., 75.

unnecessary embellishment which interferes with their use, purpose and convenience."[3] Could industry grow if it could only turn out florid products that were inferior to foreign ones? Could bad design threaten profits?

America opened its own Crystal Palace in 1853 in New York City in bald imitation of London's fair. The palace was also a glass-and-iron structure, displaying manufactured products from all nations, organized in categories. But this exhibition was much smaller. A profit-making affair, it aimed to educate Americans about modern manufacturing and to direct attention specifically to native products, which were segregated. When it came to household furnishings, the same sort of florid display and florid ornamentation that played so well in London succeeded in New York. All conceded that European manufacturers were superior to Americans design-wise. Americans were content that their unadorned, functional farm machinery and sewing machines had been praised, and they basked in the honor of hosting the extravagant show. In all the excitement, no one cared that American manufacturers had a problem with design.

But Britain knew it had a problem, and it turned to Henry Cole to solve it. London's Crystal Palace had created a climate of constructive criticism that Cole directed to reforming public art education. For more than a generation, the Schools of Design had vacillated between serving art by training artists and serving industry by training artisans. It did neither very well. Cole came down firmly on the side of training artisans to supply factories, and he forged an efficient system for doing so. In 1852, he was appointed head of the newly established Department of Practical Art, which soon superseded the Schools of Design. Under Cole's method, the pupil progressed along a twenty-three-stage course, from rote copying of geometrical forms to drawing from casts of statuary, only attaining the ability for any imaginative design at the very last stages. The aim was to produce pupils who could draw accurately and thus serve managers of industry effectively.

Square piano, by Robert Nunns and John Clark, made in New York City, 1853. This piano is probably the one the firm exhibited in New York City's Crystal Palace Exposition of 1853. With its pillared legs that do not logically support the instrument and its mash of historical styles, this is just the sort of cabinetmaking that Ruskin abhorred. (The Metropolitan Museum of Art; gift of George Lowther, 1906 [06.1312]. Photograph © 1977 The Metropolitan Museum of Art.)

Furthermore, Cole educated consumers. He set up a Museum of Manufactures to display scientific instruments, materials related to cookery, and examples of good design, along with a gallery of "False Principles"—examples of bad design. With this he hoped to improve public taste. Selections from this museum toured the provincial design schools. By the late 1850s, Cole's school was rechristened the Department of Science and Art, and it was joined with an expanding museum of the arts of design in South Kensington, London. The latter grew into the Victoria and Albert Museum, the world's most encyclopedic collection of the decorative arts. The whole matrix of education and public displays came to be known as the South Kensington system. It was to become enormously influential in the United States, both as a model to cling to and a lesson to reject.

There was one articulate critic who proclaimed that Cole was foolish to try to accommodate the machine in the production of art. John Ruskin, a prolific and magisterial writer, inserted morality into the debate about design. He began his career as an art critic. He valued art that portrayed the world "truthfully," whether the art was the swirling impastos of William Turner or the meticulous realism of the Pre-Raphaelite painters. Ruskin rejected much

-- --
[3] Ibid., 74.

art and architecture that dated from the Renaissance and afterwards, believing the symmetry and high finish of these works to be a false expression of human values. In his writings, notably *The Stones of Venice* and *The Two Paths*, he turned to the architecture and the decorative arts of the Gothic era. He found the stonework of cathedrals beautiful because the carvings expressed the artisan's joy and spirituality—his full human potential. In contrast, Ruskin claimed that industrialization severed the relationship between the worker and his work, poisoning the process and the finished product. For Ruskin, it was wrong to put a rosewood veneer on a pine cabinet, not because of technical or practical issues but because of aesthetic and ultimately ethical issues. Ruskin maintained that the furniture maker could never be happy unless he could make something that grew organically from the process of construction. And, the customer would be cheapened by living with something that was not "honest."

Ruskin recognized that the South Kensington system compounded the problems of the so-called minor arts because it segregated them from the fine arts. Painters and sculptors went to the Royal Academy, leaving the national Schools of Design to teach the "manual arts" to mechanics. Cole's Schools of Design turned out automatons who could not imagine and invent. The fine arts should depict reality and the decorative arts should be functional, but no art could be successful unless it was an honest and full expression of the labor of the artist.

Before long, William Morris began to put Ruskin's ideas into practice. As an Oxford undergraduate, Morris read Ruskin's essay on the Gothic, became fast friends with Edward Burne-Jones and the other artists and writers of the Pre-Raphaelite Brotherhood, and discovered a passion for the medieval era. With his new wife and various friends, Morris constructed furniture, wove tapestries, painted murals and made stained glass for their new

home, the Red House, designed by Philip Webb. The experience led directly to the formation of the firm Morris, Marshall, Faulkner and Co. in 1861 to make and retail household goods. By the next year, embroidered hangings, stained glass and painted Gothic-style furniture attracted much attention at the firm's booth at the London International Exposition, and the firm was launched. It quickly became known for good design and careful craftsmanship in a generally medievalizing style that expressed Ruskinian "honesty." With few exceptions, everything offered was produced by the firm's own workmen, in their own workshops. Often a single craftsman/designer was responsible for an item from start to finish, in emulation of the preindustrial guild ideal. The firm's workers included Morris's Pre-Raphaelite friends Dante Gabrielle Rossetti, Ford Maddox Brown and Philip Webb. But it was Morris who was both design genius and workhorse; he dominated the firm. By 1875, his role was acknowledged and the firm was reorganized as Morris & Co. Over time Morris's innate talents in flat design came to the fore and the firm became known for their textiles and wallpaper. Increasingly, these revived intricate weaving and dying techniques. But Morris & Co. also made furniture and various sorts of small goods like candlesticks. The firm acted as interior designers as well.

Morris had always sought to make good household articles by honest methods so that all households could be better, but his products were always too expensive for the masses. Indeed, at many moments Morris & Co. only stayed afloat because Morris subsidized it. This conundrum—that quality craftsmanship is expensive while industrial production is not—always bedeviled Morris. It led him ultimately to the conviction that socialism was the only political economy that could temper industrialization and change the world for the better. He became a militant socialist who denounced capitalism even while continuing his work making exquisite things.

AMERICA FRACTURES

The South Kensington system, Ruskin and Morris, and the state of manufactured household goods were discussed in America, but there were other distractions. The Civil War began in April of 1861, with the firing upon Fort Sumpter, and lasted until April of 1865, with the surrender at Appomattox. The war pitted the industrial, wealthier northern states against the agrarian, slave-owning, cotton-dependent southern states. Gettysburg, Bull Run and Antietam were not the only bloody battlefields of the war: New York City suffered horrific riots over the draft, while thousands died at the Andersonville prisoner-of-war camp, mostly of disease and starvation. Could the government stand? The North won, but the victory was hollow. Veterans with maimed limbs were a constant reminder of the national battle. The South was populated by freed blacks whose lot had not improved. The political process of Reconstruction in the South was riddled with corruption. There was a severe economic depression in 1873, followed by further boom-and-bust cycles. Uncertainty about the future grew.

The Civil War and its aftermath devastated the psychic health of the nation. It turned one half of the country against the other half, and each half fought within itself. In the North, the war intensified class differences between draftees and those rich enough to pay for a substitute. In the South, racial divisions deepened and ossified into a caste system that segregated whites and blacks. The war converted neither abolitionists nor secessionists to the other point of view. The antebellum authority of clerics, who had buttressed both ideologies, was challenged; morally impregnable arguments seemed no longer possible. The national psyche seemed bowed under a crisis of confidence.

facing: Detail of "Marigold" pattern wallpaper, designed by William Morris and registered in 1875, printed by Jeffrey & Co. for Morris & Co. This pattern was produced as a wallpaper and as printed chintz in many colorways. Morris's wallpapers and textiles became ubiquitous during the Aesthetic movement. (Collection of the author.)

HEALING THROUGH COMMERCE AND CULTURE

The nation sought solace by flexing its economic muscles at the Philadelphia Centennial Exposition of 1876. The federal government, the state of Pennsylvania and the city of Philadelphia each funded a share of the fair, which was to be the biggest and best that the world had yet seen.

The theme of progress was emphasized by the organization of the exhibits. There were almost two hundred buildings, including five main exhibition buildings (some with annexes); nine foreign government buildings; twenty-four buildings sponsored by the American states (each in its own architectural style); along with miscellaneous buildings of special interest, ranging from the celestial (a Bible Pavilion) to the pedestrian (a Shoe and Leather Building). In the main buildings, exhibits were grouped geographically by country, and everywhere the United States occupied the largest parcel. Within this framework, the exhibits were grouped hierarchically, in ten departments ranging from raw materials, through furniture and costume, up to tools and machinery, to the arts, ending in things that demonstrated "the improvement of the physical, intellectual and moral condition of man." Industrialized nations sent their most sophisticated products, while their colonies sent raw materials; unindustrialized, non-colonial nations were not represented at all.

By the time the fair concluded its six-month run, nearly ten million people had visited—nearly one-fifth of the population of the United States! The star of the exhibition was the Corliss Engine, a behemoth in Machinery Hall, whose mighty pistons powered all the machinery on display. Author Joaquin Miller commented on the Centennial: "Great as is seems today . . . it is but the acorn from which shall grow the wide-spreading oak of the century's growth."[4] America's capacity and potential as an industrial powerhouse was proved on a global stage.

Culture was also on display. The fairgrounds were dotted with sculpture, including the torch from Frederic Bartholdi's as-yet-unfinished Statue of Liberty. A giant allegorical fountain was erected, fittingly, by the Catholic Total Abstinence Union of America; in its base were nine drinking fonts. The finest products from the leading manufacturers were on display in the main exhibition hall, and many countries showed historical or ethnographic displays, so that one could wander from pianos, to ancient Chinese bronzes, to a diorama of a Laplander and his sled. There was also a photography building with submissions from around the world and a Women's Pavilion, where the needlework of Queen Victoria and her family could be seen. But culture reached the highest concentration in Memorial Hall and its Art Annex. Italy sent a complete survey, from ancient statuary, through Renaissance ceramics, through modern paintings. Reviewers complained that France sent only the dregs from its recent salons. Even though quality was inconsistent and content unpredictable, with so much of the globe participating, the Centennial boasted the largest art show ever mounted.

America's own cultural productivity was on display. In Memorial Hall, one could see the historical portraiture of Gilbert Stuart and John Copley. Antiquarians were pleased by the New England kitchen, where they could see John Alden's fine writing desk and the cradle used by the first child born on board the Mayflower. Other oddities could be sought out in the Connecticut cottage and the U.S. Government Pavilion. There was a comprehensive show of modern American paintings and sculpture, with landscapes, especially, holding their own against canvases from other countries. The displays of furniture makers Kimbel & Cabus and Mitchell & Rammelsberg made the argument that Americans understood Ruskinian medievalism. And, there were the beginnings of a new sort of artful craftsmanship seen in the Cincinnati room of the Women's Pavilion. Here was painted china and hand-carved wooden furniture, made entirely by amateurs, the ladies of Cincinnati, yet of a very high quality. To be sure, these were minor sidelights from the main message of America's industrial power, yet these displays pleased those who sought evidence of a native cultural excellence.

In Philadelphia, Americans saw the fruits of the design revolution that was underway in Britain. The Royal School of Needlework, an agency founded to help indigent women revive the art of needlework, sent an elaborate embroidered tent filled with smaller items for domestic use. The agency commissioned its designs from artists (including William Morris and Edward Burne-Jones) who drew from medieval, Renaissance and even Japanese art, producing a fresh set of motifs. More medievalizing "Modern Gothic" furnishings could be seen with Cox and Sons. Minton tiles and Doulton's "Lambeth Faience" line of pottery, both in a generalized attractive medieval style, were seen in large quantities. A cast-iron pavilion designed by Thomas Jeckyll and manufactured by Barnard, Bishop and Barnards incorporated bas-reliefs with naturalistic flowers, birds and insects, including a railing of sunflowers, which was to become a motif of the new artistic movement. Many of these products were shown in attractive room settings, with the tile set into hearths and the furniture arrayed around it.

---

[4] Miller, "Great Centennial Fair," 1; quoted in Rydell, *All the World's a Fair*, 16.

The mysterious, alluring country of Japan introduced itself to the world at Philadelphia. When Commodore Perry "opened" Japan by sailing into Yokhama harbor with his gunships in 1854, he began a process that culminated in Philadelphia in 1876. In some small ways, Japan was already known to the world—arts from the country had been shown in prior world's fairs, and Japanese ceramics and prints were avidly collected among a cognoscenti. In 1868, the Mejii emperor came to power and adopted a policy of modernization; the Japanese government embraced the Philadelphia Centennial as an opportunity to sell itself to the entire Western world. Japan presented itself as a feudal society with its artisanship intact, even while gearing up to industrial production. English and American advisors were recruited to help

Household Furniture, England, one of the art plates issued in a portfolio titled *Illustrated Historical Register of the Centennial Exhibition (Philadelphia 1876) and the Exposition Universelle (Paris 1878),* by the American News Company, ca 1879. A design revolution was underway in Britain in the 1870s, and various English companies sent examples of their household furnishings to the Philadelphia Centennial. This large-format chromolithograph (suitable for framing!) probably shows an amalgamation of these items, rather than the inventory of any one manufacturer.

HOUSEHOLD FURNITURE. ENGLAND.

BRONZES. SCREEN. ETC. JAPAN

top: Bronzes, Screen, Etc., Japan, one of the art plates issued in a portfolio titled *Illustrated Historical Register of the Centennial Exhibition (Philadelphia 1876) and the Exposition Universelle (Paris 1878),* by the American News Company, ca 1879. At the Philadelphia Centennial, Japan sponsored a large, carefully controlled sales pavilion of the nation's ceramics, bronzes, screens and other decorative arts. These goods were a revelation to designers in the west.

bottom: View of the Main Exhibition Building at the Philadelphia Centennial, by Centennial Views, Philadelphia, ca 1876. This stereograph view of the Philadelphia Centennial shows the profusion of goods that international commerce had produced. When viewed through a stereoscope, a kind of nineteenth-century View-Master, a three-dimensional image appears, and the quantity of items on display seems limitless. Some of the British exhibitions are in the center aisle, including the famous two-story cast-iron pavilion, designed by Thomas Jeckyll.

facing: The Ironworker's Noontime, a painting by Thomas Pollock Anshutz, 1880. Anshutz's painting shows an iron factory at lunchtime, with the workers washing up, stretching and otherwise escaping from the toil of the day. This is the industrial landscape, a male world, which is dirty and competitive but orderly and productive. (The Fine Arts Museums of San Francisco; gift of Mr. and Mrs. John D. Rockefeller 3rd, 1979.7.4.)

the Japanese produce objects to the Western taste, and thirteen hundred tons of goods were sent to the Centennial. Japan was represented in exhibits in the Main and Agricultural Buildings, in a dwelling house built by workers using traditional tools and techniques (every move watched by eager Western reporters) and in a bazaar, sited in a Japanese garden. Here fairgoers could buy paper goods, ceramics and bronzes; at the end of the Centennial, museums and collectors bought the exhibits in the main buildings.

The Philadelphia Centennial convinced Americans that a new kind of economy had emerged—and that it was glorious. As a young man, George Eastman, the popularizer of photography, visited the Centennial and was fascinated: "The ingenuity that exhibitors have displayed in arranging such things as tacks candles soap hardware needles thread pipe and all such apparently uninteresting articles is something marvelous—and they command the attention of the observer even against his will."[5] At the fair, attendees saw a greater profusion of goods than had ever been witnessed, all arranged in irresistible displays. And, many were helpfully tagged with prices! Home furnishings were set into cozy domestic settings, and even lengths of pipe were arrayed artistically. Moreover, fairgoers saw that industrialized countries were advancing in material wealth. Here was evidence that a superior economic order was developing. Clearly, the progress of America would be based on the growth of her industries that would contribute to the world's warehouse of consumer goods, which retailers could market with increasing finesse. As the workforce increased, markets for these products would enlarge. Industrial development would foster a self-sustaining dynamic—ever-increasing incomes spent on an ever-larger roster of consumer goods. Certainly not all Americans understood or embraced the new consumer capitalism, and not all shared in the wealth. At the very least, the Philadelphia Centennial helped stabilize the jumpy economy. Significant for the story of the Aesthetic movement, some Americans noticed that modern life might revolve around finding an alliance between art and industry—in the factory, in the store and ultimately in the home.

THE CHANGING LANDSCAPE OF THE AMERICAN MIND

Industrialization wrought great changes in the American landscape. After the Civil War, cities shifted from being mercantile centers for an agrarian economy to being focal points of an industrial economy. In short, America urbanized. In the 1880s, as much as 40 percent of America's rural population moved away. Cities swelled further through immigration. By 1880, over 13 percent of the population was foreign born, and, over the next decade, over five million more immigrants came to America. Large cities supported a range of industry, while some smaller cities specialized; Dayton made cash registers, and Pittsburgh made steel. The entire country was webbed with railroads and telegraph lines to facilitate the movement of people, goods and information.

Industrialization also changed the landscape of the home. As the country industrialized, fewer American men

-- --

[5] Post, ed., *1876*, 15.

worked on the farm, in the village store or in a small work-shop. Instead, each morning more men headed off to factories, offices and the growing business of merchandising. American women stayed at home, raising children and making a home life. Some of the homes were in the suburbs, made possible by the growth of train and trolley service. As access to the city and suburban markets increased, women made fewer of their household necessities at home. They no longer wove cloth, churned butter or even baked bread. Some of those in the growing middle classes had a servant. Middle and upper class women had more leisure time and access to more goods. Men and women moved in separate spheres, with men in the public world of commerce and women in the private world of home and the feminine world of shops. This divergence was seen as not only an inevitable result of the changing economy but as evidence that a higher, better world order was emerging.

Increasing prosperity and growth fostered a climate of progressivism. As any American advanced economically, he or she could also choose to advance spiritually and morally. The key to progress was a disciplined individualism. The Horatio Alger ethic was cultivated in the middle class, and its rewards were often achieved.

Out of the effort to better oneself came a new understanding of the "self." Questioning centuries of religious teachings, Americans began to believe that the soul might not be the immutable, God-given core of a human being.

Since the Enlightenment, philosophers had been investigating rational thought, while science proceeded by empirical observation. Both focused on the knowable world. A generation's worth of geologists testified that great earth forms were the products of magnetic and thermal forces working over eons. Darwin's theory of evolution suggested that humans, like all living things, were the product of random chance and natural selection. These new scientific ideas shook Christianity to the core. Apparently, the history of creation was not written in the Bible, and the order of the world might not be the result of a divine plan. Attention focused on the study of the unexplained aspects of humanity. Anthropologists earnestly studied premodern cultures, while ethnologists collected fairy tales. The irrational moved out of the sideshow and into the doctor's office, as medicine began to explore hypnotism, neurasthenia, insanity and the dream world. Gradually, an understanding of the unconscious emerged, and psychology developed as a study and a science.

Although the psyche was no longer unified and might not be God given, its fragmented parts *could* be nurtured. In fact, a self-reliant individual could make a moral choice to cultivate aspects of the psyche in order to achieve a more perfected self. It might not be duplicitous to wear one face in public and another in private; to have different public and private selves could be a responsible choice in the divided world of work and home. Many began to explore exotic spiritual paths, such as mysticism or Buddhism. In this climate, seeking beauty, for the truths it could express about the world, could be a noble quest. Beauty could elevate the soul.

THE POTENT HOME

With the new focus on the self came a new reliance on the home. One result of America's tradition of self-reliant Protestantism was a sense of the home as a sacred place. The ideal Christian home was a template of the heavenly kingdom. The western Victorian world believed that God had given women the extra measure of virtue, and they were the rightful keepers of morality, especially in their domain, the home. The hallmarks of a mid-nineteenth-century moral home were cleanliness, cheerfulness and matching parlor sets, all of which reflected God's and Mother's plan for the family. Now, the divine order was shaken. Economic struggle was being played out in the workplace, and class and racial differences were being negotiated in the ever-more-crowded urban world. The world outside the home was seen as soul withering. Home, however, could be controlled and isolated. But more than this, by shaping the home environment, one

facing: Cover of *Golden Thoughts on Mother, Home and Heaven*, 1882 ed. (NY: E. B. Treat). Americans had a sanctified view of motherhood and home, as reflected in the cover of this book of poetry, essays and illustrations. (Collection of the author. Photo: Thies Wulf and Egon Zippel.)

above: *The Duet,* a painting by Thomas Wilmer Dewing, ca 1900–10. Dewing specialized in painting ethereal, attenuated ladies who are emblems of the late-nineteenth-century absorption in the psyche, refined beauty and a perfected soul. (Courtesy of Associated Artists, LLC, Southport, CT. Photo: John Cessna.)

could shape the self that lived in it. This idea was but a deepening of the mid-century cult of domesticity, which proclaimed that the home could be a reflection of the divine order. Although Darwin had shaken faith in any ultimate divine plan, Americans still wanted to shape their own lives. The home could be a crucible that shaped the moral self.

The critical force that could shape the home was beauty. The Aesthetic movement made the leap that art is powerful and that beautiful surroundings, in and of themselves, would elevate the soul. In fact, the urge to beautify one's home was a natural moral force. In the *Manufacturer and Builder*, an American magazine read by architecture aficionados, an 1882 article proclaimed, "Every improvement in the house is an improvement in morality."[6] The magazine went on to explain that the process of making physical improvements in the home inculcated "industry, forethought and self denial." Moreover,

and in the train of these virtues, and akin to them, comes the sense of the beautiful. The man so far advanced, and partly conscious of what it is that has advanced him, wishes to adorn what is his own, and which he loves dearly because it is so precious to him. He ornaments his doors and windows. He

[6] "Morality of Home Decoration," 41.

paints his walls and ceilings. He studies the form of his furniture and of his domestic utensils. And in this way is quickened within him the germ, also, of the fine arts. The house, the home that is one's own, is as potent as it is simple and unfailing in working these humanizing effects.

In an unending process, the urge to improve and adorn the home stimulates the knowledge of beauty, which uplifts the human soul.

The sentiment was so widespread it appeared as epigrams and inscriptions. "Who creates a home; creates a potent spirit, which in turn, doth fashion him that fashioneth" prefaced the section called "Modern Homes" in *Woman's Handiwork in Modern Homes*.[7] Candace Wheeler, a textile designer and home-decorating-advice writer, built a country home in the Catskill Mountains in 1883, where she painted a frieze with an elaboration of the same motto: "Who creates a home creates a potent spirit which in turn doth fashion him that fashioned. Who lives merrily he lives mightily withouted gladness availeth no treasure."[8] Many other inscriptions also extolled beauty. Henry Fry, one of the leaders of the Cincinnati art woodcarvers, used an apt biblical inscription from Isaiah on his own mantelpiece in his Cincinnati home: "I will give beauty for ashes and the oil of joy for mourning."[9] How appropriate that this powerful idea—that beauty in the house is an unending balm—was used like a benediction, to be read and reread!

In late-nineteenth-century America, women staked the claim to beautify the home. While men worked in the public realm of office, store and factory, women took on their responsibilities as keepers of the domestic realm. Ruskin and Morris had shown that creating and using beautiful, honest objects nurtured a good and just people. Children could only benefit from being raised in a beautiful home. Working men, too, who came home to the haven of beauty, would be refreshed. A woman's purpose as a homemaker could only be ennobled by instilling beauty in the home. She was fitted by her nature to link goodness with beauty. Aestheticizing the home was women's work of the highest order.

Today, we still consider homemaking a feminine activity. Homemaking magazines and TV shows are targeted to women ages twenty-five to forty, as any advertising agency will testify. The TV show *Queer Eye for the Straight Guy* gets its humor from its gender bending: it takes a whole team of gay guys to explain homemaking and style to their hopelessly inept straight male pupils.

The idea that a home not only reflects us but also *affects* us has not waned. Today, we have imported and modernized the ancient Chinese practice of feng shui. This discipline involves manipulating and arranging the environment to attract positive life energy, or *chi*, so that it flows smoothly. Feng shui is now a thriving industry in the United States,

De Forest Interior, a painting by Walter Launt Palmer, 1878. The woman rests contemplatively; she is the centerpiece of this artful home. This is a portrait of an interior the artist knew, the home of his friends Henry and Julia de Forest, which had been decorated in a Moorish style by their son Lockwood, one of the era's most influential designers. (Smithsonian American Art Museum, Washington DC / Art Resource, NY.)

-- --

[7] Harrison, *Woman's Handiwork in Modern Homes*, 132.
[8] The author saw the inscription on a visit to the cottage in 1989.
[9] Howe, ed., *Cincinnati Art-Carved Furniture and Interiors*, 42.

supporting books, Web sites and consultants. Before she found her calling as an "innovator in life design and life coaching," Martha Beck thought that the state of her home was miserable. In the fall 2004 issue of *O at Home* magazine, she wrote, "The indifferent hodgepodge of my home stemmed from neglect of my soul, and my ill-nourished soul, in turn, was perpetuating an uninspired environment."[10] She realized that by healing her home, she would heal herself. Now she gives her clients exercises focused around changing their home decor in order to change themselves. Feng shui and lifestyle counselors elevate home decorating to a spiritual practice.

CHAIRS AND TABLES AS HUMBLE EMISSARIES OF BEAUTY

In the nineteenth-century mission of beautifying the home, the decorative arts were the missionaries. The decorative arts superseded the fine arts for pragmatic and philosophical reasons. Decorative arts, those small, useful objects, are less costly than the fine arts. When the housewife needed a new chair or table, one in the new artistic style could be introduced. It was fitting that the humble decorative arts should be the emissaries of beauty in the household because art should pervade all aspects of daily life. Though Ruskin and Morris believed that the true path to the future lay in adopting the past, and Henry Cole's South Kensington system took the opposite view, believing that the future lay in embracing industrialism, both philosophies embraced the decorative arts. Design reformers, even if they differed on method, agreed upon means. The home and life would be beautified through humble household furnishings. The role of the decorative arts was elevated.

What would these new ideas look like? If individuals were becoming psychically more complicated yet self-reliant, what style would sustain them? If industry was committed to consumer capitalism, what products should be made and by what methods? How were women to create households that nurtured their families? In short, what would the new artistic style *look* like?

THE BATTLE OF STYLES

During the first half of the nineteenth century, designers had been engaged in an extended exploration—historians say battle—of various historical styles and the meanings they could connote. Designers tried their hand at a myriad of modes, and antebellum America is graced with Egyptian-style graveyard gates, Georgian plantation houses and

Rococo-derived bentwood parlor sets. Two main currents of design were practiced: classical and romantic. The classical mode encompassed the entire Greco-Roman heritage. Classical buildings were deemed especially appropriate for public buildings of the young democracy, which was itself modeled on Greco-Roman legal and political systems. Thus, a Doric column could call to mind the virtues of the Roman republic. On the opposite side of the coin was the romantic, personified in America by the Gothic style. The high Gothic of mid-medieval Europe and the Age of Faith was implied, and the Gothic did evoke Christian virtue. The Gothic was used not only for religious buildings but also for domestic architecture, where it was executed in wood on a modest scale. At mid-century, objects and homes were stylistically unified, with the appropriate style chosen for the circumstance.

In 1856, Owen Jones proved how assiduously historical style could be investigated. His *The Grammar of Ornament*, a multivolume chromolithographed deluxe publication, showcased the styles that the world's cultures and epochs had produced. Each of the one hundred plates contained a dozen or more motifs, rendered in vivid colors and metallic inks. Jones traced a version of the history of ornamental motifs that emphasized premodern cultures (Egyptian, Assyrian and Greek and Roman), including Islamic (Jones's own study of the Alhambra was influential here), Asian (India and China), European medieval (Byzantine and manuscript illuminations) as well as forms derived from nature. Post-Renaissance ornament received short shrift, and Japanese art, not yet well-known, was barely included. The book included thirty-seven "propositions" of good design, which Jones believed were illustrated by his motifs. The book served as an encyclopedia of sources for the new artistic style.

EASTLAKE, DRESSER AND ELEMENTAL DESIGN

Charles Locke Eastlake showed one way through the thicket of historical style—he came to the style debate with a firm predilection towards the medieval. And, he had read his Ruskin. His enormously popular *Hints on Household Taste* applied Ruskin's call for truthfulness in design. In his book, Eastlake described all sorts of household goods, advocating structural integrity, simplicity, spare decoration and, above all, fitness. Stylistically, his own designs were variations on the Gothic, adapting it to modern life. The book included some eighty illustrations of antique and modern articles, including a dozen or so of his own designs, mostly of furniture. These are characterized by a severe rectilinearity,

---

[10] Beck, "What Your House Says About You," 56.

DESIGN XXVI.

A COUNTRY HOUSE IN THE POINTED STYLE.

Fig. 132.

DESIGN XXVIII.

VILLA IN THE ITALIAN STYLE.

Fig. 143.

Two illustrations from *The Architecture of Country Houses*, by Alexander Jackson Downing (NY: D. Appleton & Co., 1850). The mid-nineteenth-century battle of styles was carried out in publications like Downing's *The Architecture of Country Houses*. Downing's book, a manual for those considering building homes, offered examples in both romantic (top) and classical (bottom) styles. Downing's book popularized the type of modest wooden houses ornamented with bargeboard and other details that have come to be called "Carpenter Gothic."

obvious display of joinery, unstained woods and massive hardware. It was a bold Gothic revival.

The popularity of Eastlake's book in America was unbounded. *Hints on Household Taste*, first published in London in 1868, appeared in an American edition by 1872, and went through six American editions before 1881. By 1877, an American commentator noted, "Not a young marrying couple who read English were to be found without 'Hints on Household Taste' in their hands, and all its dicta were accepted as gospel truths. . . . The book occasioned a great awakening, questioning, and study in the matter of household furnishing."[11] In fact, the "Eastlake" style is nearly synonymous with the first phase of the Aesthetic movement.

American furniture makers, too, read the book, and "Eastlake" furniture was produced in great quantity during the 1870s. Some of the best Eastlake furniture was of ebonized wood (anathema to Eastlake!) with incised gilt lines and geometric ornament. A few firms, notably Kimbel & Cabus, produced luxurious "Modern Gothic" furniture using handsome wood, inset ceramic tiles and stout hardware applied as strapwork. The cheapest "Eastlake" furniture was little more than panels of wood nailed together, ornamented with a quick dash of incising, geometric bracket work and/or turned spindles. In the fourth edition of his book, published in 1878, Eastlake inserted this note: "I find American tradesmen continually advertising what they are pleased to call 'Eastlake' furniture, with the production of which I have had nothing whatever to do, and for the taste of which I should be very sorry to be considered responsible."[12] Nonetheless, the label stuck and today the term "Eastlake" is applied to furniture, hardware, lighting fixtures and a characteristic style of incising when it appears on picture frames, silverware, stained glass and elsewhere.

Another designer responded to the challenge of historicism by forging his own style. Christopher Dresser, a young botanist who had also trained at the School of Design in London, composed Plate 98 of *The Grammar of Ornament*. It shows various flowers and their foliage laid out in strict regimentation, making their bilateral symmetry obvious. His botanical knowledge helped him systematize natural patterns for the purposes of deriving decorative elements. In doing this, he conformed to Ruskin's insistence on truth to nature and paralleled Morris's medievalizing flat patterning. Dresser continued to find the geometries underlying plant and animal life, and he soon developed a distinctive, even eccentric style that incorporated mechanistic angular forms and anthropomorphic medallions. Plate XLVIII from Dresser's book *Studies in Design* is typical (see middle image on right on page 26): a bristling fleur-de-lis on the left, a mask form on the right—which can be read as a face crowned with a budding hat!

Dresser was a polymath. He was so prolific, especially in the 1870s and 1880s, that his designs are still being unearthed today in patent offices and company registries. A short list of the things he designed and the firms he worked for is staggering: porcelain for Minton and Company; wallpaper for Jeffery & Co.; cast-iron hall stands for Coalbrookdale; metal-and-glass tableware for James Dixon & Sons; earthenware for Linthorpe Art Pottery (which he cofounded). Among his most famous designs are

[11] Spofford, *Art Decoration Applied to Furniture*, 147.
[12] Eastlake, *Hints on Household Taste*, ix.

CRAMMAR OF ORNAMENT

PLATE LIX

CHINESE Nº1

wallpaper, textiles and ceramics decorated with flat patterning that incorporates his characteristic grotesques; strikingly angular and spare toast racks and tea kettles; and earthenwares in primitive, organic shapes. Dresser derived his patterning from botanical and animal life, but his forms come from historical sources as varied as Japanese laquerware, Bronze Age earthenware and Persian rose water bottles.

Eastlake and Dresser self-consciously moved beyond a strict examination of style. Both began by striving to imitate the purity and honesty they saw in their models. Eastlake explored the construction of medieval furniture and Dresser explored the organic construction of plant forms. Both focused on the functionality of their models and, by doing so, came to understand elemental form.

At the core of this way of seeing was the focus on form, for its own sake. Eastlake did not abandon the Gothic and Dresser did not abandon plant life; instead, each put more emphasis on the design of crocket or leaf than in making the motif recognizable. They emphasized the aesthetic qualities of each form, not the associations it might conjure up with real forms. Future artists and designers would follow this path further—it leads to abstraction. Monet's water lilies and Picasso's Cubist nudes were descended from these ideas. Although the road of abstraction winds throughout the twentieth century, its story is not the story of the Aesthetic movement. Nonetheless, the Aesthetic movement was a precondition for abstraction.

ELABORATING ON THE ELEMENTAL

The artists and designers of the Aesthetic movement made "art for art's sake" their motto. They honed in on the basic elements of aesthetic form: color, shape, line, light and texture. Each of these could be treated as a vehicle for expression and explored in its own right, even exaggerated. For example, basic blue would not be used—instead, basic blue would be muted and combined with a texture, and its associations with water would only be hinted. The gracefulness of a curve, the appeal of color—these were the qualities of form that were sought for the pure beauty they could express.

Certain traits are descriptors for Aesthetic movement objects. There was a lavish use of sumptuous materials, like precious metals, costly fabrics and rare woods. Great emphasis was placed on skillful handcraftsmanship. Many techniques were adopted from older eras or invented from scratch—new colors in stained glass, embroidery stitches that revived Elizabethan work. Designers delighted in contrasting textures (e.g., placing grainy wood against the nap of velvet and smooth ceramics). Primary and tertiary colors were rarely used; the Aesthetic movement palette was dusky and pale. Lewis Mumford's book about the era was titled *The Brown Decades*, but this is shortsighted. Favorite colors were more subtle: puce, peacock blue, "ashes of roses," rich brown, and pale ochre dubbed "greenery-yallery." The influence of Morris and Dresser on pattern design was profound. Flattened, repeated forms densely applied across a compartmentalized surface were

Chinese No. 1, plate LIX from *The Grammar of Ornament*, by Owen Jones (London: Day and Sons, 1856). *The Grammar of Ornament* was a portfolio of one hundred beautifully printed plates of ornamental motifs, which served as an encyclopedia for designers.

above, left: Writing desk, by Kimbel & Cabus, 1876–82. Kimbel & Cabus were known for high-quality furniture in the "Eastlake" or "Modern Gothic" style, and variants of this desk were shown in the firm's booth at the Philadelphia Centennial. (Collection of the author.)

above, right: Plate XLVII from *Studies in Design,* by Christopher Dresser (London: Cassell, Peter and Galpin, 1876). Dresser's book was a portfolio of model motifs to be used by designers, decorators and "those who live in decorated houses." In his preface, Dresser stated that he hoped to "bring about a better style of decoration for our houses."

ubiquitous. Asymmetry was valued over regularity. Luminous or reflective surfaces were used; it was an era of metallic threads, glinting brass and mother-of-pearl. And, most of all, these stylistic traits were used in combination. This was elegant anti-minimalism.

Motifs from certain historical epochs and geographical areas were favored, and they hinted at larger poetic stories. The barbarism of the Middle East, the rustic simplicity of the Gothic, the exoticism of India—all could be conjured by motifs drawn from those cultures. Japan was an especially fertile field. Westerners were fascinated by the ability of Japanese artists to summarize nature with a few well-chosen strokes. The bold, colorful patterning they saw on Japanese prints, kimono fabrics and Imari ceramics was irresistible. At the same time, interest in archaic Greek culture ran high, with kylix bowls and amphora jars being adopted by ceramicists and silversmiths and motifs like the anthemion and the Greek key found everywhere. European medieval cultures were also sources, with motifs and forms drawn from Viking, Teutonic and Scandinavian lands. Americans turned to their own heritage and the colonial revival began. Focusing on aristocratic New England, the colonial revival drew on America's past from the settlement of Plymouth to the early Federal period—a range of style spanning the medieval to the Sheraton. Probably the most fertile source was not history but nature. Floral and vegetative motifs were drawn from other historical epochs and nature itself but were subdued under the force of the generalized flat patterning of the era. Anything depicted—an animal posed in action, an empty chair, a bare tree limb—might evoke a longer tale.

A great Aesthetic movement object encompasses an at-first bewildering range of stylistic precedents but succeeds by unifying all in a coherent, triumphant whole. One example will serve. A gilt side chair designed by the Herter Brothers once ornamented the drawing room of the William H. Vanderbilt home in New York City. With its graceful back, stiles and legs, its form evokes a high point of English furniture design, the late eighteenth century of Thomas Sheraton and George Hepplewhite. And gilt chairs had been known in the courts of France, England and Italy since the seventeenth century, where they always connoted wealth and status.

top, left: Trade card, by an unknown printer, 1880s. The gold, silver, copper, black and pink color combination of this trade card is typical of the strange and wonderful color schemes devised during the Aesthetic movement. A dealer in artistic household goods would have bought a quantity of these cards and had his firm's name printed into the blank screen. (Collection of the author.)

top, right: A group of servers, by various American makers, ca 1880s. Aesthetic movement designers achieved many different textures of metal using fine carving, hammering casting, and chasing, especially on silver. (Collection of the author. Photo: Thies Wulf and Egon Zippel.)

bottom, right: Detail, showing the top rail of a chair, by an unknown maker, possibly Herts Brothers, New York City, ca 1890. The rail of this chair shows exquisite workmanship with inlay of brass and mother-of-pearl in wood. (Collection of the author. Photo: Thies Wulf and Egon Zippel.)

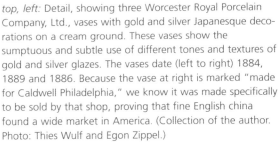

top, left: Detail, showing three Worcester Royal Porcelain Company, Ltd., vases with gold and silver Japanesque decorations on a cream ground. These vases show the sumptuous and subtle use of different tones and textures of gold and silver glazes. The vases date (left to right) 1884, 1889 and 1886. Because the vase at right is marked "made for Caldwell Philadelphia," we know it was made specifically to be sold by that shop, proving that fine English china found a wide market in America. (Collection of the author. Photo: Thies Wulf and Egon Zippel.)

top, right: Plate with Japanese swimming carp motif, by Derby Crown Porcelain Company, England, 1889. Swimming carp were adopted by Western designers as a quintessentially Japanese motif. Fine British porcelain dinner services like this one were sold worldwide; America was a major market. (Collection of the author. Photo: Thies Wulf and Egon Zippel.)

bottom, right: Detail of a vase, by Worcester Royal Porcelain Company, Ltd., England, with owl and toad decoration, 1889. The toad and the owls on this vase seem to be illustrations from a mysterious fable or legend. Many objects made during the Aesthetic movement evoke a poetic fable, without telling a specific story. (Collection of the author. Photo: Thies Wulf and Egon Zippel.)

But, the Vanderbilt chair is lighter, more luxurious and makes more allusions than these precedents. With its back rail like a choker necklace of mother-of-pearl and gold snakes, with mother-of-pearl discs that hang like pendants from the seat rail, with stiles punctuated by a string of graduated mother-of-pearl discs, with all-over gilding, the chair is itself a piece of jewelry. Yet, it is animated by the tensile strength of the front legs, which seem to spring forward on dainty hoofs, but are restrained by the straight back legs and the bowed chair back. The chair was originally upholstered in red embroidered Chinese silk, and it stood in a room whose walls were covered with red velvet that was studded with crystal and mother-of-pearl. The room was full of objets d'art of the grandest sort—many are now in museums, as are most known examples of this

left: Chair, by an unknown maker, probably American, ca 1880s. This chair was modeled loosely after examples of medieval manor furniture. Designers of the Aesthetic movement mined the past for motifs. (Collection of the author. Photo: Thies Wulf and Egon Zippel.)

right: Side chair, by Herter Brothers, ca 1881–82. This gilt side chair, made for the William H. Vanderbilt house in New York City, is a quintessential Aesthetic movement object. (Courtesy of Associated Artists, LLC, Southport, CT. Photo: John Cessna.)

chair. The Vanderbilt chair builds upon the elemental aesthetic of great ornamental side chairs, and, together with other furnishings of the room, forges its own style.

DECLINE AND RISE OF THE AESTHETIC MOVEMENT

Eventually, the Aesthetic movement ran its course and other styles came to the fore. The American Renaissance, the cultural movement that tied the United States to the Greco-Roman heritage of Europe, pushed classicism to the fore. The World's Columbian Exhibition held in Chicago in 1893 was a triumph for America's leading architects, who constructed a glorious "White City" of plaster and lathe, all temporary structures that used the Roman orders. Edith Wharton and Ogden Codman reexamined the classical styles of seventeenth- and eighteenth-century France in their book *The Decoration of Houses.* By the turn of the century, a new generation of design reformers was advocating simplicity. Heavy oak furniture suitable for bungalows emanated from Elbert Hubbard's Roycroft factory and from Gustav Stickley's Craftsman factory. Frank Lloyd Wright and the Prairie School that grew up around him emphasized earth-hugging homes made of brick and wood. Two paths led away from the

Aesthetic movement: the erudite reuse of classical forms practiced in the American Renaissance or, in contrast, the workman-like simplicity of the Arts and Crafts style. Soon, the idea that a home ought to express one's personality rather than a pure idea of art took hold. By the turn of the century the Aesthetic movement was over.

As during the Aesthetic movement, our own era is similarly plundering historical style for design effect. "The new baroque is colorful and witty, opulent without being stuffy," noted the *New York Times* on September 30, 2004, in the "Home" section. The article profiled some "new baroque" furnishings: Louis XVI chairs fabricated in Lucite; a greatly enlarged damask that is printed, not woven. Similarly, a four-page spread on "the New Eccentrics" in *New York Magazine* of April 11, 2005, shows apartments inspired by pop art, Venetian palazzos and a summer country cottage. In our era of quick communications and global sourcing, anything can be found and used. The new aestheticism, reveling in eclecticism, is redeploying the tactics of the Aesthetic movement.

NOTES ON SOURCES

The statistics and quotes on London's Crystal Palace Exhibition are drawn from Briggs, *Victorian Things.* New York's Crystal Palace exhibition is much less studied but is described well by Hirschfeld's article, "America on Exhibition: The New York Crystal Palace."

The design reform movement of the mid-nineteenth century, encompassing theory, pedagogy and objects, is complex, and various aspects of it are treated by specialized studies. These are among the best: Lynn, "Decorating Surfaces: Aesthetic Delight, Theoretical Dilemma," chapter 2 in Metropolitan Museum of Art, *In Pursuit of Beauty.* Although it mostly deals with the later phases of the Arts and Crafts movement, Boris, *Art and Labor,* is useful. Cole and the South Kensington system are described in Macdonald, *The History and Philosophy of Art Education.*

For the rise of industrialization, see Trachtenberg, *The Incorporation of America.*

The seminal book on late-nineteenth-century psychic ennui is Lears, *No Place of Grace: Antimodernism and the Transformation of American Culture, 1880–1920.*

For the Centennial, see Rydell, *All the World's a Fair.* For Japan at the fair, see Hosley, *The Japan Idea.*

Christopher Dresser's long-neglected career has been publicized by a recent exhibition and accompanying catalog by Whiteway, ed., *The Shock of the Old: Christopher Dresser's Design Revolution.*

The cult of domesticity is described in Clark Jr., *The American Family Home,* and Greir, *Culture and Comfort: People, Parlors, and Upholstery, 1850–1930.*

For our own modern views of how we shape the home environment and how it in turn affects us, see Gallagher, *House Thinking.*

Tastemakers

OSCAR WILDE—APOSTLE OF AESTHETICISM

The reporters were so eager for the story that they couldn't wait for the boat to pass through quarantine. A controversial celebrity had arrived from England—a twenty-seven-year-old dandy, an aesthete, a rowdy, who spoke in epigrams and wrote poems, some decidedly salacious. He decorated his rooms at Oxford with lilies in blue-and-white vases, and then sighed about "the difficulty of living up to one's china." (He was reproved from the pulpit for the remark.) He was supposed to be the "Apostle of Aestheticism," the new movement that had already proved to be great fun for the British press. Now, he had appeared on American shores to lecture on this craze for the beautiful; he was fair game. On the evening of January 2, 1882, the reporters hired a launch to take them out into New York harbor, where they climbed aboard the steamship for their quarry: Oscar Wilde. He appeared in a green, fur-trimmed greatcoat with matching hat.

"Why come to America?" asked a reporter.

"I am here to diffuse beauty," answered Wilde.

(From a reporter gesturing at the New Jersey shore.) "Might beauty then be in both the lily and Hoboken?"

"Something of the kind . . . it's a wide field which has no limit, and all definitions are unsatisfactory."

"Please give us your definition of aestheticism."

"Aestheticism is a search after the signs of the beautiful. It is the science through which men look after the correlation which exists in the arts. It is, to speak more exactly, the search after the secret of life."

"Do you call aestheticism a philosophy?"

"Assuredly. It is a study of what may be found in art and in nature. Whatever in art represents eternal truth expresses the great underlying truth of aestheticism."

(A reporter, attempting to bait Wilde.) "Aestheticism has been understood to be blind groping after something which is entirely intangible. Can you, as the exponent of aestheticism, give us an interpretation which shall give a more respectable standing to the word?"

"I do not know that I can give a much better definition than I have already given. But whatever there has been in poetry since the time of Keats; whatever there has been in art that has served to develop the underlying principles of truth; whatever there has been in science that has served to show to the individual the meaning of truth as expressed to humanity—that has been an exponent of aestheticism."

(Confusion among the reporters.) "Where would this movement end?"

"There is no end to it; it will go on forever."

"What are your intentions as to your American tour? Will you lecture?"

"That will depend considerably upon the encouragement with which my philosophy meets."

"Are you here to secure a copyright on your play? Some say that you are!"

(Wilde laughs.) "Whatever my business may be, whatever I may accomplish in America, whatever I may do in lecturing, whatever the success of my tragedy may be, it is enough to have seen America."[1]

The next morning, in his interview with a customs officer, Wilde said, "I have nothing to declare except my genius." Or, he may not have said it—no matter. The remark is now among Wilde's most famous. *Bon mots* were expected, and Wilde delivered.

Wilde's trip to America was not his idea. The lecture tour was instigated by Richard D'Oyly Carte, a theatrical producer who had done well in London with Gilbert and Sullivan's latest operetta, *Patience*. D'Oyly Carte had opened it in New York in September of 1881, and pirated productions were staged elsewhere. *Patience* spoofed the new young set of aesthetes. So who better to promote the play than one of England's most notorious? D'Oyly Carte knew that if he could induce Wilde to exhibit himself across the United States, Wilde would ensure the success of his national tour of *Patience*. For his part, Wilde needed the money and jumped at the chance to promote aesthetic ideas and himself.

Wilde came to an audience primed by *Patience*. The operetta concerns the rivalry between Bunthorne (described in the script as "a Fleshly Poet") and Grosvenor ("an Idyllic Poet") for the love of Patience, a milkmaid. Lyrics and lines mock the fashionable motifs of aestheticism by praising them. The ideal aesthetic poet is "A most intense young man / A soulful-eyed young man / An ultra-poetical, super-aesthetical / Out-of-the-way young man! . . . A Japanese young man / A blue-and-white young man / Francesca da Rimini, miminy piminy / Je-ne-sais-quoi young man!"[2] First one and then the other poet is followed around by a fickle chorus of lovesick young ladies. When a whole platoon of soldiers adopts the "stained glass attitudes" of the poets in order to win back the ladies, the ladies proclaim them "perceptively intense and consummately utter." Bunthorne is a sham; he only seems to scan his book "in a rapt ecstatic way," while Jane, the lady he spurns, sighs despairingly, "I am soul-fully intense." Bunthorne turns out to be the more vapid of the two poets, but Grosvenor

Oscar Wilde. (Photograph by Napoleon Sarony, 1882.)

[1] The exchange quoted here is drawn from interviews Wilde gave on the evening of January 2 and the morning of January 3, 1882. See "Oscar Wilde," 6:4; "Oscar Wilde's Arrival," 1:4; "Ten Minutes with a Poet," 5:6. Further quotes are taken from Ellmann, *Oscar Wilde*, 159–60.
[2] The lines from *Patience* are quoted from Gilbert and Sullivan, *The Complete Plays of Gilbert and Sullivan*, 194.

is eventually induced to become an ordinary young man. In the end, Grosvenor wins Patience, while Bunthorne is left with his lily. To encourage innuendo, the actors playing Bunthorne in various venues conflated the mannerisms and dress of various real-life esthetes, including Wilde and two of his friends, poet Algernon Swinburne and painter James McNeill Whistler.

One New York journalist explained the contemporary reaction to *Patience*:

> *If the man of the next century should ever see the amusing little opera of* Patience, *which has so pleased us who are his great-grandfathers and queer old ancestors, he will understand not only that this age was the renaissance of taste, and not only that it had its contemporaneous caricatures of its characteristic tendency, but that it was conscious of them and greatly enjoyed them. The droll 'aestheticism' which produced a figure like Oscar Wilde and a kind of social cult evident enough to give point to the pictorial laugh of Punch was only a raveling out of the solid and golden fabric of refined and elegant taste. The worship of the teapot is only an extravagance of the impulse which designs the beautiful house and fills it with beautiful things.*[3]

Americans loved both their sincere impulse towards the aesthetic and the mocking of that impulse that made *Patience* a success.

Audiences came to Wilde's lectures ready to embrace the same set of contradictions—or at least to gaze upon them. And Wilde delivered a spectacle. He had no beard and he wore his hair long, like a bohemian. He usually lectured wearing a waistcoat, knee breeches, silk stockings and patent leather slippers. His coat came in various versions; most were of dark velvet, trimmed with silk frills or ornamented with embossed and embroidered panels; the knee breeches matched the coat. He often wore a wide collar with an even wider cravat in a

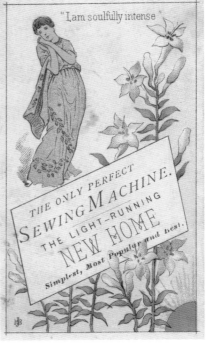

[3]Attributed to George William Curtis, in Lynes, *The Tastemakers*, 115–16.

startling color, and he sometimes wore lace at his wrists. The costume quickly attracted ridicule. In Boston, sixty Harvard students paraded down the center aisle, dressed in the requisite breeches and wide cravats, carrying sunflowers or lilies and striking languid poses. Wilde had been warned and that night he wore regular evening attire. He was able to chide the students by assuring them that there was more to the movement of aestheticism than knee breeches and sunflowers, and he amused the rest of the audience by asking them to save him from his disciples. Nonetheless, Wilde wore the breeches throughout the tour.

This raises the matter of Wilde's sexuality—it was, a contemporary lady observed, "undecided."[4] The naturalist John Burrows met Wilde and said he was "a splendid talker, and a handsome man, but a voluptuary. As he walked from you, there was something in the motion of his hips and back that was disagreeable."[5] The *Boston Evening Transcript* was more direct: "Is he manne, or woman, or childe? / Either, / and neither! / She looks as much like a manne / As ever shee canne; / He looks more like a woman / Than any feminine human."[6] On the one hand, Wilde was tall and muscular, with a burly voice (even if he did have a slight lisp) and his devotion to actresses Lillie Langtry and Sarah Bernhardt was evident. But on the other hand—those knee breeches, the lavender scarves, the lace at the wrists! Was Wilde an artistic man or irretrievably feminine? The question hung in the air. Flamboyant and unrepentant, Wilde flaunted himself and made it a part of the show.

Whatever skepticism Wilde's pose prompted, his credentials for speaking about the artistic movement were impeccable. Artists of all sorts were his friends, including the revolutionary Pre-Raphaelites, academics like Sir Lawrence Alma-Tadema, and members of the avant-garde like James McNeill Whistler and Albert Moore. He knew the poets: Swinburne, Browning, Tennyson. Ruskin was his mentor. Wilde had read widely in ancient and modern poetry and philosophy, and he had won Oxford's most distinguished prize for poetry, the Newdigate. He grew up in Dublin, son of a knighted physician/writer and a mother who held salons; he wrote poetry and campaigned vigorously for Irish independence. His pedigree and his skills as a conversationalist earned him a place in London's elite cultural circles. If an apostle for the arts was needed in America, Wilde was the man for the job.

And Wilde's lectures *were* earnest. He began the tour with one lecture titled the English Renaissance. It was a loose history of brilliant moments in art that were finding their culmination in the awakening of the art spirit in Britain. Wilde stated that new methods and techniques were being forged in this modern renaissance, that now form was becoming as important as content, and that the new appreciation for beauty would make human life richer. Only one month into the tour Wilde realized that so many newspapers were reporting on his lectures, sometimes virtually repeating them verbatim, that his audiences would demand new material. He quickly expanded his thoughts into two new lectures: the Decorative Arts and the House Beautiful. The first delved a little more deeply into the economic and aesthetic value of the revival of hand craftsmanship promulgated by Ruskin and Morris. Wilde advocated the establishment of South Kensington–type museums next to every art school and reminded everyone that no art was better than bad art. In the House Beautiful, Wilde metaphorically walked through a house, recommending specific things: the use of secondary colors rather than primaries, wainscoted and tiled halls, Dutch porcelain stoves rather than cast-iron ones, Queen Anne–style furniture. Throughout the lectures, Wilde insisted that art could sanctify everything it touched and that life would be raised to the degree that the modern world embraced art. He urged his audiences to have the courage to give themselves up to their impressions, for that was the secret of the artistic life. He summarized: "We spend our days looking for the secret of life. Well, the secret of life is art."[7]

facing: These three trade cards are part of the craze that surrounded the Gilbert and Sullivan operetta *Patience*, which spoofs the sillier aspects of aestheticism. The center shows Patience herself, a simple milkmaid, who learns about love over the course of the operetta. At left is a caricature of Bunthorne, a poet, who here suspiciously resembles Oscar Wilde. At right is Jane, an aesthetic lady. (Collection of the author.)

[4] Ellmann, *Oscar Wilde*, 179.
[5] Ibid., 161.
[6] Quoted in Blanchard, *Oscar Wilde's America*, 11.
[7] Ellmann, *Oscar Wilde*, 166.

In some venues, Wilde spoke from within an artistic setting. In Denver, the stage was set up as a parlor with Turkish upholstery and silk curtains in varying textures. In Milwaukee, the stage was ornamented with iron storks standing amid foliage and the walls had Moorish doors hung with portieres. In his costume and in such a setting, Wilde became an other-worldly prophet, an "apostle of the esthetic," as one newspaper called him.[8] No doubt Wilde agreed.

Between January 9 and October 13, 1882, Wilde lectured in over 130 cities in the United States and eastern Canada. Wilde was news wherever he went. He was taken down into a Colorado silver mine, where he dined on whiskey and spoke of Cellini, the Renaissance goldsmith. Wilde was mildly disappointed with Niagara Falls but more disappointed by the new Chicago water tower, mocking its "pepperbox turrets." Sometimes he was met by affectionate satire, as when groups of girls holding sunflowers sang the lovesick maidens' song from *Patience*. At other times, exposés on his poetry or his motives or his manliness appeared. At the beginning of his tour, Wilde sat for over twenty poses with photographer Napoleon Sarony; these were published as *carte de vistes*, an obligation of all celebrities in America. (An obligation Wilde was eager to fulfill.) The images were quickly pirated and used to advertise an amazing range of goods. In a landmark case that established that photographs were artistic images that could be copyrighted, Sarony sued one of the producers of trade cards, the Burrow Giles Lithographic Company, and won. All this publicity, whether good, bad or tangential, brought more fame to Wilde and spread the tenants of the Aesthetic movement.

Trade card for Mme Fontaine's Bossom Beautifier, probably around 1882, printed by Cossak and Co., Buffalo, NY. This is one of many advertising images that used Oscar Wilde's image to sell its product. The vignette at lower left shows Wilde, who certainly did not endorse this product. This photograph of Wilde was taken by Napoleon Sarony, who sued the printer for using his images of Wilde without permission or payment. Sarony eventually won. Meanwhile, Mme Fontaine promised that her product would "enlarge and beautify the bossom." (Collection of the author.)

JAMES MCNEILL WHISTLER—CONTROVERSIES AND HARMONIES

Wilde, an Englishman who came to America to promulgate aestheticism, paired himself with an American who lived in England as an aesthete. In his House Beautiful lecture, Wilde commended the interiors that James McNeill Whistler had fabricated for the exhibition of his art. Both Wilde and Whistler were flamboyant public figures famous for flip pronouncements, and the two shared some of the same iconic habits: collecting china, attention-getting clothing, and out-of-bounds sexual relationships (Whistler openly set up housekeeping with his models/mistresses). When Bunthorne sang of "the blue-and-white young man" in *Patience*, audiences mingled the painter and the poet in their minds, making both tastemakers for the artistic movement.

James McNeill Whistler came from an old Massachusetts family, spent formative years in Russia where his father built railroads, learned drawing at West Point and etching while working with the U.S. Coast and Geodetic Survey. He studied art in Paris and moved in the avant-garde café society of painters and writers. By 1859, he made London his base, and soon knew the Pre-Raphaelite painters and poets. He and his art were a link between the bohemians of Paris and London.

Whistler cultivated the spotlight. With his first solo exhibition in 1874 at the Flemish Gallery in London, Whistler set the pattern for his interactions with the press. In sessions that were more diatribes than interviews, the painter coached the critics, then, if the resultant review did not please him, sent out scathing letters of correction to the editor—so, Whistler received coverage twice. Several London plays were farces of the emerging art scene, and alluded to Whistler's place in it. *The Grasshopper* of 1877 concerned painter Pygmalion

-- --
[8] "Oscar Wilde, the Esthete," 2.

Harmony in Blue and Gold: The Peacock Room, 1876–77. The room consists of shutters and eighteenth-century leather wall coverings painted by James McNeill Whistler as well as his painting *Rose and Silver: The Princess from the Land of Porcelain.* The room also includes shelving designed by Thomas Jeckyll for the patron's collection of Oriental blue-and-white china as well as Jeckyll's now-famous sunflower andirons. (Freer Gallery of Art, Smithsonian Institution, Washington, DC; gift of Charles Lang Freer.)

Flippit and his canvas titled *Dual Harmony in Red and Blue*; it could be shown with either end up. In the press, on the stage and live, and around town, Whistler's lean figure could be seen, complete with a monocle, a pencil-thin cane and a shock of prematurely white hair at the center of his forehead.

With the *Peacock Room*, Whistler commandeered a patron and the press. The artist was never authorized to produce this work of art, his only surviving interior (it is now in the Freer Gallery of Art, Washington, DC). He was authorized to make minor adjustments to a dining room that Frederic Leyland had commissioned to highlight a collection of Oriental porcelain and a set of eighteenth-century gilded and lacquered leather hangings. But, Whistler thought that none of these harmonized with his own painting for the room, *Rose and Silver: The Princess from the Land of Porcelain.* So, while the patron was away, Whistler proceeded to paint the ceiling, the shutters, a panel above the sideboard, the sideboard itself and, eventually, the expensive leather in his own blue green scheme of Japanese roundels and peacocks. He also flirted with the patron's wife, invited the press and public in to view the room while he was at work on it, and charged Leyland multiples of the amount originally agreed upon. The newspaper coverage was extensive, and Leyland's anger was extreme.

But the next year Whistler constructed a media event that received even more coverage. When John Ruskin saw Whistler's nearly abstract painting of fireworks falling over the Thames River, *Nocturne in Black and Gold: The Falling Rocket*, in the Grovesnor Gallery, he wrote, "I have seen, and heard, much of Cockney impudence before now; but never expected to hear a coxcomb ask two hundred guineas for flinging a pot of paint in the public's face."[9] Whistler responded by suing Ruskin for libel. Testimony at the trial, held in November of 1878, came from London's art world and revolved around nothing less than the purpose of art. Whistler maintained that his work had no moral theme, depicted nothing more than an effect, and was merely a harmonic arrangement—art for art's sake. Whistler won the case, but he was awarded only a farthing for the "damages" caused by the libel.

In his exhibitions, Whistler applied the radical principles of his paintings to the decor that surrounded them, creating startlingly unified environments. Whistler arranged every element of these exhibitions, laying floor matting, mixing harmonizing tones of wall paint, designing frames, sometimes even supplying livery for a servant. At the show of Whistler's pastels from Venice, held in the Grovesnor Gallery in 1881, the walls were a dull yellow green color, the frieze and ceiling a pale red brown, and the moldings and picture frames were various tones of gold, described as citron, guinea and ruby. An 1883 exhibition of etchings was orchestrated in yellow and white. Visitors entered through a portiere of yellow plush and silk. Festoons of golden yellow velvet and lemon yellow muslin ornamented the walls, which were covered up to the height of ten feet with white felt that had been stenciled with yellow lines and scattered butterflies—the symbol Whistler had adopted for his signature. A yellow sofa and "perilous little cane-bottomed chairs painted canary colour" were available, and rows of tiny yellow Japanese pots each held a yellow flower: daffodils, narcissi, marguerites.[10] An attendant in yellow plush handed out the catalog; a reporter dubbed this fellow the "antimated poached egg."[11] The prince and princess of Wales attended the opening, where favored lady guests wore a butterfly pin designed by Whistler. The press and public either mocked or stood in awe of the excruciatingly tuned color sensitivity but all recognized it as Whistler's unique accomplishment.

Whistler also implemented his ideas about decor in his own houses, which were only slightly less public than his exhibitions. The most famous of these was 35 Tite Street, commissioned from architect E. W. Godwin. Its plain facade and tall gambrel roof were thought too severe by the government commission that had to approve the building permit; the architecture became another point of aesthetic contention to be parlayed by Whistler in the press. In a dining room of blue and yellow, Whistler displayed Oriental porcelain and antique silver. The roof was the shell that formed the largest room in the house, a studio on the top floor, designed both for making art and entertaining. The prevailing color scheme of terra-cotta was structured with a dado composed of battens over textured white plaster, augmented with the shadows cast by the mullions of a wall of windows; the room was to be furnished with black lacquered Japanese objects and Godwin-designed black lacquer furniture in a similar vein. In fact, the house was never fully furnished. Whistler occupied it for less than a year because the trial with Ruskin and the battle with Leyland had bankrupted him.

Whistler's interiors stood in contrast to another mode of artistic decoration developed by William Morris. Whistler constructed his interiors around harmonic arrangements of pale or bright tones, with spare furnishings, while Morris emphasized patterning, dark colors, and

-- --
[9] Ruskin, *Works of John Ruskin*, 29:160.
[10] Bendix, *Diabolical Designs*, 227.
[11] Ibid., 226.

greater density of furnishings in a medievalizing mode. So, by the late 1870s, these two styles of furnishing were available—the avant-garde, spare Whistlerian mode, and the more historical, homey mode of Morris.

ARTISTS' STUDIOS AND BOHEMIAN LIFE

The cosmopolitan artist in his studio, a potent image Whistler made famous, was taken up by William Merritt Chase in New York City in 1879. Chase was a young up-and-coming painter from Indiana, by way of Munich. He represented a new generation of artists who went to Europe to study, where formal lessons were taught in the bare rooms of academies and further tutorials occurred in the opulent private atelier of the master. The studio was an artistic salon, a place where patrons and critics were entertained, and convivial art shop talk was a regular event. As they learned to paint in their master's studios, the young Americans formed ambitions of establishing their own studios. While still abroad, Chase began collecting studio furnishings, and he declared to a fellow American student, "I intend to have the finest studio in New York."[12]

Soon, Chase proved that his boast had not been idle. Within a year of his arrival in New York City, he settled into the largest room in the Tenth Street Studio Building, a bastion of the old art guard. Chase took over the disused central exhibition room (as well as a smaller adjacent space) and arranged a vast inventory of objets d'art. Newspaper and magazine articles, photographs and visitor's accounts all record the contents copiously. One's eye raced from a stained-glass window of the 1600s, to a Puritan hat, to a set of Italian court swords, to a harem slipper, to a row of Japanese fans, to a carved cassonne, to a tangle of musical instruments and weaponry hung up as a bunch. On the walls were paintings and engravings by Chase and his friends, copies after old master paintings, Persian carpets, Chinese silks and old cut velvet. It was like Ali Baba's cave, where all wonders could be found. The studio was a semipublic place. Here, Chase taught students, including many women pupils. And, the

In the Studio, an oil painting by William Merritt Chase, ca 1882. In the 1880s, when it was new, Chase produced many paintings of his studio and displayed them in exhibitions— effectively publicizing the studio and the new aesthetic that it displayed. (Brooklyn Museum, 13.50; gift of Mrs. Carll H. de Silver in memory of her husband.)

[12] Roof, *The Life and Art of William Merritt Chase*, 51.

A Studio Home

The Ship Wrecked Hotel, an installation by Kenneth Andrew Mroczek, New York City, ca 2004. Satisfying the modern desire to see how artists live and work, Mroczek has opened his home and made it a work of art that people pay to see. He transformed a small tenement apartment in New York's lower East Side into the Ship Wrecked Hotel. The artful decor of this bohemian bed and breakfast is made from unlikely materials: scrunched-up Scotch Tape, a stuffed beaver, fabric swatches and much more. Every surface is hand decorated with riotous paint, artificial flowers, paper cutouts and traceries of inked lines. Guests are treated to a theatrical event every night at 7:05 p.m., can listen to Erik Satie while enjoying a miso soup breakfast, and can hear the fascinating fantasy histories of everything in the hotel. For the night, guests enjoy a studio that is a work of art. (Photograph Jason Schmidt / *Nest Magazine*.)

studio was always open to friends and was also open on certain days for public receptions. The best documents of the studio are Chase's own paintings and pastels of it, which were exhibited in the early 1880s.

Although Chase's studio was a hard act to top, artists all over America quickly adopted the new mode of elaborate studios. Oscar Wilde enjoyed a tea party in a studio in San Francisco in 1882, where he held an animated conversation with a mannequin, to the amusement of the other guests. By the mid-1880s, big cities had whole buildings devoted to artists' studios, and most cities of any size had an informal art district with studios scattered among the retail and office buildings of downtowns. Few art galleries existed, and those that did favored European art and more established American artists; studios acted as sales rooms for the new generation. These European-trained artists were developing an art that was based less upon realism and more upon style and form. The atmospheric studios fostered the new art and the new art life. Artists took care that their studios were known by exhibiting paintings of them and encouraging photographs and articles in the press. For the public, these studios demonstrated another mode of decorating, where the emphasis was on the display of choice furnishings, where casual arrangements of objects prevailed, and all appeared to be the result of effortless harmony.

Often, when the new generation of artists made themselves known, it was by affiliating themselves with projects that explored the decorative arts. The Tile Club was a notable example. This group of painters, illustrators, sculptors and writers met in New York City in the early 1880s for occasional evenings of tile painting and socializing. Spurred on by the fun they had, the opportunity to make art in new terrain and the possibility of publicity, they made some excursions. The first was to eastern Long Island, then a thinly settled region of sand dunes and mosquitoes. The most luxurious was a barge trip up the Hudson River and Erie Canal, all expenses probably paid by *Scribner's Monthly*. The tilers did not travel light: the barge was staffed by several servants and furnished with divans, cutlery and Chinese lanterns from Chase's studio. The escapades of these well-known artists vacationing as makers of tiles were recounted in illustrated magazine articles and later in a deluxe book on the club. Dabbling in the decorative arts was now chic.

Today, long after Chase put his Tenth Street studio on the artistic map, a fascination with how artists live and work continues. By the early twentieth century, the term "studio apartment" connoted a bohemian place that fostered a free-wheeling lifestyle. Nowadays, the studio visit has become a staple member's activity for art museums. Artists still congregate in buildings and neighborhoods, join guilds and open their studios collectively for tours. It is common to see an artist's work/living space featured in the pages of glossy shelter magazines and "Living" sections in newspapers. Modern audiences are fascinated by environments where creativity happens; *studio* is still a romantic word.

ARTISTS DESIGN INTERIORS

In the 1880s, the line between artist and designer of interiors became blurred. John La Farge and Louis Comfort Tiffany, both better known today as makers of stained glass, were also both easel painters and interior decorators. In the 1880s, their careers were dominated by interior design commissions. They both worked collaboratively, establishing workshops with fluid membership and contracting with specialized firms for specific components. La Farge was the principal designer for several of the most magnificent rooms in the Cornelius Vanderbuilt II home, a French chateaux on Fifth Avenue. There he worked with sculptor Augustus Saint-Gaudens on a monumental fireplace; Saint-Gaudens designed the caryatids and La Farge made the mosaic overmantel. In this period, the architect Stanford White designed furniture, picture frames, metalwork and more, as needed. He also went on buying sprees in Europe, incorporating the spoils into his interiors. If he could, for example, buy only one Louis XIV table, he would commission another from a New York City cabinetmaker, then design coordinated paneling. Many easel painters became mural painters, many made paintings that were incorporated into paneling, door panels and ceilings. In short, the makers of fine arts expanded their repertoire; painters made more than easel paintings, sculptors made more than free-standing figures and architects did more than produce plans.

The work of Associated Artists, a short-lived artists' collaborative dedicated to decorating, was an influential link between artists and interior designers. After some years of working as a painter (and avoiding a career with his father's silver and jewelry firm), Louis Comfort Tiffany reportedly said, "I have been thinking a great deal about decorative work, and I am going into it as a profession. I believe that there is more in it than in painting pictures. . . . We are going after the money there is in art, but the art is there all the same."[13] Tiffany was the fulcrum of Associated Artists, with textile designer Candace Wheeler also intensely involved and many other artists playing supporting roles, including painter Samuel Coleman and painter, furniture importer and designer Lockwood de Forest. The firm existed on paper only from 1881 to 1883 as Louis C. Tiffany & Associated Artists, although Tiffany had been working collaboratively as a designer for a few years before that and continued long afterwards. Candace Wheeler continued her textile work under the name Associated Artists for decades. The firm did not close until 1907. Nonetheless, then and now, the decorating firm was known as Associated Artists. The firm drew in designers as needed for each commission and formed a large workshop of embroiders, stained-glass fabricators, painters and drafts people; many were women. The firm distinguished itself with interiors that placed emphasis on the shell of the room rather than its furnishings. This shell was singularly unified by rich color and patterning, a high level of craftsmanship and imaginative use of materials. The drawing room of John Taylor Johnston and his wife, Frances, is an example. It was an environment of salmons, red, yellows and brown, with an overmantel composed of panes of clear glass and mirror, a mantel of carved teakwood panels and colored glass. At the door hung thick plush portieres and above it was a transom of wood lattice work and colored glass. The walls, brushed in various textures of paint, were the background to the Johnstons' important art collection.

-- --
[13] Wheeler, *Yesterdays in a Busy Life*, 231.

Salon in the George Kemp House, New York City. As published in *Artistic Houses*, by George William Sheldon, vol. 1, plate 53 (NY: D. Appleton and Company, 1883). The Kemp Salon was one of the earliest and most important decorating commissions of Louis Comfort Tiffany. It is a Middle Eastern extravaganza carried out in many media. The Moresque patterns on the wall are executed in stucco and white holly with panels of cut velvet; the ceiling is composed of iron tracery; and windows feature stained-glass transoms, enameled pillars and embroidered curtains. The color scheme is complex, encompassing buff, red, blue and olive, all enriched with much gold and silver. The room was probably complete in early 1880, just as Tiffany established a series of formal business partnerships and less formal working relationships with Candace Wheeler, Samuel Coleman and Lockwood de Forest. In this commission, Wheeler probably executed the various needlework and textile effects, de Forest may have supplied some imports from the Middle East, and Coleman at least supplied bric-a-brac. By 1881, the firm Louis C. Tiffany & Associated Artists was formed and the lush signature style Tiffany established with the Kemp Salon was executed in many more prestigious commissions.

Herter Brothers was the other firm that defined the new artistic style of decoration. While the workrooms of Associated Artists were filled with artists, the Herter Brothers workrooms were filled with cabinetmakers. Gustave Herter, a German emigrant, established himself as a furniture maker in New York City in 1848, working in partnership with other cabinetmakers and at least one prominent interior designer, Auguste Pottier. In this era, only a few firms were professional interior designers. At the high end of the business, the task was handled by architects and cabinetmakers. At the middle end, housewives put together their design schemes by visiting various merchants. As an expert cabinetmaker, working in all the fashionable mid-century styles, Gustave Herter was poised to ride the wave upwards as interior design became a profession. By the late 1850s, Herter's younger half-brother, Christian, joined Gustave in New York and the two formed the partnership Herter Brothers in 1864. Christian Herter spent two years in Europe, traveling and studying painting with muralist Victor Galland in Paris. The firm operated under the name Herter Brothers from 1864 to 1907, although Gustave lived in retirement in Germany during the years of the company's biggest successes, and Christian died in 1883. The company was managed and staffed by a long list of able designers, including William Baumgarten. Herter Brothers were among the first in America to adopt what was then known as the Anglo Japanese style: furniture that used rectilinear ebonized frames that contrasted solids and voids. In the late 1870s and through the 1880s, Herter Brothers made an exquisite variant that used asymmetrical elements, marquetry and inset panels of porcelain, metals or painted surfaces.

Herter Brothers was a full-service firm for America's wealthiest families. Working with an array of contractors and shops, the firm could furnish an entire mansion, supplying woodwork, tiling, draperies, carpeting, stained glass, plaster-work, mural and easel paintings, and a wide range of luxe objects, such as European clocks, Oriental porcelain and even paintings. Herter Brothers furniture and its

importations could also be commissioned separately or purchased from the firm's showrooms in New York City. The firm worked from coast to coast: from a town house for William H. Vanderbilt in New York City, a hall and dining room in the Potter Palmer residence in Chicago, and two rounds of decorating the Darious Ogden Mills mansion in Millbrea, California.

The success of tastemakers Herter Brothers and Associated Artists was publicized—discretely—with the publication of two books by George William Sheldon: *Artistic Houses* and *Artistic Country-Seats*. Both were expensive books of captioned photographs, sold only to subscribers, issued in sections over a two-year period, as unbound folio-sized sheets (*Artistic Houses* was issued 1883–84, *Artistic Country-Seats* in 1886–87). The photographs were printed from glass-plate negatives using the newest printing technologies; minute detail was captured in the black-and-white images. The owners cooperated with the author and photographer, supplied information about their houses and furnishings and helped to set up the shots. With the publication of these books, the work of architects and decorators, and the taste of owners, was recognized and specifically distinguished as "artistic."

William Dean Howells must have had the work of high-end decorators like Herter Brothers and Louis C. Tiffany & Associated Artists in mind when he described Cornelia Saunders' impressions of Mrs. Maybough's tasteful apartment in the Mandan Flats in his novel *The Coast of Bohemia*, published in 1893:

Northwest Corner of the Drawing Room, with Portions of Galland's Fête, a color plate from Edward Strahan's book, *Mr. Vanderbilt's House and Collection*, vol. 1 (Boston: G. Barrie, 1883–84). The Herter Brothers were the lead interior designers for William H. Vanderbilt's house on Fifth Avenue in New York City, which was an opulent showplace. This plate shows their work, largely conceived by Christian Herter, which included the architectural and decorative scheme and the furniture. The wall panels were composed of stretched velvet embroidered with cut crystals of various colors, the woodwork was inlaid with mother-of-pearl, as was some of the furniture. (Courtesy of Associated Artists, LLC, Southport, CT. Photo: John Cessna.)

> The drawing room was a harmony of pictures so rich and soft, that the colors seemed to play from wall to floor and back again in the same mellow note; the dimness of the dining-room was starred with the glimmer of silver and cut-glass and the fainter reflected light of polished mahogany; the library was a luxury of low leather chairs and lounges, lurking window-seats, curtained in warm colors, and shelves full of even ranks of books in French bindings of blue and green leather. There was a great carved library table in front of the hearth where a soft coal fire flickered with a point or two of flame; on the mantel a French clock of classic architecture caught the eye with the gleam of its pendulum as it vibrated inaudibly. It was all extremely well done, infinitely better done than Cornelia could have known. It was tasteful and refined, with the taste and refinement of the decorator who had wished to produce the effect of long establishment and well-bred permanency; the Mandan Flats were really not two years old, and Mrs. Maybough had taken her apartment in the spring and had been in it only a few weeks.[14]

The apartment shows off the decorator's achievement: an impression of refined luxury, with no one style predominating. Howells was right: professional interior designers were enablers, who allowed America's elite to become tastemakers by buying interior design.

-- --

[14] Howells, *The Coast of Bohemia*, 126–27.

WOMEN IN THE STUDIO—AESTHETIC EVANGELISTS

In 1878 William Brownell, writing in *Scribner's Monthly*, suggested an entirely different route that would produce tastemakers. "*Take care of the art-schools*. It is to these schools that one looks, both for accomplishment of good work and for the dissemination of aesthetic taste. Out of the schools should come, not only artists, but aesthetic evangelists."[15] In a short ten-year period, from the late 1870s to the late 1880s, America's varied art schools *did* play a crucial role in turning out "aesthetic evangelists." This happened in formal art academies, in schools that trained designers for industry, in classes for an impoverished genteel class, and in the art making and art collecting at America's nascent art museums. Americans learned how to make art and, in the process, cultivated their taste. Most of these pupils were women, and their education was bound up with thorny issues surrounding how the fine and decorative arts were going to develop in America in the wake of the Centennial.

[15] Brownell, "The Art-Schools of New York," 765.

The opportunities for education in the fine arts of painting and sculpture expanded in the 1870s. Chicago, San Francisco, Providence and St. Louis established schools while new schools appeared in the older art centers of Philadelphia, New York and Boston. The curriculum at older schools was also reinvigorated, with students following a systematic path from drawing, to modeling, to independent creative work, eventually under the tutelage of a master. These instructors were most often young men, just home after forming their own cosmopolitan art ideas through study and work in Europe. These were the very men who were establishing their own well-furnished studios. Women and men enrolled in the schools, but there was a tension between those pupils who hoped for careers in art (mostly but not entirely men) and the amateurs who had leisure and money enough to study art for its own sake (mostly women). For example, by 1883 over half the students at the Art Students League in New York City were women, many of them devoted pupils of William Merritt Chase. The Cowles Art School in Boston was modeled after the Art Students League with similarly coed classes. Typical of their social class, most of Chase's pupils married; and most never developed active careers as painters. Nonetheless, as women enrolled in art schools in increasing numbers, the schools became dependent upon their tuition and grew even larger.

Training for makers of decorative arts followed a different model, the one set by the British with the South Kensington system, of a matrix of school and art collection. At these schools, artisans were trained to take their places in industry, designing goods to be manufactured. By serving as models of excellence, the collections would be silent adjunct instructors. But here, too, women made inroads—and in some places they became the road builders. The classic pattern was cut by Helen Metcalf in Providence. As one of the forces behind Rhode Island's Women's Centennial Commission, in 1877 she took charge of the surplus from the Centennial to establish an independent school that would train artisans to work in industry and prepare those seeking to enter the fine arts. The new Rhode Island School of Design also collected art, including an ancient Italian amphora, seventy-one etchings by Salvator Rosa and a painting by Hudson River School painter Asher B. Durand. In these early years, the museum acquired plaster casts of famous sculptures, as did most museums in the era; the casts represented the world's great art and served as models for drawing and modeling classes. Classes in specific crafts were taught in addition to a fine arts curriculum, and Metcalf herself was a china painter of some distinction. The Metropolitan Museum of Art, founded in 1870, soon had an important collection of original art, casts and reproductions. It did not add its art school until 1880; the school emphasized industrial art education for men entering the trades. Classes for women in painting on silk, leather and glass were soon offered. An interior designer, Vincent Stiepevich, offered at least two classes in the design and rendering of interiors. Soon, the collections of the Metropolitan Museum of Art came to the fore and the commitment to teaching faded. But in the 1880s its museum school and the schools at other museums were major educators of handworkers, especially women.

There were other places where women got training in the decorative arts. Massachusetts led the nation when in 1870 it passed a law requiring that public school students learn mechanical drawing so they could help manufacturers. The Normal Art School offered free tuition to potential art teachers and soon its enrollment was 65 percent women. It trained a generation of art teachers and artists. The Women's Art School was established in 1859 as one branch of the Cooper Union in New York City. Through the 1860s it offered women a course of fine arts instruction to prepare them for practical careers in the arts, especially as illustrators and art teachers. In 1872, under the direction of Susan Carter, the

facing: An anonymous lady working in an art school, ca 1880s. During the Aesthetic movement, great numbers of women sought art training. Some received rigorous training in the basics of drawing and modeling; many also learned more specific skills in the decorative arts, such as painting on china or wood carving. This lady is drawing plaster casts of sculpture. (Collection of the author.)

school began a curriculum emphasizing the applied arts, including china painting and photograph processing and coloring. Within a few years, she also hired some of New York City's new generation of European-trained artists to teach courses in cast and life drawing. The Philadelphia School of Design for Women, an institution founded in 1844, pursued a similar course of applied-arts revamping after the Centennial. Both places were established for potential professional artists but were increasingly populated by amateurs.

Women art students in Cincinnati were especially fruitful; they were the force behind the founding of the museum and most decorative arts production. By 1873, two Englishmen, Benn Pitman and Henry Fry, were teaching courses in wood carving and china painting at the University of Cincinnati. Their pupils were so adept that their productions merited a special room in the Women's Pavilion at the Philadelphia Centennial. That project had been conceived and implemented by the students, who were mostly married ladies, pillars of society. Buoyed by their success at the Centennial, they formed themselves into the Women's Art Museum Association to found a combination museum and art school. In just over two years, they raised enough money and collected enough objects to ensure the success of the project. Woodcarving, decorative designing and metalwork were taught as well as painting and

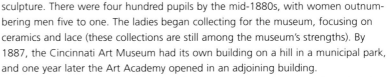

sculpture. There were four hundred pupils by the mid-1880s, with women outnumbering men five to one. The ladies began collecting for the museum, focusing on ceramics and lace (these collections are still among the museum's strengths). By 1887, the Cincinnati Art Museum had its own building on a hill in a municipal park, and one year later the Art Academy opened in an adjoining building.

And the women's legacy continued. The women wood-carvers of Cincinnati produced a multipaned monumental organ case for the new Queen Anne–style Music Hall. One of the ladies who exhibited ceramics and woodcarving at the Centennial, Mary Louise McLaughlin, pioneered a process for underglaze slip painting and wrote a treatise about it. She remained an active ceramicist, metalworker, woodcarver and printmaker. Maria Longworth Nichols exhibited her china at the Centennial and the next year her husband, George, published *Art Decoration Applied to Industry*, which advocated for artistic training to raise the quality of America's manufactured goods. As Cincinnati's power couple for cultural matters, they were *facing, top:* Dresser, by Benn Pitman, Adelaide Nourse Pitman and her sister, the painter Elizabeth Nourse, 1882–83. This dresser is one of the masterpieces of the Cincinnati art-carved furniture movement. Benn Pitman, an Englishman who came to Cincinnati to teach woodcarving, designed the dresser. His new wife, a Cincinnatian, carved it. And, her sister, the painter Elizabeth Nourse, executed the panels. Cincinnati art-carved furniture is noted for naturalistic carving, and here the naturalism is heightened by the painted scenes of daisies in spring and birds in the snow. The painted scenes may allude to the May-December marriage of the Pitmans; Adelaide was a generation younger than Benn. (Cincinnati Art Museum; gift of Mary Jane Hamilton in memory of her mother, Mary Luella Hamilton, made possible through Rita S. Hudepohl, guardian. 1994.62.)

facing, bottom: Vase, decorated by Maria Longworth Nichols Storer, for the Rookwood Pottery Company, 1882. This vase is an early piece by Maria Longworth Nichols (who later married Bellamy Storer). She made it shortly after she founded the Rookwood Pottery Company. She was among the leaders in a very active circle of women ceramicists in Cincinnati. Some worked as amateurs at home and in small clubs, others as professionals in the many small commercial kilns of the city. The vase is technically and aesthetically sophisticated. It uses the under-the-glaze technique that had been unveiled by Haviland, the French firm, and re-created by another Cincinnatian M. Louise McLaughlin. Nichols's vase, with its sea life caught under a net, takes its inspiration from Japanese illustration and ceramics. The long-lived Rookwood Pottery Company became a leading ceramics firm during the Aesthetic movement and the later Arts and Crafts era. (Cincinnati Art Museum; gift of Florence I. Balasny-Barnes in memory of Elizabeth C. and Joseph Balasny. 1992.86.)

above, right: The showrooms of the Society of Decorative Art in New York City, as seen in an article on the society published in *Scribner's Monthly Magazine,* vol. 22 (1881): 704. The Society of Decorative Art was organized to raise the quality of the decorative arts in America. One of its projects was a consignment salesroom that accepted only objects of high artistic quality. The bulk of the items for sale were designed and made by women.

squarely behind the new museum. In 1880, Maria founded a new pottery: Rookwood. Under her artistic leadership (she left the business side of things to male managers), the Rookwood became one of the country's leading makers of artistic pottery.

But what could be done for respectable women who had to earn a living by making art? Factory jobs, even painting china or hand coloring illustrations, were not suitable for such ladies. Candace Wheeler and a group of like-minded lady philanthropists gathered in 1877 to solve this problem by forming the Society of Decorative Art. The society would educate art workers, sell women's works and seek to elevate the quality of household decoration. This ambitious agenda spawned a complex menu of endeavors. The society taught classes, focusing especially on art needlework and pottery decoration. A committee of distinguished artists decided which art needlework designs would be put into production in the workshop. The workshop also produced needlework and decorative textiles that had been designed by leading interior designers. For example, in 1879 Louis Comfort Tiffany asked the society to execute a design for the stage curtain for Madison Square Theatre; this was the first major collaboration between him and Candace Wheeler. The society opened a salesroom for their own goods and accepted consigned goods that had passed muster with its artists' committee. The society formed a

Creating Artful Markets

A group of Aid to Artisans products from Bolivia, Colombia, Macedonia, Peru and South Africa. During the Aesthetic movement, the Society for Decorative Art created markets for artful goods, especially things created by women; today, Aid to Artisans does something similar. The group brings first-world retailers and marketers together with third-world artisans. The organization, headquartered in Hartford, Connecticut, with offices in eight countries, and programs in a dozen more, offers technical training in product development, business skills and marketing to artisans. One program brings artisans to the New York International Gift Fair, a huge trade fair for home furnishings. Grants for tools and supplies are also made. The artisans produce a range of products: batik pillow covers from Tanzania, woven wire bowls from the Zulu tribe of South Africa, palm baskets from Haiti, and the famous blue pottery of Istalif in Afghanistan. In fiscal years 2000–04, artisans generated retail business equivalent to $100 million U.S. dollars. Aid to Artisans calculates that during that period it aided ninety thousand artisans, and two-thirds of them were women. (© 2005 Jack MacConnell; courtesy of Aid to Artisans.)

membership and opened chapters—by 1880 there were thirty across America. To raise funds, the New York City chapter organized a loan show of antiques, drawing treasures from the city's best families; the event was repeated in New York and replicated in other cities. The society launched the *Art Interchange*, a national illustrated magazine on household craft, art and decoration. By 1882, the New York chapter ran a comprehensive lending library of books on all aspects of the decorative arts; it sent books through the mail all over the United States. These outreach activities were designed to help the average woman who had, as the annual report issued by the Boston chapter explained, "the instinctive desire to decorate their home" but lacked "the culture to do so with grace and charm."[16]

The Society of Decorative Art had a long life, but Candace Wheeler left it by 1880 to develop her expertise and business in textile design with Associated Artists and also to help found the Women's Exchange, a purely philanthropic organization that sold all sorts of women's productions. She found it difficult to reconcile the two aims of the society: promotion of artistic excellence and support of indigent middle class women. The Society of Decorative Art continued on its course, increasingly using their expertise as makers and consumers of decorative arts as a vehicle for enlarging women's cultural authority.

The era was deeply divided on the issue of whether art education should simply train art workers or labor more broadly to elevate aesthetic knowledge, especially among the women who would shepherd the cultural activities of the genteel middle class. Formal art schools trained potential professionals in the fine arts and those in aligned industries, like illustration. The South Kensington–type

[16] Boston Society of Decorative Art, *Annual Report*, 6; quoted in McCarthy, *Women's Culture*, 52.

museum schools—like the Rhode Island School of Design—were supposed to benefit industrial workers, while organizations like the Society of Decorative Art were supposed to assist genteel lady workers. The ladies entered these institutions with their own purposes. Some went looking for a profession: as art teachers, as illustrators—only a very few aspired to be easel painters or sculptors. Some were collectors and institution organizers, making decorative arts for their own homes even as they helped form the institutions that collected historic decorative arts. The young lady who had not yet found her talent or her husband could enroll in any of these schools. In the end, art education benefited everybody; it certainly produced ladies who felt better qualified to exercise their taste in their own homes.

HOUSEHOLD ART LITERATURE

The lady who simply hoped to make her home artful, but did not have the inclination to go to art school, or the money to hire a professional interior decorator, could instead read. In the wake of the Centennial came a tidal wave of books and magazine articles on the new topic of household art. These writings told the reader that she could, indeed, make a tasteful, beautiful, artistic home for herself. The books and articles spoke of general design principles, specific decorating tips and everything in between. Most were profusely illustrated. At least fifty household art titles were published in English between 1876 and 1890—and certainly hundreds of magazine articles were published in specialist art magazines, ladies magazines and magazines for a general readership. Not coincidentally, as the number of middle class homes and literate Americans grew in the late nineteenth century, the publishing industry boomed. The household art writings were one aspect of home advice literature that encompassed etiquette, cookery, domestic economy, child rearing, home entertainments—anything to do with the physical home and the activities that took place there. The household art literature was aimed squarely at the middle class homemaker, "the lady of the house," who sought to bring art into her home.

Four of the most popular household art manuals (left to right) *Beauty in the Household* by Maria Oakey Dewing (1882 edition), *The House Beautiful* by Clarence Cook (1881 edition), *How to Furnish a Home* (part of the Appletons' Home Books series) by Ella Rodman Church (1881 edition), and *Woman's Handiwork in Modern Homes* by Constance Cary Harrison (1881 edition). (Collection of the author. Photo: Thies Wulf and Egon Zippel.)

The best seller among the household art books was *The House Beautiful,* by Clarence Cook. The book, published in 1877, collected a series of essays published two years earlier in *Scribner's Monthly* titled "Beds and Tables, Stools and Candlesticks." The chatty tone of that title was carried over into the book. Cook walks through a house, from hall to bedroom, supplying suggestions along the way. Dozens of useful tips are offered (where to buy pretty rag rugs, a plan for a bookcase with removable shelves), anecdotes are told, poetry is inserted, and 111 evocative illustrations work like stepping stones in following Cook's line of thought. Cook is something of a name-dropper: he commends certain architects and artists and thanks the leading art-furniture retailers who had supplied his illustrations. Cook's book amplified many of the principles that

Much in Little Space.
No. 40.

Much in Little Space, by Alexandre Sandier, figure 40 in Clarence Cook, *The House Beautiful.* The attractive illustrations in the book helped to make it a best seller. Many of the images were supplied by Cook's artist friends, like Alexandre Sandier, who was a furniture designer (and eventually an artistic director at Sèvres), later employed by Herter Brothers in New York City. Sandier's illustration shows the Aesthetic movement talent for putting "much in little space."

Charles Locke Eastlake had advocated a few years earlier in his book *Hints on Household Taste*. We have already met Eastlake; his 1868 book inspired designers on both sides of the Atlantic to produce the angular "Modern Gothic" furniture that was quickly named after him. *Hints on Household Taste* was the pioneer household art book; *The House Beautiful* began to settle the territory. Like Eastlake, Cook advocated "honest" construction, convenient spatial arrangements and fitness of purpose in all articles. Unlike Eastlake, Cook endorsed many different historical styles. Both books went through many editions in America, and through the 1880s they led the household art book market.

Cook's writing was directed at urban dwellers in rented houses, but many suburban dwellers sought advice on construction, from the ground up, and architects stepped into the breach. With two books, Henry Hudson Holley supplied them with plans and elevations of suitable houses. Holley's *Country Seats* was another in a long line of architectural pattern books that stretched back to the eighteenth century, but it illustrated the new style that Edith Wharton was to dub "Hudson River Bracketed," a kind of American vernacular Queen Anne. Holley's next book *Modern Dwellings in Town and Country* named the new Queen Anne–style of domestic architecture and showed its suitability for the American landscape. Part two of his book dealt solely with furniture and decoration and included many room views. The format caught on, and by the early 1880s other architectural books informed the potential homeowner of the new artistic styles. William Tuthill's *Interiors and Interior Details* had elegant line drawings of Queen Anne interior detailing, while Albert Fuller and William Wheeler's *Artistic Homes in City and Country* (first published in 1882) offered drawings and photographs of exteriors.

Another group of writers drew upon history to offer authoritative household art advice. Harriet Prescott Spofford explained herself: "The private home is at the foundation of the public state, subtle and unimagined influence moulding the men who mould the state; and the history of furniture itself, indeed, involves the history of nations."[17] Cognizant that Americans were poised to shape themselves through their furniture, her *Art Decoration Applied to Furniture* gave a systematic history of furniture types, ending with chapters on the various rooms of the house and how they might be furnished. Bruce Talbert, an English architect/designer, wrote *Gothic Forms Applied to Furniture, Metal Work and Decoration for Domestic Purposes*, which did not itself have wide circulation in America, but it was copied widely. The book showed how the Eastlakian sensibility for Gothic design could be carried through to interiors and furniture. The entire text was pirated and augmented by American publishers while some furniture designs were used as templates by American makers. Uniting scholarship and commerce, American printmaker Louis Prang teamed with Austrian scholar Jacob von Falke to publish a deluxe color-illustrated edition of *Art in the House: Historical, Critical and Aesthetical Studies on the Decoration and Furnishing of the Dwelling*. Von Falke's historical accounts of the home combined with his recondite theories of interior design made a weighty contrast to the seductive illustrations.

By the early 1880s, a flood of affordable and readable household art manuals hit the American market. William Johnson Loftie edited a series called Art in the Home for MacMillan, a London publisher. Each small volume cost $1. Many of Loftie's titles, like *The Drawing Room*

-- --
[17] Spofford, *Art Decoration Applied to Furniture*, 232.

INTERIOR OF THE FIFTEENTH CENTURY.
From a French MS.

and *The Bedroom and the Boudoir*, addressed the English town house but all circulated in America. One of the earliest, Rhoda and Agnes Garrett's *Suggestions for House Decoration in Painting, Woodwork and Furniture* was picked up in 1877 by Philadelphia publisher Porter & Coates and went through many American editions. One of New York's premier publishers countered with its own series: Appleton's Home Books. These, too, were attractive and cheap, with handsome covers, useful ads and numerous illustrations. Ella Church's *How to Furnish a Home* was the quintessential utilitarian Appleton's book; its aim was "to indicate how a house may be made cheerful, home-like, and at the same time tasteful and artistic without large expenditure."[18] Most of the books proceed chapter by chapter through the rooms of house, offering tips and general rules. A few attempted instruction in aesthetic principles applied to design. Maria Oakey Dewing, a talented painter, began *Beauty in the Household* with chapters on color and form and an essay encouraging individualism in household taste. Most, however, operated on a more pedestrian plane but with enthusiasm. Almon Varney's *Our Homes and Their Adornments* (subtitled *Happy Homes for Happy People*), published in 1883, was a team effort by specialist authors. Its forty-six chapters were a step-by-step guide on how to make an artistic home, beginning with a consideration of architectural style, down to patterns for the crocheted tidies for the sofa arms. His preface states that his book will yolk "as in a *marriage tie*—this venerable and comprehensive word 'HOME' with that other word of classic mold, but of modern application,—'ADORNMENT' " (emphasis his).[19] Marrying home and art is indeed what the book sought.

After the flood of inexpensive generalist household art books came books on art crafts that could be mastered by the homemaker. In 1881, the author of one of these apologized for her contribution, noting, "The slate has been written and rewritten, and to a conscientious community like ours, that knows its Clarence Cook, there is little new to say." But Constance Cary Harrison did have something to say, with *Woman's Handiwork in Modern Homes*. About half of this book concerns needlework, with extraordinarily detailed diagrams, while another section, "Brush and Pigment," concerns painting on china, fans and fabrics. Another of the Appleton's Home Books, *Home Decoration*, by Janet Ruutz-Rees, covers virtually the same ground, but at a lower price and with fewer illustrations. And there were many, many more.

Interior of the Fifteenth Century, one the many historical interiors included in Jacob von Falke, *Art in the House*. Many of the household art manuals illustrated historic interiors, to be used as sources, or even models, for interior decor. The color plates for this edition of the book were printed by L. Prang and Company.

---

[18] Church, *How to Furnish a Home*, 8.
[19] Varney, *Our Homes and Their Adornments*, v.

INTERIOR - MORNING ROOM,
BY LOUIS C. TIFFANY

As a class, the household art books quickly disseminated the principles of artistic home design. The style of the artistic interior was described and illustrated. The room should be treated as set of structural planes: walls, floors and ceilings. These planes should be broken up by horizontal lines of chair rails, friezes and the like. The room should be darker at the base and lighten to the ceiling. The ideas of reformers from Morris to Eastlake were affirmed: the design of furnishings ought to accord with their use and the structure of furnishings should be evident. Like a conductor in charge of a polyphonic chorus, homemakers should achieve a sweet, complex harmony. Patterns should blend, rather than contrast. Sophisticated color harmonies should be established. Furnishing should be eclectic, but within limits. A Modern Gothic cabinet might be combined with wallpaper with a Byzantine motif, but Chinese elements would be too much. The books all had much to say on *the* critical element of an artistic interior: taste. Cook was the most assertive: "The point is: has the buyer taste? If he have, this book may perhaps be of some service to him in showing him how to use his taste in furnishing his house. If he have not, the author confesses, with humility, that he knows no way of inoculating him with it."[20] Other authors were a little more sympathetic. They felt that taste was a talent; it could be identified and cultivated. All the authors separated taste and money, insisting that it cost no more to buy lovely things than to buy ugly things. And, that was the point of their books—to encourage the reader to cultivate her own sense of beauty and put it to work in her own decor.

Does any of this sound familiar? House advice is now dispensed by dozens of television shows. Home-makeover shows can be found on prime time, on the lifestyle channels and on HGTV, a cable channel entirely devoted to the home. Like the

Interior—Morning Room by Louis Comfort Tiffany, color lithograph by Hatch Lithography Co., New York City, frontispiece to Constance Cary Harrison, *Woman's Handicraft in Modern Homes.* An artistic room would be a carefully composed symphony of many parts. This room features a transom undoubtedly designed by Louis C. Tiffany and curtains designed by Candace Wheeler (two of the partners in Louis C. Tiffany & Associated Artists) as well as a chair by fashionable British architect and designer E. W. Godwin. The small chair in the window bay is upholstered in green.

-- -- -- -- -- -- -- -- -- -- -- -- -- --
[20] Cook, *The House Beautiful,* 16.

Home Advice on the Airwaves

The bedroom of Kassandra Okvath, a project of the television show *Extreme Makeover: Home Edition*, from ABC, was shown in an episode that aired March 14, 2005. Home-makeover TV shows reach the same audiences served by Aesthetic movement household art manuals—middle class homeowners. Like the manuals, they teach good design and how to achieve it. Okvath's home was entirely rebuilt, reno-vated and redecorated over a seven-day period. *Extreme Makeover: Home Edition* combines good design with good works; the show makes over the homes of needy, deserving families. (© American Broadcasting Companies, Inc.)

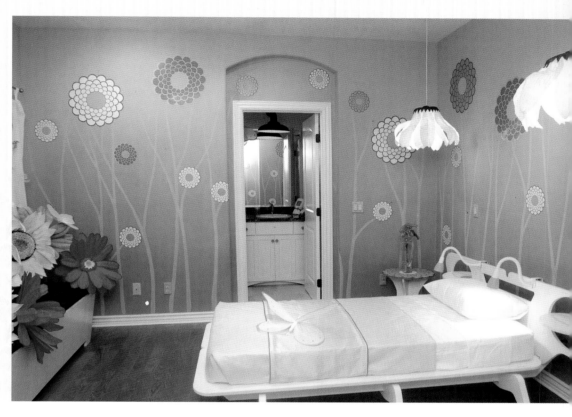

household art books, these shows offer instructions and inspiration to average middle class home-owners. Hosts demonstrate down and dirty tips like pouring concrete for garden walkways or building your own headboard (hosts often wield massive power tools). Many of the shows are pitched to specific audiences: *Designed to Sell* demonstrates quick and easy renovation tips that will make your house salable, *Rooms That Rock* lets teenagers work with designers on homemakers (parents can veto only one design element), and *Design on a Dime* appeals to anyone on a budget. All sorts of new style terms are invented: Cowboy Retro, Country Kitsch and Bachelor Funk. Many of the shows generate mild controversy (will the homeowner like the work of the celebrity host designer?) or pull on the viewer's heartstrings (will the nursery be done before the baby gets home from the hospital?). Almost all of the shows have a moment of high drama, "the reveal," when the newly redecorated space is unveiled and the audience gets to see the homeowner's reaction. Often, the moral of these shows seems to be that good taste may be relative but that bad taste is obvious.

CRITICS OF THE AESTHETIC MOVEMENT

At the same time that tastemakers were doing their work, critics were bashing it. There were playful jokes about the new movement, sensible objections, irrational complaints and even homophobic and racial slurs. Like many unfamiliar things, the new artistic movement was a lightning rod for the culture's insecurities. Notably, these caricatures appeared early; it did not take long for the artistic to have critics as well as fans.

Many thought that the new artistic movement would be merely a craze, with no intellectual rigor and certainly no staying power. Cartoonists launched attacks. In *Punch*, a British magazine, George Du Maurier (former roommate of Whistler in Paris) kept up a running attack on aestheticism in general and Wilde and Whistler in particular. His cartoons, published from 1874 until the mid-1880s (and reprinted in American newspapers and magazines) concerned Jellaby Postlethwaite, a poet, drawn to resemble Whistler, and Maudle, a painter, drawn to resemble Wilde. (Mixing up the two was yet another way to diminish them.) The cast expanded to include sycophants, especially Mrs. Cimabue Brown and her snobbish offspring. The cartoon characters live in Nincompoopiana, admiring sunflowers and using the buzz words of aestheticism: *consummate*, *intense*, and *too utterly utter*. In another long-running series for *Harper's Weekly*, Soloman Eytinge Jr. (surely a pseudonym?) used African Americans to satirize many aspects of the larger culture. One

Uncle Sam in an Aesthetic Parlor, a trade card copyrighted 1882 by E. B. Duval. This card implies that in America everything can be bought and the Aesthetic movement was part of the sales scam. This card was part of a series for collectors titled *National Aesthetics*. Here, a shrewd Uncle Sam sells all the clichéd Aesthetic movement objects: sunflowers, blue-and-white ceramics, a wobbly antique chair. Other cards in the series use aesthetic motifs to satirize the Irish, Germans, Chinese, French and Black Americans. (Collection of the author.)

cartoon *Decorative Art Has At Last Reached Blackville* aimed at aestheticism. It shows a black family in their own Nincompoopiana: a young man lunges at the wall with brush and maulstick in hand, an old man polishes a piece of bric-a-brac to ruins, and a proud man exclaims to two admiring ladies, "Dat Small Japan Jug Cum From De Ruins of Pompi." Gilbert and Sullivan's *Patience*, as we have seen, offered a whole evening out that spoofed the fad for the artistic. These were chuckles, knowing winks that communicated that aestheticism was just a harmless affectation.

Some criticism revealed more consequential bias: because aestheticism was a women's movement, it was ergo inferior. Editorials lamented "the vast horde of disorderly females who daub over plush and paint lilies of the valley on guitars."[21] Descriptions of this sort of heartfelt but hideous artistic decoration became stock-in-trade for writers poking fun at ineffective artistic women. Tellingly, the promotional tome issued by the Tile Club undermined the whole venture of male painters turning to the lady's work of tile painting. With tongue firmly in cheek, the book claims that the "decorative mania" of the era compelled the artists to steal tile-making equipment from their sisters, sweethearts and wives and constrain their great art ideas by painting tiles. All came out well in the end, though, because by sinking so low, the male artists were able to recapture the attention of their distracted patrons and reclaim the high ground of painting. Everywhere snide tone and humorous description conveyed the message: the concerns of female artist-decorators were simply not very important.

More informed critics worried that productive upper class artistic ladies had an unfair advantage in the marketplace. These amateurs took up space in art schools, competed with

-- --
21 Kurtz, "Women in Art," 10.

> They would gaze upon a lily, so "un-
> utterably utter,"
>   With eyes distended wide as if the
>   blossom they'd devour;
> 'Twas easy to believe they had relin-
> quished bread and butter,
>   And really lived on nothing more sub-
>   stantial than a flower.

An illustration by Walter Satterlee from "The Decorative Sisters," a poem by Jesse Pollard (NY: Anson D. F. Randolph & Co., 1881). The illustrated poem recounted the fate of two sisters, one doomed to a life as an artist's wife, the other saved by her marriage to an honest farmer. This page shows the beginning of the story when both sisters are captivated by aestheticism and gaze spellbound at a lily, one of the leitmotifs of the Aesthetic movement.

men in exhibitions and glutted venues like the Society of Decorative Art and the Women's Exchange. Those who needed to make their living through art—impoverished genteel ladies and honest laborers—were pushed out of the marketplace by these ladies who had education and productive leisure time on their side.

Many worried that the craze for the artistic was turning women into shopaholics. An 1880 editorial in *Lippincott's Magazine* (which developed a decidedly anti-aestheticism stance) warned that "this present epoch of artistic dress and household decorative art has brought on a dangerous craze. It is difficult to have a 'margin' with large milliners' bills and the habit of buying every 'sweet thing' in pottery and brass which offers."[22] A very unthrifty,

-- --
[22] L. W., "How We Spend Our Money," 122.

MOORISH ROOM. DECORATED WITH THE BIRGE VELOURS.
MANUFACTURED BY
M.H. BIRGE & SONS BUFFALO, N.Y.

silly lady appeared in an 1880 *Punch* cartoon, *Chinamania Made Useful at Last*; her fashionable dress is encrusted with plates and she wears a very cunning teapot hat. By 1899, Thorstein Veblen was to link women, aestheticism and wasteful spending in his theory of conspicuous consumption, *The Theory of the Leisure Class;* but for now the criticism was on the jocular plane.

A faint undertone in this chorus declared that the artistic life could draw women away from their natural duties as wives and mothers. An 1881 poem "The Decorative Sisters" contrasts the fate of two sisters who abandoned their comfortable home life when they became infatuated with aestheticism. One marries an artist and too late realizes she has consigned herself to a lifetime of artistic posturing; the other marries a farmer and lives inartistically but happily. Among the many trade cards showing women at home are a few with lady artists—one paints a portrait of her toddler, oblivious to his crying. Many cartoons satirized the lady studio visitor who lacked taste, implying that serious art patronage was beyond women; they belonged at home. But "The Decorative Sisters" was not a best seller, the trade card was one among many more favorable depictions of women artists, and ladies did go on visiting in studios. These sorts of complaints were few and faint.

To some, aestheticism was downright dangerous. It could be linked to drug addiction, neurasthenia and the era's tendency to degeneracy through over-evolution. A connection between artistic temperament and narcotics had long existed—Tennyson had romanticized it in "The Lotus-Eaters." The era of aestheticism was also the era of indoor culture and a leisure class that used alcohol, opium and morphine therapeutically. (Opium and its derivative laudanum were sold at drug stores.) But, some believed that the sensual parlors and smoking rooms produced by the new artistic movement were too easily coupled with drug use. The result was an indolent, sedated, unhealthy class. An 1882 poem in *Century Magazine* jokingly contrasted the vigorous life of a medieval knight with the modern aesthete: "All is now so faint and tender that the world has lost its gender / and the enervate Aesthetic is the model of the Age!"[23] Aestheticism could lead to gender confusion, making ladies too overbearing but, more dangerously, men too feminine. Witness Oscar Wilde's knee breeches and velvet jackets! A wonderful artifact plays upon the era's gender ambiguity, fears of unchecked Darwinian evolution and attraction to aestheticism. A double-faced teapot patented in 1881 by the Worcester Royal Porcelain Company shows, on one side, a Bunthorne-esque man with a sunflower, and on the other a Patience-bonneted young woman with a lily; whichever side is used the tea pours out through a limp wrist. The inscription on the teapot reads, "Fearful consequences through the laws of Natural Selection of Evolution of living up to one's teapot."

For these critics, the "I told you so" moment came in 1895 when Oscar Wilde was convicted in a London court of "gross indecency." Although Wilde married and fathered children, he had male lovers, including Lord Alfred Douglas. To end the affair, Douglas's father insulted Wilde publicly and Wilde took him to court for liable. The truth came out, and Wilde's homosexuality—criminal activity under English law—made the headlines. He was sentenced to two years of hard labor. His health failed, and he died in 1900 in exile in France. Wilde's trial was part of a larger cultural backlash against the artistic life that included publication of Max Nordeau's *Degeneration*, which argued that genius lay too close to neurosis. These events seemed to remove all doubts that aestheticism could lead to degeneracy.

But Wilde's disgrace was the very last chapter in the story of aestheticism. In the 1880s, the critics were minority voices. The culture at large clamored for more news of the artistic and how to achieve it. Tastemakers had done their work. The marketplace was ready to supply the need for the artistic.

facing: Moorish Room, decorated with the Birge Velours, a color supplement advertising wallpaper produced by M. H. Birge & Sons, from the Decorator and Furnisher, December 1885. One criticism of aestheticism was its tendency for hedonistic self-absorption and self-indulgence. Orientalist decor, with its overtones of life in the Middle East, connoted drug use, harems and other unspoken illicit behavior. In spite of these risqué associations (or because of them), Orientalist decor came into vogue during the Aesthetic movement; it was thought especially appropriate for smoking rooms.

23 "The Yearn of the Romantic," 959; quoted in Yount, " 'Give the People What They Want,' " 287.

NOTES ON SOURCES
Biographical information on Wilde is drawn from the excellent biography by Ellmann, *Oscar Wilde*, and the more recent cultural study by Blanchard, *Oscar Wilde's America*.

For Whistler's interiors, see Bendix, *Diabolical Designs*.

For a discussion of the reasons artists used elaborate studios, see Zukowski, "Creating Art and Artists." For an alternate viewpoint, see Burns, "The Artist in the Age of Surfaces," a chapter in *Inventing the Modern Artist*.

For a visual survey of high-style Aesthetic movement interiors, see *The Opulent Interiors of the Gilded Age* by Lewis, Turner and McQuillin, which reprints the photographs in *Artistic Houses*. For a discussion of the interiors, see an essay by Johnson, "The Artful Interior," in the Metropolitan Museum of Art's *In Pursuit of Beauty*. The careers of the tastemaking interior designers of the Aesthetic movement can be pieced together only through examining disparate monographic sources. Among the best are Frelinghuysen, "Partonage and the Artistic Interior," in Howe, et al, *Herter Brothers*; Peck and Irish, *Candace Wheeler*; Mayer and Lane. "Disassociating The 'Associated Artists.' "

Recent scholarship on art education during the Aesthetic era focuses on female students. See Swinth, *Painting Professionals*, and Prieto, *At Home in the Studio*.

The household art books are surveyed in an article by McClaugherty, "Household Art: Creating the Artistic Home, 1868–1893." See also the books themselves, cited in the footnotes for this chapter and in the bibliography.

Critiques of the Aesthetic movement can be found in Lambourne, *The Aesthetic Movement*, and in a study of the era as a consumerist impulse by Yount, " 'Give the People What they Want': The American Aesthetic Movement, and Art Worlds and Consumer Culture."

Selling *the Style*

facing: First page of an article on Cincinnati, from *Harper's New Monthly Magazine*, vol. 67, July 1883, 266. Pictures and words together conveyed ideas in the pages of the new illustrated magazines like *Harper's*. The illustrated magazines, an invention of American publishers, thrived in the post–Civil War period. For the first time, middle class readers could absorb images and texts simultaneously, and articles on the arts appeared in unprecedented numbers.

PICTURES IN EVERY HOME

After dinner, Mrs. Kenner settled into her easy chair to look over the new issue of *Harper's*. She treated herself to this evening every month. There were always interesting articles with excellent illustrations, several poems—old ones and new—book reviews, some political news and a few jokes and anecdotes from the Editor's Drawer. With a soft summer rain falling outside, in the light of her well-regulated oil lamp, she scanned the issue. She admired the full-page frontispiece by F. S. Church: an inquiring owl and a thoughtful woman perched together on a half-moon. Here was an article on the picturesque London suburb of Hampstead, another on the boomtown of Cincinnati, another on the Puritans and Quakers and another on old New Englanders—this last article had charming illustrations by Howard Pyle. She would return to the opinion piece on what education women ought to have in America—she wanted to read it carefully, as she had a definite viewpoint on the matter. She was happy to see the next chapters of "A Castle in Spain," a long, funny tall tale that she'd been reading aloud to Fred, her ten-year-old son. She examined Rosina Emmett's illustrations for Robert Browning's poem "Song"—the panels illustrating the young queen and her lovelorn servant boy did make a handsome page. She put a bookmark in the article on the Romanoffs; she would show it to Mrs. Federova, her downstairs neighbor who still had relatives in Russia. She thought her husband, who had just joined the civil service to work for the city of Chicago, would enjoy the article on political honors in China. It was a satisfying issue, as usual.

But it was the article on the principles for conventionalizing ornament that absorbed Mrs. Kenner's attention completely. Here was something of practical value! For some years, she had been designing her own embroidery patterns. Some had turned out very well, and her doilies and dresser runners had been accepted for sale at the New York showrooms of the Society of Decorative Art. But some of her embroidery had been rejected as "not show-ing the proper understanding of botanical forms." Looking carefully at these offending pieces, she had to admit that they looked clumsy. Perhaps this article would help her under-stand. It had diagrams and showed details of the lovely ornament in different objects: a Persian rug, a Japanese woodcut, a Renaissance bas-relief. One plate showed how a logical overall pattern had been derived from a drawing of peaches on a bough. She would surely get some good tips from this article.

All these articles appeared in the July 1883 issue of *Harper's New Monthly Magazine*. With a circulation of 175,000 annually in 1883, many Mrs. Kenners digested their monthly issues of *Harper's*. The magazine and others—*Century, Lippincott's,* two versions of *Scribner's, Frank Leslie's Illustrated Weekly* and *Harper's Weekly*—formed a new phenomenon: illustrated magazines pitched to the educated general reader. They offered a mix of literature, feature articles and poetry enlivened with black-and-white illustrations. The magazines covered the kind of not particularly timely but more in-depth news that the newspapers skipped. Editors

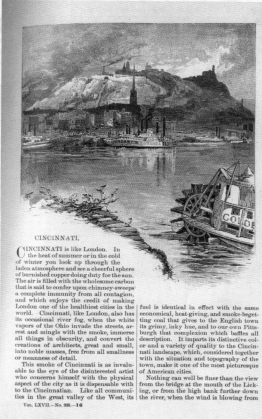

CINCINNATI.

CINCINNATI is like London. In the heat of summer or in the cold of winter you look up through the laden atmosphere and see a cheerful sphere of burnished copper doing duty for the sun. The air is filled with the wholesome carbon that is said to confer upon chimney-sweeps a complete immunity from all contagion, and which enjoys the credit of making London one of the healthiest cities in the world. Cincinnati, like London, also has its occasional river fog, when the white vapors of the Ohio invade the streets, arrest and mingle with the smoke, immerse all things in obscurity, and convert the creations of architects, great and small, into noble masses, free from all smallness or meanness of detail.

This smoke of Cincinnati is as invaluable to the eye of the disinterested artist who concerns himself with the physical aspect of the city as it is dispensable with to the Cincinnatian. Like all communities in the great valley of the West, its

VOL. LXVII.—No. 398.—16

fuel is identical in effect with the same economical, heat-giving, and smoke-begetting coal that gives to the English town its grimy, inky hue, and to our own Pittsburgh that complexion which baffles all description. It imparts its distinctive color and a variety of quality to the Cincinnati landscape, which, considered together with the situation and topography of the town, make it one of the most picturesque of American cities.

Nothing can well be finer than the view from the bridge at the mouth of the Licking, or from the high bank further down the river, when the wind is blowing from

expressed mildly progressive and not particularly surprising opinions in their columns. Racial and ethnic jokes, shocking to us, merely leavened the dough.

For days and months after she read *Harper's*, Mrs. Kenner recalled the pictures. She had a corner of her mind's eye filled with images from the illustrated magazines. She drew upon them for her embroidery. The images came back to her as she walked in the park or kneaded the bread. Mrs. Kenner was in the first generation that experienced this gentle barrage of pictures. Images were now everywhere. Not only in the magazines, but in the graceful flowers curling along the edge of the soap box, in the clever sketch of a lobster battling an octopus that ornamented the menu card in the department store café—images were even printed onto china. Nearly everyone she knew had a handsome color print in a gold frame, hung above the sofa. Whenever she left the house, especially when she went shopping, she saw pictures. So many pictures, and so many in the graceful new artistic style! Really, these days one could not avoid

seeing pictures. All these pictures added a lovely note to daily life.

During Mrs. Kenner's life, the technologies for making and multiplying images were revolutionized. For centuries, images had appeared on prints, but these had been expensive productions, based on hand printing from metal engraving plates or wood blocks. Photography had been around since Mrs. Kenner's childhood, but now it was much cheaper and many families could afford a trip to the photographer's studio. The 1880s was a decade of experimentation with photomechanical processes. With the invention of the halftone, images could be transferred to the printed page cheaply, quickly and in quantity. Durable zinc plates replaced lithography stones, which themselves had been easier to manipulate and more durable than metal and wood plates. By the 1890s, the process of transferring a photograph to printing plates was perfected, and the electrotype made the number of impressions from a single plate virtually limitless. With the introduction of steam presses, printing became mechanized. Copyright law was being written and enforced; illustrations and texts that publishers commissioned would not be at the mercy of piraters. Thanks to the new emphasis on art schools, a cadre of well-trained image makers existed. They joined the staffs of the magazines or worked freelance. Painters, sculptors, photographers and designers of all stripes contributed to the magazines. Montezuma, the pen name of editor/writer Montgomery Marks, patted himself on the back when in 1881 he described the network of publishers, editors, printers, engravers and artists who had made America the leader in the industry of illustrated periodicals.

ACCESSING THE ART WORLD

Through the illustrated periodicals, Mrs. Kenner and her fellow readers were the first Americans to have full access to the art world. Also in the 1883 issue Mrs. Kenner could read about traditional Indian metalwork and wood carving in an article written (and apparently illustrated) by J. L. Kipling. It showed a shield, spoons, bed chains and water vessels of many varieties, in fine detail. The final image was a carved teak screen by the Ahmedabad workshop organized by New Yorker Lockwood de Forest, whose woodwork was being used by Louis Comfort Tiffany's Associated Artists decorating firm. The letter "T" that began the article on "Recent Building in New York" was a drawing of a wrought-iron gargoyle. The article itself, by leading architectural critic Montgomery Schuyler, included elevations of town houses. The article on Cincinnati showed incidents of daily life, including a woodcut by Harry Fenn of a woman playing the magnificent new organ with its art-carved panels. Illustrations could be realistic: an engraving of a photograph of George Boughton's studio captured the reflections on his polished wood floor; or atmospheric: Edwin Austin Abbey's drawing of a prisoner's cell showed gloomy shadow and spotlighted paving stones. Each issue included a frontispiece of an artwork of some fame, engraved by another artist of note. The news of art was current, the illustrations showed what could be achieved in black and white by modern printing methods. Together, texts and images let the readers see art.

As daily and weekly newspapers flourished, art news and art images reached everyone. Weekly newspapers for towns with populations fewer than one hundred thousand tripled between 1870 and 1900. By the 1890s, the illustrated Sunday edition was in full swing. Cornelia Saunders, the heroine of William Dean Howells *The Coast of Bohemia* was an aspiring art student from a small Ohio town. She had learned all about the New York art world from her local paper, which carried features like "Gossip of the Ateliers," and "Glimpses of the Dens of New York Women Artists." Howells makes Cornelia a discriminating reader of the Sunday features section: "She did not believe it all; much of it seemed to her very silly; but she nourished her ambition upon it all the same."[1]

National weeklies, many offshoots of the large book and magazine publishing houses, were lively and well illustrated. Besides the usual news and illustrations, the weeklies had cartoons and sometimes color supplements. The news of Oscar Wilde's lecture tour, the grand new art museums (and the private houses that were the equal of them) being built in the big cities, the works of the world's leading painters and decorators—all the tastemakers were reported. There were other big "art" stories: the treasures brought out at the 1885 Pedestal Fund Loan Exhibition, major industrial expositions (the Cotton Centennial in New Orleans had a large section of Japanese art), the premier of Gilbert and Sullivan's *Mikado* in New York in 1885. A group of articulate and well-connected art critics published in magazines and newspapers: Richard Watson Gilder edited *Century* (and was married to artist Helena de Kay), Charles de Kay (Helena's brother) wrote for the *New York Times*, and Clarence Cook, advocate for aestheticism, was better known as a writer on the fine arts. In short, art and decorative arts were topics that lent themselves to illustration—in fact, good pictures could sell papers.

By the 1890s, at least fifty magazines on the visual arts were being published in the United States. This compares to six in the years 1840–50. The *American Art Review* was a dignified journal, with etchings bound in, while the *Studio*, edited by Clarence Cook, had more of the flavor of a New Yorker's insider opinion. The *Magazine of Art* and the *Art Journal,* two of the leading publications, were British, but offered broad overviews of European art developments and, for parts of their runs, American editions. The American circulation of the *Art Journal* was fifteen thousand. The art magazines covered both modern art and historic art and reported news of sales and exhibitions. There was much on the decorative arts. There were also combination literary and art magazines, portfolios and instructions of artworks for student copyists, and magazines for special audiences, like the publications issued by the larger art schools. These art magazines appealed to a generalist audience of collectors, practicing artists and art aficionados.

THE FIRST SHELTER MAGAZINES

For the homemaker seeking to make her home artful, there were household art magazines. These aimed to inform the homemaker about art made by artists and, more importantly, art she could make herself. They delved deeply into the issues treated by the household art manuals, like decoration, home crafts, connoisseurship and taste. These magazines were profusely illustrated, with expensive color supplements. All directed at buying, making, arranging and using household furnishings—artistically.

Many titles were available by subscription or at newsstands. The *Art Interchange*, a biweekly, was "An Illustrated Guide for Art Amateurs and Students, with Hints on Artistic Decoration" (as its masthead declared). The *Art Interchange* began as a publication of the Society of Decorative Art, but was continued under for-profit publishers. Part of each issue was devoted to readers' concerns about decoration. Beginning in January of 1886, this section was published independently as *Home Decoration*, leaving the original magazine to concentrate on art and art making. Another leader was the *Art Amateur*, a monthly devoted to "the cultivation of Art in the Household." The *Decorator and Furnisher* was begun in 1882 as a publication for homeowners and professional designers, and it lasted for five crucial years but apparently was too specialized and too costly to survive longer. There were also special-interest magazines for amateurs: *Clayworker*, the *Builder and Wood Worker*, the *Modern Priscilla* (for needleworkers). There

[1] Howells, *The Coast of Bohemia*, 80–81.

Cover of the *Decorator and Furnisher*, December 1883. Household art magazines, like the shelter magazines of today, were packed full of articles and pictures that offered decorating examples and advice.

were also trade publications read widely outside the trades: *American Architect and Building News* and even *Crockery and Glass Journal*.

The household art magazines had a predictable structure. There were feature articles, news notes, columns and responses to readers' questions. Typically, a third or more of the editorial space was devoted to illustrations. Some illustrations stood alone; others accompanied a text. If she bought the *Decorator and Furnisher*, Mrs. Kenner might find a long article on Celtic ornament. In the *Art Amateur*, she would see articles on the masters of traditional pictorial genres, such as flowers, animals and marine scenes. She could count on reviews of important art books and art exhibitions. There would be news on art issues, like how tariffs were hurting American expatriate artists. She would have looked to household art magazines for their specialty: detailed instructions and full-scale patterns for complicated projects, like china painting, embroidery and painting on cloth. After some years of faithful reading of the sections on home decorating, she would have become thoroughly educated on decorating issues. Over time, all various elements of a room would be discussed individually and the decor of new, exemplary houses illustrated. There was much space devoted to extraordinarily specific questions from readers: "What shade of wall and ceiling paper would be most suitable for a room carpeted with light-colored Brussels, of which the most prominent colors are red and olive shades, and the furniture of which is black walnut upholstered with crimson plush with trimming of olive green plush?" (The answer: walls to be olive, ceiling a much lighter shade of olive.) The household art magazines were generally large format, with small type that was relieved by much white space around the illustrations.

Household art magazines usually had color supplements—these were a big draw. These were high-class chromolithographs, many of which were nice enough to keep and frame. One month the *Art Interchange* cautioned its readers to look out for the upcoming color supplement of pink roses; past experience had shown that their popular supplements, packaged in their own wrappers, were easily purloined. (The author notes that the trend continues; few color supplements are today still with their parent issue—though we know they existed because they are listed in the table of contents.) The value of the color supplements, beyond their sheer decorative appeal, was pedagogic. They were to be studied and copied, often into a different media. Elsewhere in the magazine the reader would find detailed instructions for how to render the image, perhaps in watercolor, perhaps in embroidery, perhaps in oils. Particular tints of paint, specific tones of embroidery thread and step-by-step instructions would be given. The most popular topic for color supplements were probably floral arrangements, but animals, portraits of children, ornamental patterns and realistic (if romantic) images by modern artists were also given. Historical art and allegorical devices were rare.

The advertisements in household art magazines revealed the nature of the reader. And these ads, unlike the ads in the illustrated periodicals, were often illustrated. There were ads for standard art supplies, such as drawing pencils, watercolors and modeling clay. There were

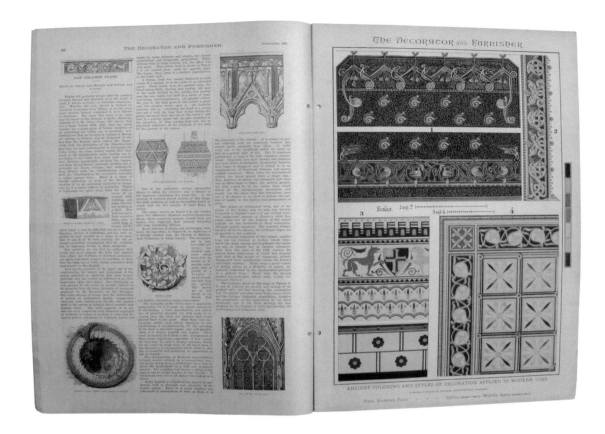

An article on Celtic ornament, with its accompanying
color supplement by Rafael
Gustavino, from the
Decorator and Furnisher,
December 1883. Household
art magazines included lavish
color supplements like this
one. This supplement was
part of a series on historical
ornament. Each month
readers were treated to a
color plate featuring a different epoch. Readers could
use the plates as takeoffs for
their own designs. The supplements were suitable for
framing all by themselves.

ads for specialized art supplies, like home kilns and wood-carving tools and all sorts of
embroidery flosses and crochet yarns. There were many ads for stamping patterns (which
allowed a pattern to be transferred onto another surface). There were ads from instructors and art schools. General-interest magazines took ads that listed their art-oriented
articles. There were ads for narrative art books, instructional art books and even other
household art magazines. Decorators, art dealers and antique dealers advertised.
Manufacturers of stained glass, artistic metalwork, tiles and picture frames advertised.
There were a few ads for household articles, like the ubiquitous Pear's Soap. A picture
emerges: the reader of household art magazines was a middle class woman who wanted
art information and made art for her home.

SHELTER MAGAZINES TODAY

Statistically, the reader of today's shelter magazine is also likely to be a middle class
artistic woman. This a boom time for shelter magazines, as a trip to the magazine
section of any superstore bookstore will show. Industry analysts guess that the popularity of shelter magazines stems from the post-9/11 nesting instinct and the subsequent
real estate market boom. Now, a huge percentage of everyone's net worth is tied up
in real estate—specifically, their houses. It makes sense to invest in house remodeling and

household furnishings, to develop house envy and even to harbor house fetishes. The shelter magazine market has segmented to meet these desires. Old-school house envy is satisfied by the doyennes among the shelter magazine: *Better Homes and Gardens* (established in 1923, with a circulation of 7.6 million in March 2004) and *House Beautiful* (begun in 1896), a survivor from the end of the Aesthetic era. A more dignified and pricier sort of house envy (mansion envy, really) is satisfied by *Architectural Digest, World of Interiors* and a host of foreign imports, such as *Elle Decor Britain* and *Abitare*. All these magazines weren't appealing to the younger downtown-oriented homemaker, who has less to spend. So, new-school house envy magazines were born. *Elle Decor* was first to enter the field, in 1989, and it now competes with *Metropolitan Home, O at Home* (Oprah Winfrey's offering), and the newest entry, *Domino*, a self-declared "magalog"—a combination magazine and catalog featuring home furnishings. Numerous niches have established themselves. The homeowner on a strict budget is served by *ReadyMade, Real Simple* and (what else?) *Budget Living*. Americans' urge towards informality has made "country" style a big seller—thus *Country Living, Country Home* and *Cottage Living*. The renovator is served by *This Old House*. Lifestyle magazines often have shelter features; a yoga magazine will run a feature on a particularly Zen-like bathroom. *Better Homes and Gardens* publishes a fleet of special-topic magazines: *BH&G Kitchen, BH&G Garden Deck and Landscape, BH&G Do It Yourself*. It is a fluid statistic, but somewhere in the neighborhood of one hundred design magazines are now published in the United States. Many of these shelter magazines are part of larger shelter media market that includes TV shows, books, Web sites, blogs and the Home section of most major metropolitan newspapers.

During the Aesthetic era, magazines hounded potential subscribers, just as they do now. The *Art Amateur* sent postcards to potential subscribers, offering four trial issues for a discounted price if they returned the special offer card. The *Decorator and Furnisher* offered valuable prizes for signing up subscribers; if a reader persuaded ten friends to subscribe, she got a stained-glass panel or a sofa pillow. Flash forward more than a century: "Dear Friend: If I'm right about you, you're different. You're one of the few who strives for the authentic. . . . You reject style for its own sake. You're design savvy and unabashedly modern." This is from the subscription letter from *Dwell*, a magazine focusing on modernist homes. Bribes, flattery and desperate tactics have always been used to sell shelter magazines.

COLOR, COLOR EVERYWHERE

The color supplements that appeared in household art magazines were one of the most visible manifestations of the color-printing revolution that occurred during the Aesthetic movement. Color lithography, along with photomechanical processes for black-and-white images, became quicker and cheaper. The mechanization of printing processes and the development of new inks and design strategies made multicolor, many-stone lithographs possible. These chromolithographs could be printed onto paper (and menu cards, decals for ceramics and soap boxes) in any scale. Painting-sized chromolithographs became cheap enough to give away. Color supplements began appearing in art periodicals and main-line illustrated magazines. Samuel Clemens (Mark Twain), always the perspicacious cultural commentator, described his East Hartford home: "You couldn't go into a room but you would find an insurance-chromo, or at least a three-color God-Bless-Our-Home over the door—and in the parlor we had nine."[2] Some growled that a chromolithograph was simply a cheap substitute for a real artwork; in 1874, an American commentator used the term "chromo civilization" to make an analogy between this sort of sham art and the country's distressing satisfaction with an easygoing moral value system.[3] Nonetheless, for better or worse, chromolithography was the key technology that brought color images into American homes.

ARTFUL ADVERTISING FOR THE ARTFUL HOMEMAKER

Art news in illustrated periodicals, household art magazines, shelter magazines—then and now these put the new aesthetic front and center for readers, right where readers expected to find news of the new aesthetic. But, design trends also reach people who are not looking for them. Americans encounter everyday graphic design everywhere. In the late nineteenth century, the design formulas of aestheticism, elegant and *new*, likewise appeared everywhere: in the rich colors of the trade card that came with your thread; in the borders and background pattern of the theater poster for the *Mikado*; on the stylized cattails adorning the cover of your child's new arithmetic textbook. Even on the curtains, carpet, plates and drinking glasses in the railroad cars. Just by living, people experienced this new aesthetic; it presented itself at every corner; it was inescapable. Now, every flat surface could be ornamented with imagery. Color was now available cheaply; the shadow world of

[2] Schlereth, *Victorian America*, 194.
[3] Godkin, "Chromo-Civilization," 201–2.

black-and-white design was suddenly vivified. Aestheticism simply and subtly permeated graphic design.

This was no coincidence. As American industry ramped up, manufacturers wanted to reach buyers, so the profession of advertising invented itself. Before the Civil War, advertising was scarcely necessary because few commodities were sold directly to consumers. Flour, sugar, soap, textiles and sewing notions were all bought in bulk by retailers and sold unpackaged (if they were not made at home). With the expansion of American manufacturing, uniform products were ensured, and with vastly improved transportation networks, these products could be brought to market; quality and distribution were accomplished. The now-familiar concept of a "brand name" as the key to product identity came into being. Brand names multiplied. Manufacturers turned to adverting to make their brands known. Between 1870 and 1900, the volume of advertising vastly expanded; some historians measure a ten-fold increase. Graphic design became a handmaiden to advertising. So, motive (manufacturers want to reach buyers) and means (advertising by means of eye-catching graphics) were in place.

The final leg of this three-legged stool was the audience—the homemaker. Much of what was being advertised were household goods, and women ran the households. The whole enterprise of advertising—the hard sell, the dickering, the near falsehoods—was faintly scurrilous and distinctly unfeminine. But, aesthetic graphic design could overcome this hurdle. Aestheticism could be pitched to the superior taste of ladies. It could be used to connote that a product was morally superior. It could distinguish a product as classy. It was deployed accordingly. The confluence of motive, means and message led to aesthetic graphic design.

INCIDENTAL AESTHETICISM—TRADE CARDS, SCRAPBOOKS AND GREETING CARDS

All the stars aligned by the early 1880s to make trade cards the exciting new method of advertising and one especially suited to aesthetic graphic design. Few alternatives existed—there were not many advertising vehicles. Most newspapers ran ads as small blocks of un-illustrated black-and-white typography. Many periodicals did not accept advertising at all; they did not want to deliver commerce to their subscribers. Outdoor advertising (signs painted on rocks, posters, men with signboards) was déclassé and reached a limited audience. Small, free-standing, easily distributed advertisements made sense. It was now possible to print illustrations, and, best of all, print them in color. Manufacturers and retailers could afford to use multicolor lithography for bulk quantity printing. There was a precedent: business cards illustrated with engravings. Distribution was easy: stacks of cards could be distributed by the jobbers who called on retailers and took stocking orders. The trade card was born. These giveaway premiums were attractive enough to save and collect. Aesthetic designs in living, vivid color distinguished a product. An artistic trade card could sell something.

The typical trade card was printed in color on stiff paper and measured about half the size of a modern postcard. The trade card manufacturers built upon the technological knowledge gained by printing large-scale, many-color chromolithographs suitable for the parlor. The leading chromolithograph printer, Louis Prang, also led the way in trade cards by entering the field early and by making stylistic innovations. Immediately, other printers entered the trade card field. Boston, New York City and Philadelphia had numerous firms, and other cities with large German populations (German workers dominated the color printing industry), such as Cincinnati and Pittsburgh, also had important printers. Most cards were designed by printers, who left a blank space where the manufacturer or retailer's name could be added, usually long

facing: Five trade cards from the late 1870s and early 1880s. These are part of the first wave of trade cards that flooded America during the Aesthetic movement. The card with Chinese acrobats is an early trade card produced by the firm of Louis Prang; it is trademarked 1878. The firm may also have produced the card for Mme Demorest's Reliable Patterns—it has the deep, rich colors typical of Prang's printing. The card with the blank blue field has not yet been imprinted with an advertiser's name. (Collection of the author.)

Cover and a page from a scrapbook compiled by Elmer L. Wengren, Portland, ME, 1882. Pretty pictures, now ubiquitous in culture of advertising, were assembled in scrapbooks during the Aesthetic era. This scrapbook was proudly inscribed by its owner who collected trade cards and pasted them into the book in artistic patterns. (Collection of Lester Barnett. Photo: Lester Barnett.)

after the first round of color printing. Thus, the same design could be used to advertise different products—a card showing a few chicks in a wooden shoe floating down a river was used by a butcher and, with the addition of the slogan "We are Bound for the Land of Promise," by a railroad. Cards could be ordered for as little as $3.25 for a thousand. The price depended on the amount of color and typographic complexity.

Louis Prang noted, "Hardly a business man in the country has not at one time or another made use of such cards to advertise his wares."[4] Prang was in a position to know; he printed a significant percentage of them. The vast majority of trade cards advertised household goods, and the most competitive companies produced the most cards. Thread, patent medicines, packaged food, stoves, garments (men's collars and cuffs, shoes, corsets)—all appeared on trade cards. Some manufacturers distributed both artistic and nonartistic cards, hedging their design bets. Retailers also used them, as did some makers of goods marketed to men (wagons, tractors, nails, tools) and a few service-oriented businesses (hotels, railroads). Trade cards were collected by adults and children. They provided a powerful incentive to buy one brand over another.

The growing business of trade cards coincided with and even fueled the popularity of scrapbooks; printers began producing "scraps" for collectors. Scraps were bits of paper printed with some picture. They were destined for scrapbooks, homemade cards and all sorts of imaginative

-- --
[4] Jay, *The Trade Card in Nineteenth-Century America*, 36.

Three greeting cards. The card with a silhouette is by Bufford, a Boston publisher; the other two are unmarked. Greeting cards, rare before the Aesthetic era, took advantage of all the new printing and decorative methods, including metallic inks, fringe, embossing and cutwork. (Collection of the author.)

uses, like doll houses and decoupage projects. Scraps were usually small-scale, color-lithography-printed, die-cut pieces of paper; they were often in complex shapes. Flowers, birds, children and ladies in historic dress were common themes, and any one of these could be rendered artistic by its design. Some scraps were printed in series and meant to be collected. The line between a trade card and a scrap was indistinct since both were collected for reuse. Many trade cards never had their advertising slogan imprinted, so they functioned as scraps. Scraps were distinguished because of their especially fine printing that used a wide range of colors and metallic inks.

While trade cards are no longer produced, the hobby of scrapbooking is alive and well today. In 2004, scrapbooking was a $2.5-billion-a-year industry in America; analysts estimated that one in four households participated in the hobby. It supports hundreds of Web sites, mail-order houses and stores that offer advice and supplies. It is a feminine hobby, centered on the endeavor of memory-making. Women of all ages meet in houses and scrapbooking stores for an evening of composition—selecting, cutting, flattening, pasting. Many scrapbooks commemorate an event or a person. They use photographs, invitations, ticket stubs, pressed flowers—the ephemeral things of life that might otherwise be tossed. This stew of personal ephemera is organized onto special papers, headed with text and supplemented with narrative. Scrapbookers learn graphic design as they go along, and artistic expression is poured out on these memory books.

Cheaper chromolithography launched another industry that depended on artistic graphic design: greeting cards. Here, too, Louis Prang led. In 1874, he printed a Christmas message on one of his trade cards in the space intended for the advertiser. The cards sold well. Many printers followed suit. Prang, known for his especially artful printing, aggressively pursued the market through artistic designs. From 1880 to 1884, Prang sponsored a competition for the design of Christmas cards. The prize money was generous, the judges were well-known artists (including John La Farge, Louis Comfort Tiffany and Edward Chandler Moore, the chief designer at Tiffany & Company), leading poets were paid for their verses, and, best of all, the winning drawings and paintings were reproduced by the thousands as cards. No wonder that America's leading artists and illustrators competed! Whether Prang specified it or the judges chose it, Prang's greeting cards of these years were distinctly aesthetic, with stylized imagery set in cartouches, asymmetric touches and the artistic palette. The winners constitute an honor roll of practitioners of the new aesthetic look: Rosina Emmett, Alexandre Sandier, Elihu Vedder, Dora Wheeler, Charles Caryl Coleman. Prang and others produced cards for Christmas, New Year's Day, Valentine's Day and Easter as well as cards with generalized well wishes that were good all year round. The better cards required twenty different lithography stones to produce all the colors and tones. Some were multi-panel affairs that stood up on their own, or were fringed, tasseled, cut-worked or otherwise ornamented.

A group of books with artistic design. (top to bottom) *A Family Flight Around Home*, by Rev. E. E. Hale and Susan Hale (Boston: D. Lothrop and Company, 1884); *Flowers from Dell and Bower*, by Susie Barstow Skelding (NY: White, Stokes & Allen, 1886); two pages from *Leisure Hours*, an illustrated poetry book, edited by Daphne Dale (Philadelphia and Chicago: Elliott & Beezley, 1889); and *Practical Arithmetic* by H. Duemling (St. Louis: Concordia Publishing House, nd). Many books published during the Aesthetic era used the new graphic style on their covers. Even *Practical Arithmetic*, a book of arithmetic exercises, could look more attractive if the cover was treated artistically.

Artful Graphic Design and Everyday Life

Artistic graphic design was used so often in printed matter, it became an everyday fact of visual life. Artistic graphic design could add *caché* to premiums: calendars, bookmarks, Sunday school certificates of merit; it could cut through the hubbub of the urban scene: posters, shop signs, circulars. When the publisher of *Beautiful Homes: How to Make Them* reissued this 1878 book in 1885, he gave it a handsome new mustard-colored cloth cover, ornamented with decorative bands and a Japonesque cherry branch in a pot. The text remained exactly the same; its old-fashioned advice did not match the cover. Vast numbers of titles published in the 1880s have aesthetic covers—the strategy must have sold books. More and more of the incidentals of daily life were made elegant with artistic designs.

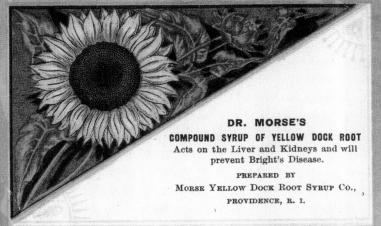

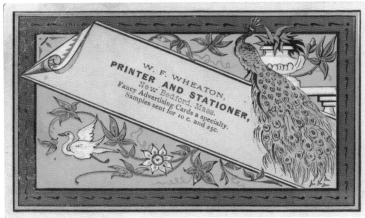

Six trade cards, by various printers, all dating ca 1885–91. These cards, produced at the height of the Aesthetic movement, are a catalog of artistic graphic strategies and motifs. Asymmetrical compositions, grayed colors and metallic inks—all are seen here, as are many of the clichés of the aestheticism: a peacock, a flying crane, a sunflower. Many of the trade cards even treat their products a bit irreverently (note the spool of thread transformed into a paper lantern), but the final design is undeniably artistic and attractive. (Collection of the author.)

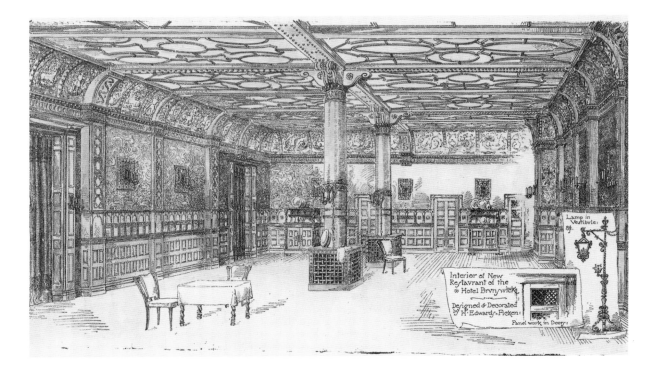

Interior of New Restaurant of the Hotel Brunswick, illustration by H. Edward Ficken, from *American Architect and Building News* 12, no. 353 (September 30, 1882), later hand-colored by an unknown artist. Many people first encountered the new aesthetic style in public spaces, like hotel restaurants. The Hotel Brunswick, located on Fifth Avenue, between Twenty-sixth and Twenty-seventh Streets, was one of many fashionable hotels in the Ladies' Mile area of New York City. Its artistic dining room was designed by H. Edward Ficken, who also designed the interior of the American Art Galleries. This illustration was published as a supplement in a magazine and then hand-colored by a reader; the colors more or less match the published description of the room.

Periodical illustrations, trade cards, book bindings, greeting cards—the explosion of printed matter with the new style of graphics codified the conventions of artistic design. The picture plane was flattened and broken into asymmetrical segments, and images were rendered as stylized forms and set into the segments—as pictures within pictures. Much imagery was derived from the Orient: fans, kimonoed ladies, cranes, patterns taken from Japanese textiles. Certain motifs became clichés of the aesthetic graphic design: the sunflower, the peacock, and Oriental imagery. Artistic graphic design began to pass into the realm of the abstract. The imagery on trade cards often had scant relationship to the product advertised. There were weird juxtapositions of scale, bizarre imagery, abandonment of logical perspective and unnatural color. Aesthetic graphic design rendered whatever it ornamented as modern, sophisticated and advanced.

The Americans who lived through the end of the nineteenth century were the first people to be visually literate, and the conventions of aesthetic design became a part of their vocabulary. The reach of illustrated periodicals, household art magazines, trade cards, greeting cards and other printed matter into the range of the average American's vision was breathtaking. For the first time on a large scale, images and texts were linked in printed materials. Together, pictures and words conveyed meaning. As a team, pictures and text communicated quickly—useful in a country full of immigrants who were not yet literate in English, a country with a large young population, an urbanizing country where the pace of life was ever quickening. And, artistic images were everywhere. These images amplified the meaning of popular poetry and literature in illustrated periodicals. The artistic images on trade cards could induce you to buy a product. The artistic images in household art magazines could provide instruction in a practical art or educate the eye in the ways of good design and beauty. Artistic images gave pleasure and provided diversion. Artistic imagery grabbed the eye and made it linger. The color, line, patterning, textures, reflective surfaces and strange imagery were seductive. Americans could enjoy artistic imagery as pure design, as art for its own sake. Artistic imagery turned Americans into a visual people.

THE NEW AESTHETICISM IN PUBLIC PLACES

Mrs. Kenner's long-awaited trip to New York City was finally here. Today, she planned to take her husband around town on a day devoted to the fine arts. Her first stop of the morning was the American Art Galleries, which specialized in American paintings. There were several different rooms displaying art, including a circular reception parlor lined with gold velours and cherrywood display cabinets. The decor was vaguely Moorish, with woodwork in dull gold, and various shades of red in the carpet and curtains. All in all, she felt it was a bit too gaudy. This year, the American Art Galleries had instituted a "Prize Fund" scheme, which, through a fund solicited from wealthy connoisseurs, bought American paintings and distributed them to American museums. Mrs. Kenner saw paintings and watercolors that had been entered in the Prize Fund competition, gathered back from prior exhibits in Louisville, St. Louis and her hometown, Chicago. The art was simply splendid—and, she was proud that it was all produced by Americans. Just down the street they went to the National Academy of Design, its Venetian Gothic architecture said to be influenced by Mr. Ruskin's writings. Here, they saw more work by American painters in the autumn exhibition of members' work. The next stop was the Union League Club for its ladies' day; the gallery and an assembly hall would be open. The new clubhouse, opened in 1882, was quite a showplace for the new decorators. The gallery was indeed very pretty, but Mrs. Kenner was chagrined she could not see the rest of the building. Mr. Kenner could—he took a tour of the whole place, escorted by his cousin, who was a member. As planned, Mr. Kenner took mental notes, and then immediately

Spreading the New Style

The bar of Nobu 57, Manhattan, New York City. During the Aesthetic era, restaurants attracted customers with up-to-date decor; restaurants still use this strategy. The Nobu franchise of restaurants began in the Tribeca neighborhood of New York City and has since exported that "upscale downtown" style of decor to Las Vegas, Milan, Miami and now uptown to Fifty-seventh Street in Manhattan. Nobu 57, designed by the Rockwell group, features an onyx-and-walnut bar, walls shingled in reclaimed wood, a ceiling of abaca rope wrapped around wire frames and thousands of abalone shells dangling from the chandeliers. (Photograph © Scott Frances.)

met Mrs. Kenner at lunch and told her all about the rest of the building. The clubhouse was quite extravagant and unorthodox: a green-and-silver color scheme in the hallways (by Mr. Tiffany); a classical library, with its paneling and Queen Anne chairs (by Mr. Cottier); a barrel-vaulted dining room on the top floor (overseen by Mr. La Farge). The dining room was the most impressive, with a great deal of oak, gilt and blue glass tiling. Mrs. Kenner was especially disappointed to miss the dining room curtains, a famous set by Mr. Tiffany and Mrs. Wheeler, all of embroidered plush upon plush, each a different set of flowers and fruits. Mr. Kenner was full of praise for a little window on a little landing, by Mr. Tiffany; its simple design had luminous colors.

After lunch, Mr. and Mrs. Kenner went to a matinee at the Madison Square Theatre. The play *Saints and Sinners* was quite fine, but Mrs. Kenner was most impressed by the stage curtain, which she examined minutely during the intermission. This was another grand needle-work production of Mrs. Wheeler and Mr. Tiffany and their firm of Associated Artists. The curtain depicted a rich tropical river scene, with the river composed of blue velvet and water flowers in plush appliqué. Satin was also used liberally, and the textures and stitchery made the whole curtain shimmer. And, best of all, Mrs. Kenner discovered that the curtain itself was shown on the program; she could put this keepsake in her scrapbook. After the play, Mr. and Mrs. Kenner had just enough time to take a hack up to the Metropolitan Museum of Art, to its headquarters all the way uptown in Central Park, to look at the extensive collection of lace. Mr. Kenner was exhausted, and Mrs. Kenner was exhilarated. They both agreed that a quiet dinner in the hotel would be in order.

Mrs. Kenner and her fellow Americans became a visual people when they went out into their world and looked around. Mrs. Kenner's world, like most of her fellow Americans, was urban; she was presented with a panoply each time she left home. As an embroiderer, Mrs. Kenner planned her trips, whether to New York City or just downtown Chicago, to see the latest artistic needlework. But she saw many other things whenever she went downtown to shop or to go to a restaurant, exhibition or the theater. Other Americans might not have had the new artistic design in mind when they went downtown or to a fair, but they would have seen it nonetheless. The new design could be seen in the architecture and furnishings of fashionable clubs and restaurants, and it stocked the shelves in stores. The new taste for antiques and exotic art was inescapable in art exhibitions. The new artistic movement was a part of urban life.

BAZAARS, FAIRS AND LOAN SHOWS

In a repeat of the pattern set at the Philadelphia Centennial, the new art movement was on display when Americans went to the fair—and go to the fair they did! The artistic era was a time of huge international expositions, larger fairs organized by mechanics institutes and trade groups, medium-sized loan exhibitions, small county fairs and tiny ladies' bazaars. At the major international fairs, the latest industrial processes (many applied to household goods) could be compared across global markets. Handmade ethnographic curiosities from around the world were always on view, and the displays of contemporary and historic art amounted to international competitions. America hosted the World's Industrial and Cotton Exposition, which was held in New Orleans in the winter of 1884–85; Paris held an Exposition Universelle in 1878 and 1889; and, in 1893, Chicago held the biggest and grandest—the World's Columbian Exposition. The new art movement was also to be seen at fairs organized by trade groups, mechanics institutes and business leaders. The 1883 Cincinnati Industrial Exposition, for example, showcased the city's fertile ceramics scene, which was rapidly advancing through the efforts of both amateurs and businesses. These local fairs, often annual events, offered a selection of the world's products and could spotlight significant local achievements. The arts, horticulture and ladies' work were usually classed and judged along with the machinery and other products. At an even more local level, county fairs had halls on agriculture and household production; new strains of corn and new embroidery stitches won blue ribbons. Fair going was common, even for rural folk, but if you couldn't get to the fair, it was amply documented with words and pictures in newspaper articles, illustrated magazines, stereographs and all the other burgeoning media of the era.

Loan shows were held in big cities. The leaders of charitable organizations and civic causes, always prominent citizens, found that they could borrow art and antiquities from their friends and thus produce a spectacular exhibition. These loan shows became common during the 1880s and through them the paying public saw much art that was otherwise kept behind closed doors. In 1885, the cream of New York's art world organized the Pedestal Fund Loan Exhibition to raise money to build the base to Bartholdi's Statue of Liberty. Art was borrowed from collectors, dealers and directly from the artists themselves. The variety was staggering: paintings, old prints, illuminated manuscripts, costumes, stained glass, lace, musical instruments, old china, arms and armor, Oriental art, American Indian objects, old jewelry and silver, modern and antique embroideries and tapestries. It was an opportunity to see the most avant-garde European and American painting, including works by Edouard Manet, Edgar Degas, Jean-François Millet, and Jules Bastien-Lepage. Bric-a-brac outnumbered fine arts three to one and constituted a representative sample of New York's best collections. The exhibition was kept open on Sundays, and a special fund was set up to allow craftsmen artists and students to visit the exhibition.

Ladies' bazaars stand out in the artistic era because ladies organized them and they showcased ladies' work. Ladies had proven themselves spectacularly successful at raising money to aid soldiers' hospitals and relief organizations during the Civil War; it is estimated that these Sanitary Fairs had brought in $5 million. Ladies took this expertise and applied it to countless charity bazaars that raised money for churches, hospitals, schools, orphanages, old-age homes and even for political issues like temperance. The typical ladies' bazaar had a series of themed booths that sold merchandise, much of it handmade. The goods sold couldn't be found in stores: cloth items (embroidered potholders and handkerchiefs), useful household items (decorated wastebaskets), whimsies (papier mâché butterflies) or outright artworks (paintings, hand-painted ceramics). Special events, such as pageants, dinners or dances might be held during the run of the bazaar. An art gallery of borrowed items was often a component. Fairyland, Around the World, or the Holy Land—whatever the theme, it was carried out in the hall decorations, in the booths and in the costumes of the attendants. The bazaars gave ladies the opportunity to produce and administer a major event, to make artistic goods and to bond with each other and their communities. With the decor to admire, merchandise to touch, music and food, ladies' bazaars were a feast for all the senses.

Historical events merited fairs, and, at these, historical relics, especially American relics, were the focus. The organizers of the Albany Bicentennial Loan Exhibition of 1886 made their wish to display history and art explicit: they aimed to display "the treasures of our homes, to exemplify our perception of taste, our artistic culture, our veneration for the past."[5] At the Centennial Celebration of the Inauguration of George Washington, the contents of the exhibition held at the Metropolitan Opera House in New York City in 1889 were strictly limited to portraits and relics tied directly to Washington and his cabinet. Sometimes charity fairs would contain a historic component; the Homeopathic Hospital Fair in New York City in 1875 had "Lady Washington's cottage." Eighteenth-century costumes or at least "old fashioned" dress was de rigueur.

Mrs. Kenner was captivated by the new decorations of the American Art Galleries and the Union League Club in New York City. The new art spirit was evident in other public venues. Churches, clubs, office buildings, apartment houses—these public or quasi-public venues were important disseminators of the artistic style. The trend had begun when Trinity Church was opened in Boston in 1877, with a decorative scheme of murals, stained glass and architectural ornament orchestrated by John La Farge and a small army of artists working there as artisans. The Boston Art Club, in a bold style of bricks, masonry and carved-stone panels, opened in 1882—just around the corner from the Museum of Fine Arts, which had opened in stages in the late 1870s. In 1881 McKim, Mead and White finished the new shingled and ornamented Casino in Newport, Rhode Island. It stood at the head of fashionable Belleview Avenue, where new artistic houses sprung up seemingly monthly in the early 1880s, witnessed by

5 Barnes, ed., *Catalog of Albany's Bicentennial Loan*, xvii-xviii; quoted in Stillinger, *The Antiquers*, 46.

VANTINE'S CURIO ROOM—NEW YORK

fashionable Bostonians and New Yorkers as they summered and promenaded. The trend took hold; in 1888, the Minnesota Club in St. Paul was an artistic interior, complete with large wicker chairs and giant Japanese vases. Many Mrs. Kenners—and Mr. Kenners—discovered the new artistic style of interior decor when they visited a club, restaurant, theater or even a progressive church.

ARTFUL SHOPPING

On her trip to New York, Mrs. Kenner set aside one day for shopping. She began at Tiffany and Company, on Union Square. She wanted to buy a wedding present for her cousin; she hoped she could afford one of the Japanese-style silver vases that the firm was making so well known. She saw one ornamented with copper spiders, but it was very costly: $50 for a rather small vase. She would have to try elsewhere. She went into the showrooms of Herter Brothers a few blocks north, on Broadway, but only to look. She had seen illustrations of the exquisite furniture and upholstery fabrics that the firm supplied but had not seen any of it with her own eyes. She was captivated and respectful; it was altogether the most artistic and tasteful showroom she had ever seen. She left the shop, her mind's eye filled with color and pattern and walked back down Broadway, glancing at the famous Atlas clock at Tiffany's—she was late! She hurried past Elliot & Bulkley on the south side of the square. There was no need to go there to look at the Morris papers; all of them were available back home in Chicago at J. J. McGrath. She kept her eleven a.m. appointment at Mitchell, Vance and Company to look at a light fixture; she saw a suitable one in brass and gilt immediately— what luck! Now she had time to stop in at Degraaf & Taylor, a large furniture store. She felt more comfortable here than at Herter's; the prices matched her purse. She looked at a magazine rack and a new style of wire mattress. She met Mr. Kenner for lunch at the Vienna Model Bakery, at Broadway and Tenth Street; together, they revisited Mitchell, Vance and Company and purchased the light fixture.

On her own again, Mrs. Kenner went to R. H. Macy's at Sixth Avenue and Fourteenth Street, to look at the china displays. Although she had not intended to, she bought a teapot, in a new Blue Willow style from England; it would match the teacups she had found at that country auction. Walking back to her hotel with her find, she chanced upon a small shop with an intriguing display of vases, jugs and large round platters all with a soft, iridescent glow. The sign said "John Chadwick. Dealer in Spanish, Moorish and Portuguese Pottery." This would do for her cousin, who was an artistic young lady; she went in and bought a large water pitcher, which could be matched with a charger, so that the two could serve on the washstand. She went into Vantine's, the famous Oriental store. Here she bought paper fans for all the ladies in her church club back home. All her shopping finished, she made

Postcard for Vantine's, postmarked 1909. This postcard shows the range of goods available at Vantine's, one of New York City's largest Oriental stores and a leading artistic retailer.

Cottier's, on Fifth Avenue, the object of the rest of the afternoon. Here she spent a happy hour examining the curious old European furniture, the new black Anglo Japanese furniture designed by E. W. Godwin and imported from England and flower paintings by Maria Oakey Dewing, a talented needleworker and author of *Beauty in the Household*. She drifted back to her hotel, on Union Square, to change for dinner at Delmonico's.

Mrs. Kenner's day of shopping took place in New York, the center of artistic consumption. Ladies' Mile was just coming into its own in 1885, the date of Mrs. Kenner's trip. Ladies' Mile was really a district, stretching along Broadway, from around Tenth Street to the upper Twenties, and extending, tentacle like, into the neighboring side streets and avenues. The growth of commerce in New York City in the 1870s and 1880s was fueled by female shoppers. Clothing, household furnishings, gifts, books: these were things ladies bought. Women also used Ladies' Mile as an entertainment district, eating unescorted in respectable restaurants, attending the theaters and looking at art.

THE CHIC SHOPS

The very epicenter of New York's artistic shopping was a handful of small style-setting shops headed by tastemaker entrepreneurs. First on the scene was Sypher and Company, established in 1867, and, for some years, "the only real bric-a-brac magazine we have in New York,"[6] according to *Scribner's Monthly* in 1874. Sypher's could be credited with making the colonial style fashionable—its trade card showed a couple in "George and Martha Washington" costume, in a room complete with a fireplace with delft tiles. That arbiter of all things fashionable, Clarence Cook, mentioned Sypher's Chinese teak-and-marble hall furniture and Italian black wood chairs inlaid with ivory in *The House Beautiful*. Sypher's sold antiques of all sorts and "articles of vertu," and it provided full decorating services.

Daniel Cottier opened his New York store in 1873. A gregarious redheaded Scotsman, he trained in Glasgow and London (where he probably knew William Morris) as a color-boy for a house painter and as a stained-glass maker. Though he designed stained glass and interiors, he is remembered more as a disseminator of artistic taste through his shops, first in London, then New York and eventually Sydney and Melbourne. He lived mostly in New York, and Clarence Cook relied on him and his shop staff for advice and illustrations for *The House Beautiful*. "The great majority of people, who are bent on being in the fashion, and up to the times, and who have no weak sentiment about grandmothers, must be cared for—and the place for them is Cottier's."[7] There you could buy old things and new things: "faienceries" (hand-painted chargers by Minton and Company), Venetian glass, Oriental carpets, lacquerwork, bronzes, and furniture in Old English, Japanese and Queen Anne styles. Cottier exhibited French Barbizon School paintings, Rembrandts and modern Dutch landscapists. In 1875, he hosted the first exhibition of renegade painters and sculptors who were to form the Society of American Artists. Cottier was an active decorator; he facilitated collaborations between patrons and artists. When he died in 1883, the New York art scene lost his presence, but his shop went on until 1915.

Cottier's was perhaps the ne plus ultra in artistic stores. One of Cook's readers wrote him: "You talk about Cottier's, and you publish the most provokingly pretty pictures of elegant and costly things, and you describe them and descant upon them, and aggravate us so . . . that we can't rest till we have tried to get things like them, and then we find they are far too dear; and then when we ask you how to get them cheap, you tell us can't be done! What makes you show them to us if you know we can't get them? What's the use?"[8] Could there be a more vivid description of consumer desire for artistic goods?

And, of course, there was Herter Brothers. The famous, prestigious decorating firm kept an elegant shop that was open to the public. Here, a stock of their furniture was always on display, as well as a huge selection of textiles. Herter's textiles, Cook said, were a testament that the textiles of this era could match any in history. And, other things could be found in the showroom: rare old embroideries; wallpapers; stained glass; mosaics; old Chinese porcelains, jade and lacquer.

Boston had its own style setter: Charles Wyllys Elliott and the Household Art Company. Like Cottier, Elliott must have been a colorful figure. From an old New England family, Elliott wrote a history of the region's ghosts, a book about the settling of America by Norsemen, a novel or two, and a more conventional history of pottery. He was a proselytizer for the new style, and he opened the Household Art Company in 1873. "Unlike Sypher's and Marcotte's, whose collections of costly antique and modern articles are solely within the means of the wealthy, this store is designed to bring to people of moderate incomes decoration and furniture for their dwellings, based on honest taste, which shall supercede the imitation of meretricious

[6] Metropolitan Museum of Art, *In Pursuit of Beauty,* 501.
[7] Cook, "Culture and Progress," 501.
[8] Cook, *The House Beautiful,* 320.

Corner cabinet made by Cottier and Company, New York City, ca 1875. Cottier and Company was one of the city's fashionable purveyors of the new artistic style. Daniel Cottier, a Scottish stained-glass maker, all-around designer and entrepreneur, played a big role in disseminating the new style on three continents; he had shops first in London, in New York by 1873 and later in Australia. A cabinet very much like this one was illustrated in Clarence Cook's *The House Beautiful*. The bust on the shelf is by Olin Levi Warner, and it depicts Cottier himself. (Collection of Post Road Gallery, Larchmont, NY. Photograph by Helga Photo Studio.)

French ornament, and furnish only sensible and substantial manufacture."[9] Elliott was among the first in America to carry Morris wallpapers, that signpost of advanced taste.

Then there were the specialist stores that clustered in the Ladies' Mile area. Tiffany and Company, already an august vendor of tasteful and costly gifts, entered the artistic arena guided by Edward Chandler Moore as head of design. Moore kept a reference library on archeology and the history of decorative arts. He also collected Japanese and Indian textile sample books as well as medieval Oriental and Islamic objects. All these were available to the design staff. A stream of silver flatware and hollowware, presentation pieces and jewelry flowed from the workshops; much of it drew on the exotic goods in Moore's library and collection. Besides the mainstay of the store (jewelry, silver, watches and clocks, leather goods, stationery, precious stones), Tiffany and Company also sold imports. In 1876, Charles Tiffany commissioned Christopher Dresser to bring art back from Japan. Direct from the 1878 Paris Exposition came "Placques by Minton . . . Salviati's latest reproductions of the Venetian Glass of the Sixteen Century. Fac-similies of the Trojan iridescent bronze glad exhumed by Dr. Schliemann. . . . Reproductions, by Doulton, of old Flemish stone ware" (according to an ad of the day). On the store's second floor there were always bronze, enamels, marble and ivory. There were many other shops in Ladies' Mile. Davis Collamore & Company specialized in china, cut glass and Rookwood pottery. Meriden Brittania Company, the huge manufacturer of silver plates, kept a showroom in the area. The showrooms of the major decorator/furniture makers, including Marcotte, Herts Brothers and many others, were to be found along with Herter. There were also the showrooms of the Society of Decorative Art and the Women's Exchange.

-- --
[9] "Art, Music and Drama," 123.

There was a plethora of antique and curio stores. H. O. Watson made old tapestries a specialty. P. Stevens guaranteed the authenticity of his old china, silver tapestries, bronzes, furniture, "direct from European art centers." L. A. Lanthier sold a high class of old master paintings, arms tapestries, rugs, old silver, marbles, ivory and "bric-a-brac generally." He sold (and probably compiled) a four-panel screen composed of paintings of costumed ladies, allegories representing the senses, to Hudson River School painter Frederic Church and his wife, Isabel. (Their house is now the museum Olana, where the screen and the bill for it survive.) Robert Fullerton's Old English Curiosity Shop in New York City carried oil paintings, bric-a-brac, jewelry, bronzes, swords and daggers and other curios. For a time, Siegfried Bing, the man who was to christen and promote a style through his Paris shop L'Art Nouveau, had a store in New York City that sold Chinese and Japanese art objects.

Artful Emporiums

The very stylish stores selling expensive furnishings weren't the only options. There were furniture stores that sold a range of more moderately priced goods and provided some interior decorating services. On her walk, Mrs. Kenner wandered into Degraaf and Taylor near Union Square but she recognized the model because it existed elsewhere. Bruschke & Ricke sold "Artistic Furniture" to the public and the trade in her native city of Chicago on Division Street, and Pitkin and Brooks, also in Chicago, was a large china and glass wholesaler with public showrooms, where they offered smaller furnishings, like tables and stands. The furniture dealer Linus T. Fenn, in

Artful Shopping Today

Main floor of ABC Carpet and Home, in Manhattan, New York City. By coincidence (or serendipity), the area around Union Square is once again a hotbed of artistic household design, as it was in the Aesthetic era. The flagship retailer is ABC Carpet and Home, which began as a discount carpet and rug store and evolved into a high-end souk. Fittingly, ABC took over the structure built in 1881 by W. & J. Sloane, a rug emporium, as its Ladies' Mile headquarters. Now, the six loft floors sell artistic luxury home furnishings in boutiquey departments. ABC spawned other eccentric retailers of home furnishings. Fishs Eddy sells overstocks of restaurant-supply china, Renovation Hardware sells retrograde hardware. Housewares, candle stores and eco-friendly cosmetic stores line the streets. There are many stores selling tile, modern furniture and designer kitchens. Nowadays, the old Ladies' Mile neighborhood is good place to furnish a whole artistic house. (Photo courtesy of ABC Carpet and Home. Photo by Amy Melson.)

Hartford, Connecticut, advertised "assortment the largest" and "prices the lowest"; these were typical claims. Paine's, in Boston, invited the public to the showrooms in its factory, which occupied a square block. Its trade card showed a room with fashionable furniture, including an Eastlake hanging wall cabinet, art pottery on the lintel, and—a new class of furniture—a pier mirror and drawers that folded down to become a bed. At these stores, serviceable artistic furniture was available at a good price and in all the styles.

Mrs. Kenner shopped for fans at Vantine's, one of the first and one of the biggest of the country's so-called Japanese novelty stores. In the late 1870s, Vantine's was among a handful of stores in the United States specializing in Oriental art, especially Japanese scrolls, screens and ceramics; such stores served wealthy connoisseurs. By the mid-1880s, however, Vantine's was among hundreds of stores that carried a vast array of Oriental goods, many of them at moderate prices. The stores stocked Japanese objects, but also things from China, Turkey, and other points east of Europe. The stores were everywhere. Some were owned by Oriental entrepreneurs, some by Westerners. K. Nicolaides kept a Japanese emporium in New Haven, Connecticut; Yung Lee sold Chinese and Japanese goods in Silver City, New Mexico; San Francisco (not surprisingly) had dozens. At Japanese novelty stores, you could buy paper fans, umbrellas, lanterns; ceramics for use or display; silk brocades and printed cottons; scrolls and kits for making scrolls; and, often, such miscellany as Middle Eastern rugs and weaponry, inlaid tabouret tables, hookahs and peacock feathers. The stores became a staple for household-art-advice writers and the organizers of ladies' bazaars. Constance Cary Harrison's household advice book *Woman's Handiwork in Modern Homes* quoted the costs of various sorts of Japanese dessert china: ranging from a Wakayama bowl, in pale yellow, decorated outside with a checker work of black and copper, for $15; to dessert plates at $12 to $18 per dozen. Articles on how to make things to sell in ladies' bazaars often specified the matting and papers that could be purchased at Japanese novelty stores. These stores provided staples for the artistic middle class customer.

Mrs. Kenner looked in at Macy's because, as the *New York Times* noted in 1887, "There is probably no better place in the country to study the character, the gracefulness of outline, the delicacy of blending shades and quiet and brilliant colorings in pottery and glassware than at R. H. Macy & Co.'s."[10] Macy's and other department stores became retailing giants and innovators in the artistic era. Before the Centennial, only a few dozen department stores existed in the United States, but by the turn of the century there were hundreds. The major cities had the leaders of the 1880s: in New York City, it was Macy's, Lord and Taylor, and Arnold Constable (A. T. Stewart, the granddaddy, closed in 1882); in Philadelphia, it was Wanamaker's; in Chicago, it was Marshal Field's. Their stock in trade was "soft goods," from cloth on the bolt to ready-made clothing. They offered plenty of artistic merchandise and other things, too: magnificent architecture, ladies' tea rooms, fixed prices, delivery by parcel post. The department stores distinguished themselves by various strategies. Macy's had

above: Trade card for Saratoga Japanese Emporium. Hundreds of Japanese novelty stores dotted the American landscape. This trade card for a store in New Haven, Connecticut, was probably printed in Japan. (Collection of the author.)

facing: A small department store around 1890. All sorts of artistic goods can be seen in this dry-goods store, including a display of tassels arranged as a portiere and a Middle Eastern rug. This unidentified store was probably located in a mid-sized city. (Collection of the author.)

-- --
[10] Spenlow, "Decorating and Furnishing," 5.

"Ceramics, for the Million. Ceramics for the Millionaire." Wanamaker's had stylish clothing. Department stores displayed their goods artistically and, of course, issued artistic trade cards. Artistic goods were available in general stores in smaller cities, where one store might carry furniture, upholstery goods, Oriental rugs, Wilton carpets and even transom panels of turned decorative wood and decorative tassels.

The Newest Old Thing

In the Aesthetic era, it became fashionable to shop for the newest *old* thing. Antiques became a concern of artistic people. While some Americans (especially the well-traveled and deep-pocketed) collected European objects, most focused on American antiques. There were many reasons for this. "Anti-modernism," the term one scholar has used to describe the undercurrent of nostalgic yearning in late-nineteenth-century America, found many sorts of expressions. The colonial kitchen exhibits at the Sanitary Fairs and the Centennial celebrated America's past and made it

quaint and fashionable. The successful and well-publicized crusades of the 1850s to preserve Mount Vernon and Washington's headquarters in Newburg, New York, ennobled these sites and arguably started the industry of cultural tourism. Histories, such as Benjamin Lossing's reverential biography of Washington and Alice Morse Earl's anecdote-packed *Home Life in Colonial Days*, romanticized the artifacts of early America. A cadre of connoisseurs (including painter E. L. Henry and antiquarian Ben: Perley Poore) fixated on American furnishings, or at least things bought and used by Americans. They filled up their homes and opened the door to guests; their collections became quasi public. The era's tendency towards new takes on old hand-crafted forms (the Morris chair reworked a vernacular cottage armchair; Eastlake tables and cabinets reworked medieval furniture) naturally caused people to look more carefully at the originals. At the same time that the English started collecting Jacobean, Queen Anne and Sheraton furniture, Americans started collecting "Pilgrim" furniture

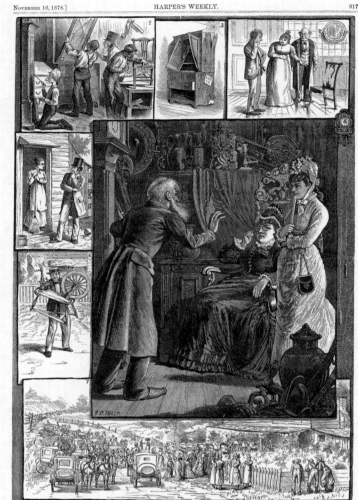

1. The Sale of a Veritable Antique.   2. How "Veritable Antiques" are made.   3. A Bargain.   4. "There, Mr. Mortice, I think if you put new Legs, a Back, and Seat on that, it will make a lovely Chair."
5. "Lor', no, Mister! I 'ain't seen no old Clocks hereabouts."   6. A Prize.   7. A Rumor having spread that an old Lady on Long Island has some old Chelsea China, a few Collectors go down to see it.

THE RAGE FOR OLD FURNITURE.—Drawn by A. B. Frost.—[See Page 718.]

The Rage for Old Furniture, a cartoon by A.
B. Frost, from *Harper's Weekly,* November
16, 1878. This cartoon satirizes the craze for
antiques and antique hunting. The center
scene shows an antique store where a "veritable" antique is being sold to ladies, while
other panels show antiques being created in
the back room and antique hunters invading
an old farmhouse.

(i.e., seventeenth-century objects) and
colonial and Federal furnishings.

Household art writers explicitly connected artistic with antique. Constance
Cary Harrison discussed Shaker chairs and
"Grandmother's crewel work," along with
an old Louis XV screen and a new
"Cromwell" chair. Cook was perhaps the
most insistent promoter of American
antiques. He claimed that an interest in
old American furnishings was not mere
"centennial mania"; it was sensible, for
this furniture was never ugly or awkward,
it showed the cultured taste of our for-
bearers, and was "proof that our taste is
getting a root in a healthier and more
native soil."[11] In fact, household art advisors did not insist upon "genuine"
antiques. Numerous writers in household
art magazines and books agreed: if you
can't afford the real things, buy good
reproductions. The *effect* of age, not actual
historicity, was important. Responding to
demand, dealers refurbished, restored and
re-fabricated dilapidated objects. Their
work could be so extensive that a shadow
of the former object remained, but this sort
of restoration was considered masterly, not
deceptive. "Pilgrim," colonial, colonial-
revival and "cottage" objects proliferated
(see image on left on page 29).

Americans became antique collectors. The expensive stores, like Sypher's
and Cottier's, served the wealthy. If the
right quantity and quality of antiques
could not be found, they could be made.
For example, cabinetmaker Ernest Hagen
was commissioned by Louis Comfort
Tiffany to produce a set of twelve ladder-
back chairs. Those who could not shop at
Sypher's or commission "Pilgrim" furniture
through decorators, began the hunt.
Ordinary household goods, once considered used furniture, were resuscitated,
and grandparents were enjoined to recall
the whereabouts of castoffs. Attics, base-
ments and barns were ransacked.

-- -- -- -- -- -- -- -- -- -- -- -- --
[11] Cook, *The House Beautiful,* 187.

Clarence Cook told an "Antiques Roadshow" story: on the recommendation of an antiquarian friend, Cook bought an old, abused table and found it was a handsome antique that could be easily re-hauled. "This was, of course, a piece of good fortune, but after all, not of very rare good fortune; those who seek such things are continually finding them, for the garrets and barns in the older parts of the country are rich in this furniture of a by-gone time, that has been set aside to yield place to that of a more fashionable make."[12] People took to the country for a day of picnicking and antique hunting. Antique furniture began to fill the homes of artistic people.

ARTFUL IMAGES EVERYWHERE

New printing technologies, the invention of advertising and marketing, the development of a shopping culture—all combined to make the artistic era a newly visual world. Images became incidental, part of the fabric of life. This was a dialectic: the technology of images was perfected because there was the desire for images and the desire for images was perpetuated by the increasing number of images. The more images pervaded everyday life, the more visual people became. Whether or not an individual paid any attention to things "artistic," images were inescapable. They were a part of the culture of consumption. Mrs. Kenner's life at home and out in the city was filled with images. So was every American's. Many of the images were artistic. Artistic images were in magazines and on trade cards. Artistic goods were found in the department stores. Household art magazines and illustrated periodicals, sold on newsstands, were filled with artistic images. Artistic culture, a culture filled with a particular style of imagery, was a part of everyday life. Aestheticism was sold through everyday visual culture.

---

[12] Cook, *The House Beautiful*, 77.

NOTES ON SOURCES

The background for Mrs. Kenner's experience of reading the illustrated periodicals and her days in New York City were informed especially by these period sources: *Harper's New Monthly Magazine*, for July through December, 1883, vol. 67, and three issues of *Decorator and Furnisher Magazine* 3, no. 3 (December 1883); 5, no. 3 (December 1884) and 7, no. 3, (December 1885).

The chapters on "Consuming" and "Communicating" in Schlereth, *Victorian America,* are a good overview of the mechanisms that sold the Aesthetic movement to Americans.

The development of advertising and the influence of trade cards and scrapbooks are discussed in Garvey, *The Adman in the Parlor,* and Jay, *The Trade Card in Nineteenth-Century America.*

Shopping and the development of a consumer culture are masterfully described by Leach, *Land of Desire.* Ladies' Mile is thoroughly surveyed in Boyer, *Manhattan Manners.* The astonishing number and variety of Japanese novelty stores is made clear by an article by Brandimarte, "Japanese Novelty Stores." Biographies of some important retailers, including Daniel Cottier and Charles Wyllys Elliott, are supplied in the Metropolitan Museum of Art's *In Pursuit of Beauty.*

The specialized shopping available at ladies' bazaars is discussed by Gordon in *Bazaars and Fair Ladies.* The rising popularity of American antiques is described by Elizabeth Stillinger in *The Antiquers.* For a look at one important loan show, see O'Brien, *In Support of Liberty.*

Artful Objects at Home

THE FACADE

Imagine walking down a street in one of the new Chicago suburbs, looking for Mrs. Kenner's house, in the year 1885. What style would the house be? Imagine entering the front door and looking around. What would you see? Mrs. Kenner kept an artistic house, in a middle class neighborhood. If an inventory of her house was drawn up, how would it differ from that of her less artistic neighbors? And, how would her house differ from the wealthy families on Lake Shore Drive? Who were the superstar manufacturers and artisans, the names that Mrs. Kenner would proudly mention when describing her furnishings? In short, what sort of artistic objects filled American houses, and what did they *look* like? We can draw a mind's-eye picture.

Aesthetic movement houses are alive and well and populating American streets today. An archetypical American streetscape is lined with Aesthetic movement houses: Stick Style cottages with muscular roof trusses and exposed timbering; many-colored painted ladies with gingerbread porches; rambling wood cottages with patterns of shingles delineating their various turrets and gables; rows of brick Queen Anne houses with their bay windows; and, perhaps, a dignified stone house with massive Romanesque arches. There were other stylistic modes in the nineteenth century (Italianate, Second Empire), but the architecture that we think of as most typically and characteristically "Victorian" is some aspect of the Aesthetic movement. Collectively, these houses made up neighborhoods, towns, whole cities—and they still do. The Aesthetic movement left a legacy of built housing and shaped our conception of the middle class home.

More important than the literal brick or stone forming the foundation of the Aesthetic movement home was its metaphorical foundation: the dream of a single-family home. Everyone wanted their own home, with a garden, in a neighborhood. Many could attain this dream because America enjoyed a generation of relative prosperity and technological advances. The era witnessed a spectacular rise in population, a growth economy and improvements in transportation. Americans could choose houses located some distance from the work done by the breadwinner, who commuted by trolley, omnibus or train. Construction was facilitated by building and loan associations that pooled the savings of its members to earn interest, wrote mortgages, and often supplied plans. These associations were often organized around religious, professional and ethnic lines and sometimes helped form neighborhoods along these same lines. Housing was also a big business; on an unprecedented scale, developers built their conception of the American dream house, ready for occupancy. America might have become urban in the decades before the Civil War, but it became a place of urban and suburban neighborhoods in the decades after the war.

In this rising tide of prosperity, comfort and taste, Americans used the various permutations of Aesthetic movement architecture to signal their individualism. With the expanding opportunities in manufacturing, managing and merchandising, a professional white-collar class was created. Laborers and mechanics also earned a comfortable wage. To reflect all these proud and differing segments that composed this vast middle class, Americans wanted not just more housing but new housing forms. And, these Americans had the purchasing power to influence the housing forms they inhabited. As a commentator wrote in 1898, through its architectural form the house became a means of expressing the identity of the family as a living cell in the larger organism of community.

The picturesque villa in a small estate, built in some numbers in America at mid-century, was a helpful precedent for Aesthetic movement houses. Alexander Jackson Downing designed and, with *The Architecture of Country Houses*, publicized many variants on the Gothic (especially the Carpenter Gothic cottage, with bracketed eaves) and the classic (especially the Tuscan villa, with a handsome masonry tower). (See images on page 24.) Downing's catholic taste for many sorts of houses in many styles was continued in other books written by practicing architects: Samuel Sloan's *Model Architect*; Gervase Wheeler's *Rural Homes*; Calvert Vaux's *Villas and Cottages*; and at least nine titles by George Woodward, beginning with *Woodward's Country Homes*. The plans and elevations in these pattern books—most for actual houses that had been built on sizable and sometimes scenic lots—established certain architectural features in the landscape. These houses showed off irregular massing and a broken skyline. They often replaced the earlier set of square parlors with open living halls and large windows that provided views and cross ventilation. Most had eye-catching detail, be it diamond-paned casement windows or an iron railing outlining a ridge beam. The effect was stylistically eclectic and most definitely picturesque.

Avant-garde British architecture also had its influence in America. As part of the design reform undertaken in the 1860s, the English looked back to their architectural roots. Among the first built manifestations of this interest was William Morris's own house, which he and Philip Webb designed in 1859. Called the Red House, its set of brick masses and half-timbering details, topped by a steeply pitched red clay tile roof, evoked the history of vernacular rural farmhouses, from late medieval to Georgian. It was not meant to exemplify any style; it was meant to be plain and sincere. In late 1860s, Richard Norman Shaw designed several elaborate country houses that used picturesque irregular massing and an extensive vocabulary of Tudor, Jacobean and Elizabethan detailing—even the classical modes of those

phases. Nonetheless, the houses were not at all archeological; they were picturesque and impressive. At roughly the same time, E. W. Godwin was designing simplified, severe houses that referred minimally to Georgian architecture; Whistler's White House was the most famous example.

Americans also looked to their own architectural roots. The Centennial offered fanciful glimpses of the past, from the Colonial kitchen and its antiquarian furnishings to Mississippi's pavilion, a log cabin with Spanish moss hung at its eaves. As Americans pursued the wonders of their natural landscape through scenic tourism, looking at old buildings became fashionable. In 1877, the young architects Charles Follen McKim, William Rutherford Mead, Stanford White and William Bigelow took a walking tour along the coasts of Massachusetts and New Hampshire. They sketched colonial buildings, and the portfolios that resulted informed their work for decades. Focused writing on American buildings began to appear, led by Arthur Little's *Early New England Interiors*. Articles on aspects of colonial architecture began to surface in the popular press, and in 1881 the architectural journal *American Architect and Building News* began regularly publishing photos and measured plans of old buildings. Americans began to understand that "colonial" architecture was a rich mix, from the late-Elizabethan wooden-frame Fairbanks house of Dedham, Massachusetts (profiled in *American Architect and Building News* in 1881), to the handsome Federal-style house of Henry Wadsworth Longfellow and his family, a house that Washington really did sleep in.

Japanese buildings were also intriguing and influential. As a crew of Japanese workers built two pavilions for the Centennial in Fairmont Park, using tools and techniques unknown in the West, their every move was pictured and described in the press. This was followed by a steady stream of articles on the pavilions themselves, joining a body of literature in the popular press on Japanese art and architecture, which were recognized as inseparable (see top image on page 18). When Sylvester Morse's well-illustrated *Japanese Homes and Their Surroundings* was published in 1886, it became a best seller. The influence of Japanese art and architecture could be subtle and pervasive, manifest as a new respect for blocks of horizontal spaces interconnected by wide pocket doors that functioned like shoji screens. Or, the influence could be incidental and diluted, manifest on an upturned eave edge or as a band of carved sunflowers so stylized that they resembled a row of Japanese Imperial mon crests.

Aesthetic movement architecture was transmitted quickly from coast-to-coast and overseas by the English-language architectural press. The leader was the *American Architect and Building News*, begun in 1876. Besides its historical writing, it sponsored competitions and profiled good design. There were a number of British journals with wide American circulation: *Architect*, *Builder*, and *Building News*. Some of these journals, like *Scientific American, Architects and Builders Edition*, published from 1885 until at least 1901, were read by laymen. These journals benefited

from the new technologies for reproducing images and were profusely illustrated.

Note should be taken of the role that resort towns played as germinators of Aesthetic movement architecture. In their vacation homes, patrons felt freer to be playful, to build spaces that promoted social interaction along with the circulation of fresh air. Superannuated seaports and disused market towns, which had a stock of quaint architectural models, found new life as resorts. Newport, Rhode Island, was a veritable library of eighteenth-century housing. Some of the earliest and most innovative Aesthetic movement houses were built on the Jersey Shore (a cottage for Ulysses Simpson Grant Jr. in Asbury Park, designed by Bassett Jones, 1878; the Emlen Physick House in Cape May, designed by Frank Furness, 1881), along Maine's rocky coasts (a cottage for an unnamed client, designed by Henry Paston Clark, Kennebunkport, 1880; Redwood, a cottage for C. J. Morrill in Bar Harbor, designed by William Ralph Emerson, 1879), and in Newport (many examples, noted below).

Probably the first architectural manifestation of the Aesthetic movement to appear in wide numbers in the landscape was the Stick Style. Though the name was not used during the Aesthetic movement and it only appears as a distinct style in hindsight, Stick Style is still a useful designation. It describes wooden-frame houses with much timbering that suggests (but might not actually match) the underlying balloon-frame construction. The style drew from the rustic half-timbered architecture of the Alps, Normandy and Tudor England but added carved and spindled brackets, trusses, barge boards, deep eaves, decorative siding and cross timbers. Commonly, each of the various wooden elements would be painted their own earth-toned color, making a lively polychromatic surface. In its own day, the simpler variants of the style tended to be called "Modern Gothic" or "Eastlake," though Eastlake himself would have disclaimed any responsibility for the style, which, unlike his own furniture, strayed far from simple, rugged late-medieval precedents. In the 1860s, Richard Morris Hunt designed several Stick Style houses that were built in Newport, including the Griswold House, still standing and operating as the Newport Art Museum. By the time of the Centennial, it was the fashionable style for the various state pavilions; New Jersey and Wisconsin built especially flamboyant examples. Plentiful wood and well-trained carpenters as well as good press in journals and exposure in pattern books ensured that the Stick Style was built all over America.

The next stylistic variant of the Aesthetic movement to appear on the scene was the one that took the widest range of forms: the Queen Anne style. The term was applied to buildings by Richard Norman Shaw, an English architect. His buildings did have tangential affinities with British architecture of the early 1700s and Queen Anne's reign. But, characteristically, Americans took this stylistic ball and ran with it. In Britain, the Queen Anne usually refers to urban houses of brick, with window frames neatly painted white. In America, Queen Anne houses could be built of brick, wood or stone, could be faced in stucco or shingle, and could be roofed in slate or shingle. Typically, an American Queen Anne house maximizes its visual impact by using many of these materials in combination. In America, the Queen Anne style appears in urban row houses, small suburban houses and grand estate mansions. The facades of Queen Anne houses feature projecting bay windows, turrets for staircases, a roofline punctuated by chimneys, attached terraces, verandas, second-floor sleeping porches, ornamental terra-cotta panels, stained glass or scroll-sawn wood. The different components of wood Queen Anne houses were commonly painted contrasting earth tones; these are the houses that were later termed "painted ladies." Specific decorative motifs might be borrowed from virtually any historical phase, but eighteenth-century America, Elizabethan and Tudor England, Japan, and the lighter moments of Hellenic classicism were favored. Contemporary abstracted geometrical ornament, à la Christopher Dresser, was also ubiquitous.

Queen Anne architecture began with a bang in America in 1875 with the completion in Newport of a house for William Watts Sherman. It was designed in the office of Henry Hobson Richardson, where the young Stanford White worked. Both architects contributed to this lively, very American house with strong ties to Richard Norman Shaw's version of the Queen Anne. A variant within the Queen Anne, the Shingle Style, is exemplified by the Isaac

facing: John Noble Alsop Griswold House, Newport, RI, Richard Morris Hunt, architect, completed 1864. The Griswold House was one of the first Stick Style buildings in America. It was designed by Richard Morris Hunt, the first American to attend the architecture school of the Ecole des Beaux Arts in France. The Stick Style, known at the time as Modern Gothic, is loosely related to wooden medieval buildings with half-timbering, especially Swiss chalets. The wood skeleton of Stick Style buildings is articulated on the frame of the building by timbers painted a contrasting color. The Griswold House was built as a vacation house, but the style was soon adopted for full-time domestic structures. (Photo: James L. Yarnall.)

Bell House in Newport (constructed 1881–83) by the newly formed firm of McKim, Meade and White. Diamond-point, fish-scale and other kinds of patterns of white cedar shingles ripple across the facades, interrupted by windows of various Georgian styles. Japanese elements are seen here, too: the porch uprights are lathe-turned to resemble monumental bamboo poles, and on the interior pocket doors span large expanses and function like shoji screens to create and reshape space (see image on page 143).

Seemingly all of America's great architects of the day worked in the Queen Anne mode, with style and grace. Wilson Eyre designed the Charles A. Potter house, Anglecote (1881), in Chestnut Hill, Pennsylvania, in a Shingle Style, with distinct seventeenth- and eighteenth-century detailing. The style reached a climax at Tuxedo Park, a rambling, well-landscaped development north of New York City. (The development gave its name to the men's evening attire that was de riguour in the clubhouse.) Bruce Price was engaged to design a gate house, a clubhouse and some forty cottages. A remarkably abstract, ahistorical set of Queen Anne buildings resulted. Fred Savage, a carpenter who trained in the office of Peabody and Stearns, designed some three hundred Shingle Style structures on Mount Desert Island in Maine. Savage's career was not uncommon; countless lesser-known architects were proficient in the style. The work of many local heroes remains standing but largely unsung.

One stylistic variant within the Aesthetic movement has perhaps the fewest built examples, but it is so distinctive and its chief practitioner turned out so many strong examples that it has been given his name: Richardson Romanesque. Henry Hobson Richardson made his mark on the Aesthetic movement early, with the design of Trinity Church, which opened in Boston in 1877. This structure, whose massive tower was based on the Spanish Romanesque pilgrim church of Salamanca, brought painters, stained-glass makers and wood-carvers together under Richardson's magnificent trussed roof beams. It began the era's interdependence between architecture and the decorative arts. The Romanesque of the Aesthetic movement was commonly expressed in masonry, nearly always in stone. The Romanesque arch is the dominant motif, but squat, round columns, deeply recessed windows and carved ornament loosely derived from some medieval precedent, especially Celtic or Byzantine ornament, also enliven the style. Richardson produced many houses throughout New England; his libraries in the style are also numerous. The Romanesque was taken up by William Ralph Emerson and

given a light aesthetic touch in his design for the Boston Art Club (designed 1881–82). For the Robert Treat Paine family, Richardson designed a large addition for an 1860s house. The upper stories of different patterns of shingles rest on a rubble stone base, and this construction encloses a set of interconnected free-flowing spaces.

All these stylistic subcategories strive for the same visual effects. Variety and surprise are achieved through asymmetry and irregular massing. Aesthetic movement houses often have flexible floor plans that can be compartmentalized with sliding doors or thrown open to adjoin. The individual units of massing in a single house stand independently, so that different sections of the house might have different floor levels. Aesthetic movement houses ornament the structural and make ornament structural, so a bay window can be both decorative and load bearing. Flat planes are broken into segments of highly textured and contrasting materials: shingle against stucco, against carved wood, against brick. Earth colors predominate. Details show enough facility with historical precedents to transcend them. Ornament can become incredibly inventive. A fanciful coat of arms composed of red, green and blue glass bottle bottoms appears in the stucco of the Samuel Tilton House in Newport, designed by McKim, Mead and White. Above all, Aesthetic movement houses are playful and complex—just for the visual fun of it.

Artistic Architecture for Everyone

The typical potential homeowner learned about this new architectural style not from architects, but from books, magazines, contractors, builders and carpenters. Few houses were the product of one-on-one commissions from client to architect, at least in part because there were few architects. Training was still largely by apprenticeship, and, commonly, architects were engaged only for costly commercial and institutional buildings. Most domestic building was done by contractor/builders. These were men trained on the job in the trades, as carpenters, masons, roofers and plumbers. Many of these builders read professional architectural journals and pattern books and so did their potential patrons. Builders and homeowners had an ever-growing library of pattern books to use. The number of architectural pattern books doubled in the 1870s and nearly doubled again in the 1880s. The new style of architecture was disseminated through these books.

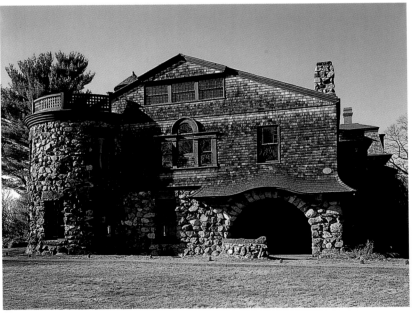

top: John H. Ammon residence, Cleveland, OH; Julius Schweinfurth, architect, completed 1881; unknown photographer, from George William Sheldon, *Artistic Country-Seats* (New York: D. Appleton and Company, 1886–87), plate 59. The Ammon residence exemplifies the Queen Anne style, which is characterized by irregular massing and rooflines, varied materials (here, wood, brick and stone) and much picturesque detail. The house boasts varied porch balusters, stained glass and half-timbering. Enough different types of shingles are used as siding to earn the house a place in the subcategory of the Shingle Style. The Queen Anne moved rapidly west across the United States, and in this case the diffusion was direct. The Ammons were Cleveland natives who lived much of the year in New York City; John Ammon was head of publishing for Harper and Brothers and later became a rare-book dealer. The architect was Julius Schweinfurth, another Clevelander who trained in the Boston office of Peabody and Stearns.

bottom: East facade of Stonehurst, the Robert Treat Paine House, Waltham, MA, designed by Henry Hobson Richardson, completed 1886. Richardson originated a bold style of architecture that now bears his name: Richardson Romanesque. Like the medieval style upon which it is based, Richardson Romansque is characterized by the use of masonry, especially heavy stone, and round arched-door and window openings. Unlike medieval Romanesque architecture, Richardson Romanesque makes use of inventive, irregular groupings of volumetric space and combines masonry with wood and other materials. Stonehurst is built around a large central living hall with a massive staircase, with adjoining parlors and a dining room, making the first-floor public rooms all interconnected. (Photo: Paul Rocheleau.)

A small portion of the books discussed historical styles, technical issues of building or architectural theory. Eugene C. Gardner asked the homeowner to consider the function of architecture. He wrote several books in the 1870s, including *The House That Jill Built, After Jack's Had Proved a Failure,* that discussed the purpose of various rooms and connected the design of house to the character of its inhabitants. Gardner's chatty books illustrated moderately Stick Style houses with units based on the square.

Most books focused on style and the rationale for it—and they were profusely illustrated. Henry Hudson Holley's *Modern Dwellings in Town and Country* opened with a chapter titled "The Queen Anne Style" that voiced the attractions of it, and William T. Comstock's *Modern Architectural Designs and Details* offered "Queen Anne, Eastlake, Elizabethan and other Modernized Styles." Such books typically included floor plans and some elevations—enough information to understand the overall style and form of the house. Many of the books had chapters of technical advice concerning drainage, heating, ventilation and construction. A subset of the books included large-scale drawings of details, such as brackets, cornices, baseboards, moldings and more.

This generation of pattern books and the new architectural magazines opened up lines of communication between client and builder. The potential homeowner could understand the drawings, and yet the books were specific enough to serve the builder. A client and a contractor could sit down with an attractive plan in a book; specific ornamental embellishments; and lists of wood, tile, brick and other materials to order. These were the raw materials from which a final plan and a contract could be drafted. Thus, pattern books facilitated the era's building boom.

There was a middle route for the middle class: mail-order architecture. The leader in this field was George Palliser, a master carpenter who owned a sash and door factory and who had built speculative housing for P. T. Barnum in Bridgeport, Connecticut. His *Model Homes for the People* was an inexpensive pattern book that offered a couple of twists. First, detailed plans could be purchased outright. Or, upon receipt of a fee and the answers to a set of seventeen questions about the proposed building, the firm would return, by mail, an original and unique set of plans and elevations, full-sized working drawings, lists of material required and all necessary contractual material needed by the client and a local builder. Further correspondence could be conducted if the client wanted more detail, and more

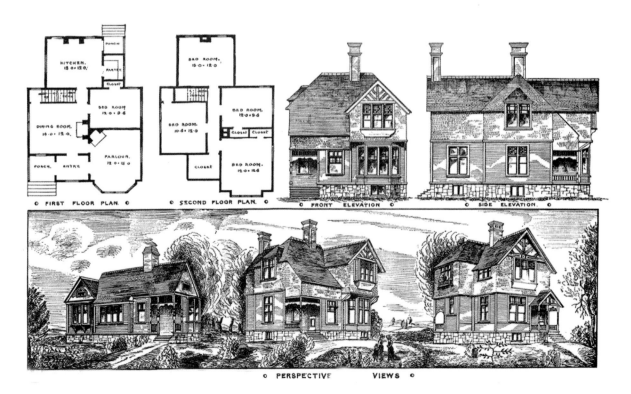

o FIRST FLOOR PLAN. o   o SECOND FLOOR PLAN. o   o FRONT ELEVATION o   o SIDE ELEVATION. o

o PERSPECTIVE   VIEWS o

fees would be charged. Naturally, this architecture by mail was cheaper than hiring an on-site supervising architect. The idea of mail-order architecture was not entirely new; a few prior pattern books had invited readers to refine the published plans by mail. But, Palliser systematized and publicized the mail-order architecture business, and he flourished. His brother Charles joined the business, and by 1878 they published *Palliser's Model Homes*, which had eighteen new designs, nearly all in the new Queen Anne style. In all, the Palliser brothers published twelve titles between 1876 and 1883, including *Palliser's Specifications* (model documents and drawings for domestic systems, like central heating) and *Palliser's Useful Details* (designs for gates, gables, bookcases and more). Fifty thousand copies of the last book were sold; apparently there was scarcely a contractor in America that did *not* have a Palliser book on his shelf. Other architect/authors offered plans by mail, including Henry Hudson Holley and Robert W. Shoppell, working with a coalition of architects called the Co-Operative Building Plan Association.

With a mail-order plan, a homeowner could go to a builder, hand over plans and sign a contract—theoretically, little was left to chance. Builders could also buy plans and architectural services by mail and supplement them by consultation with other architectural pattern books. Thus, designs could be amalgamated and customized to the needs of the client. By 1887, the Palliser brothers boasted that "there is not a city, town or village of consequence in the country but what contains from two to twenty buildings" that had been erected according to their plans.[1] One scholar studying an upstate New York town in depth has indeed traced connections between many extant houses and published designs. The Palliser brothers and their competitors in the mail-order architecture business were a great force in popularizing Aesthetic movement architecture.

Another route was to buy an Aesthetic movement home already made from a developer. The large-scale builder came into his own in this era. He advertised. He managed a construction crew. He used mass production to his advantage, buying machine-milled lumber, ornament and hardware and getting quantity discounts on large purchases of construction materials. To enable mortgage payments, developers became their own building and loan associations. A few artistic housing developments had been built even before the artistic era. Riverside Park, outside of Chicago, designed by the firm of Vaux, Withers and Olmsted in 1868, was one of America's first picturesque suburban developments. Between 1876 and 1881, British investor Jonathan Carr built Bedford Park, a subdivision in an outlaying area of London. Designed by R. N. Shaw and E. W. Godwin, the houses were in a brick Queen Anne style with clean white casement window frames, and they sat in carefully walled lots. Bedford Park attracted artists and writers as well as stockbrockers and was much praised and pictured by the British and American architectural press.

So, American builders certainly noticed Riverside and Bedford Park but found these precedents too expensive and too regimented to imitate. The single-family home on its own plot of lawn was too strong of an ideal. Homeowners were too individualistic to conform to any one style, and builders wanted to build what their customers wanted. American developers reached out to the potential homeowner by offering dozens of stylistic and functional models. Architects did work directly for developers, producing plans or finished houses; for example, in 1887, J. Lyman Silsbee designed a handsome Shingle Style house for developer John L. Cochran in Edgewater, a suburb of Chicago. Samuel E. Gross offered houses in dozens of variants in the Aesthetic mode—by 1892 he had built in some sixteen towns and one hundred and fifty subdivisions near Chicago. In San Francisco, Fernando Nelson planned and sold whole subdivisions. Developers certainly imposed conformity on the naturally nonconformist Aesthetic movement,

-- --

[1] Palliser, *Palliser's New Cottage Homes and Details*, np; quoted in Reiff, *Houses from Books*, 107.

Honeybee frieze and field wallpaper, originally designed by Candace Wheeler, 1881; reproduction manufactured by J. R. Burrows & Company, Rockland, MA, 2006. In 1881, leading wallpaper manufacturer Warren, Fuller & Company sponsored an international contest for original wallpaper design, and Candace Wheeler's entry won first prize. Her design for frieze, field wall and dado patterns used images of honeybees, clover, beehives and honeycombs; some elements were rendered realistically while others were conventionalized. The design gained further recognition when it was published in the second edition of Clarence Cook's *What Shall We Do with Our Walls?*, a tract advocating aesthetic wallpapers published by Warren, Fuller & Company. Wheeler's design was put into production, with some modifications, by 1884. The frieze and field papers pictured here are reproductions based on surviving wallpaper in the Ionia Community Library in Ionia, Michigan, formerly a private residence. J. R. Burrows & Company painstakingly copied the scale of the original wallpaper and replicated the colors found in unfaded sections of the wallpaper preserved under architectural moldings and in seams. (Photo: J. R. Burrows & Company.)

but by doing so built street upon street of houses and spread the gospel of artistic houses.

As contractors, builders and developers did their work and people chose their houses, style distinctions became foggy and somewhat irrelevant. Buyer and builder aimed for the same goal: an attractive, affordable house that could be heated and did not leak. Although everyone wanted a lovely house, no one cared much if a house could be termed "Queen Anne," "Eastlake," "Modern Gothic" or even "Free Classical." Nonetheless, the labels did have some meaning. Eastlake and Modern Gothic usually denoted wood construction with obvious timbering and probably decorative spindles. The catchall term "Queen Anne" was often used to describe houses with wood, stone and brick exteriors, especially ones that combined all these materials. Queen Anne houses often had decorative half-timbering, large casement windows and grouped Tudor chimneys. High style advocates claimed that the Queen Anne style was passé by 1884, but distinctly Queen Anne prefab houses were still being sold by Sears in 1908. More important than stylistic fidelity was the impulse to display the most inventive vocabulary of architectural form that could be achieved within the budget. All the styles can be called collectively "Aesthetic movement architecture," or, as the 1888 edition of *Palliser's New Cottage Homes and Details* put it, the new "National Style." The Aesthetic movement was the prevailing style, so it was used, and used with gusto. It is these builders', developers' and contractors' houses, all vaguely Queen Anne, Shingle, Stick or Eastlake that have populated so much of our architectural legacy and still form the backbone of America's most picturesque housing stock.

FINE FITTINGS: WALLPAPER, WINDOWS, WOODWORK AND MORE

The architects, builders, developers and homeowners that lavished attention on the architectural shell of houses did not stint on the interior. They all saw the architectural fittings of a house as yet another opportunity to orchestrate visual delight. The functional elements of a structure—walls, windows, light fixtures, hardware, fireplaces—offered surfaces to elaborate. It helped that machinery made things cheaper; power drove the presses that printed wallpaper, the looms that wove carpets, the saws and lathes that made intricate woodwork. Everyone took heed of the exhortations of Wilde, Morris and Cook and all the household art book writers: beautiful surroundings beautify life. And beauty could be attained through architectural ornament.

The broadest canvases offered were the walls—these were very often wallpapered. Wallpaper was so closely identified

Wallpaper Reprised

Jacob, wallpaper designed by Wook Kim, New York City, 2004. Wook Kim is a textile and wallpaper designer, an installation artist and a teacher at the Rhode Island School of Design. Like William Morris, he consciously makes consumer goods based on thoughtful design and fine craftsmanship. Many of his designs are new takes on motifs used in 1880s: thistles, peacocks and dragonflies. After a generation of comparative neglect, designers are again turning to the field of flat pattern design. Lively colors and intriguing motifs are again seen on wallpaper. (Photo: Wook Kim Wallcoverings, New York City Designer.)

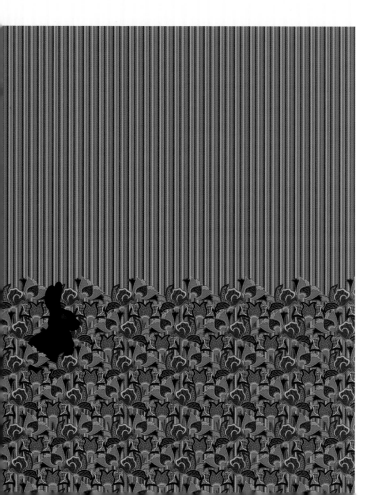

with the new preference for all things artistic that one commentator dismissed the whole new artistic style as "this wallpaper movement."[2] Tastemakers at the highest levels discussed wallpaper. Novelist William Dean Howells, then editor of the *Atlantic Monthly*, wrote a letter in 1873 to his friend Henry James: "We have done some aesthetic wallpapering, thanks to William. Morris whose wallpapers are so much better than his poems; and my library is all in chestnut, with a three-story mantel-piece, after Eastlake—set with tiles, and standing very solidly on a tiled hearth, while overhead is a frescoed ceiling. I try not to be proud."[3]

In 1880, Clarence Cook, working for Warren, Fuller and Company, wrote a preachy little book titled *What Shall We Do with Our Walls*? Wallpaper them, of course, and his book included tipped-in wallpaper samples. Perhaps no other topic received as much coverage in the household art books and decorating magazines. Artistic Americans were devoted to their wallpaper.

Artistic wallpaper adhered to a rigid design canon: it avoided three-dimensional effects and strove for a sense of a flat overall pattern. Illustrations in design manuals and popular journals showed "false" wallpaper patterns (for example, a bouquet of flowers hovering above clouds, all rendered illusionistically) and "true" wallpaper patterns (flattened, conventionalized sunflowers laid out in strict symmetry, within a grid work of abstracted trellising). Americans showed a definite Anglophlic taste in wallpaper; they bought imported British wallpapers, patterns by British designers, derivatives of their work and outright plagiarisms. Even though they were expensive, Morris wallpapers set the style (see image on page 14). There is some evidence that Morris wallpapers became passé for the most sophisticated homemakers by the mid-1880s, but long after that prominent stores proudly proclaimed themselves as agents for the papers. Besides Morris (who designed over fifty patterns in his lifetime), Christopher Dresser, Peter Bonnet Wight, Walter Crane, J. Moyr Smith and E. W. Godwin, all British, designed wallpaper that was sold in America. Dresser designed at least thirteen patterns for Wilson and Fenimore, a Philadelphia manufacturer. A few superstar American designers, namely Louis Comfort Tiffany, Candace Wheeler and Samuel Colman, turned their talents to wallpaper. But, the designers of the vast majority of artistic American wallpaper patterns remain unknown. Even the manufacturers of many are not known, since many extant samples are not marked. There are thousands of patterns preserved in archives that are known to

-- -- -- -- -- -- -- -- -- -- -- -- -- -- -- -- -- --
[2] "Mr. Wilde and his Gospel," 14.
[3] Arms and Lohmann, eds., *W. D. Howells*, 2:34.

have been used in American homes, dozens of American firms are recorded, and dozens more foreign manufacturers whose products were marketed in America. There were rich choices, from the medievalizing naturalism of Morris, the rigid geometries of Dresser, the quaint historicity of J. Moyr Smith, the abstract elegance of Colman. A similar aesthetic range was available in American-designed and -made wall-papers, from the subtle spiderweb and clematis printed in burnished metallic colors in creamy ground (designed by Tiffany) to a gaudy novelty paper showing scenes of Niagara Falls and the Brooklyn Bridge interspersed with Japanese vases (by an unknown, presumably American maker).

The era dictated (as God did to Adam) that it is not good to be alone; wallpapers had companions. Rarely was only one pattern of wallpaper used in a room—they were used in combination. The most common configuration was a three-part wallpaper set consisting of a frieze, fill and dado. This set could be supplemented with borders, ceiling ornaments and medallions. Usually, the dado (the portion of the wall between the floorboard and roughly the height of a chair rail) would have the densest pattern and most saturated color, the field wall (above the dado, usually the largest space) would have the lightest, least-dense pattern, and the frieze (a band just below the ceiling) would have the most figurative or even allegorical design. A set would be com-posed of wallpapers with similar palettes and motifs. Hundreds if not thousands of patterns were on the market at any one time. Wallpaper could be used with painted walls, wood wainscoting, fabric, straw matting or any num-ber of other wall coverings. Sometimes decorators provided access to papers, but often the homeowner shopped her-self, mixing and matching patterns by different manufacturers. To help envision how wallpapers would look in combination on the wall, merchants could load their stock onto a wallpaper-and-border exhibitor, a machine that allowed the buyer to scroll through several rolls of wallpaper simultaneously. Many homemakers surely delighted in the limitless combinations.

A few companies and processes stand out. Jeffrey and Company manufactured William Morris wallpapers until well into the twentieth century, and they were the most aggres-sive in commissioning Britain's elite designers to make wallpaper. Warren, Fuller and Company (which became Warren, Fuller and Lange by 1883) likewise commissioned important American designers Samuel Colman, Candace Wheeler and Louis Comfort Tiffany (who, perhaps not coin-cidentally, later were the winners of the design competition

Cook's book celebrated). At least some of the leading American manufacturers of artistic papers can be discerned from period ads and surviving marked samples: Frederick R. Beck and Company and Robert Graves (both of New York); M. H. Birge Company (Buffalo, New York); Howell and Brothers (Philadelphia). Hand processes (such as wood block printing) and machine processes (such as roller printing) were used, sometimes in combination. Distemper inks, which are water based, but mixed with sizing to make them thick, matte and adherent, were used. Metallic inks, espe-cially bronzes in all tones from bright gold to dull coppery red, were very, very common, even as ground colors. Special effects were achieved through special materials, like sparkly pulverized mica or thick, textured flocking. Embossing in very high relief became fashionable; flowers and foliage could stand up from the ground an inch or more. The most elaborated form of embossing was a special process known as Lincrusta Walton that used gilded composition materials to imitate tooled leather. It has proved extremely durable; much of it survives today where it was originally hung. Although "true" Lincrusta Walton was patented by Frederick Walton and manufactured by Frederick R. Beck and Company, it was imitated under many brand names by many companies. Another sort of embossed paper, known as Japanese leather, was actually made of thick paper that was pounded, colored and varnished to resemble leather. Most Japanese leather papers were really made in Japan, but the American company Rottman, Strome and Company also made them. Even plain one-tone papers were made, but most were enlivened by the nubs and flecks left in roughly processed paper pulp.

Tiles were almost as important as wallpaper to signify an artistic household. As the housing market expanded, so did the market for tiles. Sanitary, durable and heat resistant, tiles were must-haves for bathrooms, kitchens and hallways, and as a base for stoves and other hot and high-traffic areas. Tiles formed borders to wood floors. They were used as baseboards and at the top edge of dados and on the uprights of stairs. They were rarely omitted from mantel-pieces. Tiles for the fireplace were often designed as a set, with corner pieces and center medallions, verticals and hori-zontals. For example, a set could consist of two coordinating floral vertical pieces for either side of the fire-place opening, with fauna along the lintel and a medallion showing a portrait head, all bound together with a coordi-nating border (see image on page 94). Tiles were also incorporated into andirons and metal fireplace surrounds.

top, left: J. & J. G. Low Art Tile Works, Chelsea, MA, 1881–85.
top, center: Unknown maker, probably American, ca 1880s.
top, right: Minton's, Ltd., Stoke-on-Trent, England, probably late 1870s.
bottom: Minton's, Ltd., Stoke-on-Trent, ca 1880s.

The tiles manufactured by Minton were transfer-printed on a light ground. This technique was used as an industrial process, especially by the large English factories; it allowed large-scale production of colorful, attractive, relatively inexpensive tile. During the Aesthetic era, Mintons, Ltd., and its sister company Minton, Hollins & Company became the world's leading producer of architectural tile. In contrast, American "art" tiles were made in workshop settings, which could only achieve small-scale production. Typically, American art tiles were molded by hand and rich, sophisticated glazes were applied. (Collection of Sarah Eigen [American art tiles], New York City, and the author [English tiles].)

Tiles for less trafficked areas could have printed or painted figurative designs. The English manufacturers perfected long-wear "encaustic" tiles, composed of layers of colored clay so that the pattern was as thick as the tile itself and could not be worn away. Americans imported both tiles and tile makers, hiring away British craftsmen. But the big English manufacturers, such as Minton, Maw and Company, Wedgwood and T. and R. Boote, supplied much of the American market for durable architectural tiles.

An "art tile" industry sprang up in America. At the very top end were tiles hand painted by working painters, like those of the Tile Club. Only a few verified examples of the work of the Tile Club survive, but ads in household art magazine and listings in directories indicate that hundreds of professional tile painters were active in America. Besides hand painting, decoration on tiles was transfer printed, molded and impressed. Rich, earth-toned glazes were preferred, and they puddled into depressions to create artful and realistic effects. J. and J. G. Low Art Tile Works of Chelsea, Massachusetts, were especially innovative, and the "plastic sketches" by Arthur Osborne, delicate low-relief scenes, often of pastoral or mythological themes, are especially notable. Isaac Broome, a prolific designer, worked for both Trent Tile Company

right: Fireplace surround; tiles painted by Edwin Austin Abbey, ca 1879, and manufactured by Minton, Hollins & Company; fireback by an unknown manufacturer, ca 1880s. The tiles were painted by Edwin Austin Abbey, a well-known easel painter, muralist and, at this date, a member of the Tile Club. A portion of the fireplace was illustrated in an 1879 article about the Tile Club. The tiles are a recent find; few documented works by Tile Club members are known. Club members included avant-garde painters, illustrators, portrait photographer Napoleon Sarony and others in the New York City art world. (Collection of José Arias—Martin Cohen.)

facing: Fish, Flowers, and Fruit, window transom designed by Louis Comfort Tiffany, New York City, ca 1885. During the Aesthetic era, stained glass moved out of its traditional religious setting and into the home. By the late 1870s, Louis Comfort Tiffany turned his attention to stained glass for domestic interiors. Like other makers of the era, he rejected painting on glass, a common practice. Instead, he worked with small glass furnaces to achieve new tonal effects in glass, and, by 1881, he had patented certain types of glass. Tiffany's glass achieved novel illusionistic effects. This window, originally a transom in the dining room of Mary Elizabeth Garrett's Baltimore house, conveys the look of fish in water. (The Baltimore Museum of Art: BMA 1979.173.)

and Providential Tile Works in Trenton, New Jersey, making subtle patterned and figurative tiles. American Encaustic Tiling Company made both encaustic tiles and printed tiles with designs from Walter Crane's *Baby's Opera*, a children's song book. Americans also collected old tiles; tin-glazed monochromatic Delft tiles were especially popular for fireplace surrounds (see images on pages 132 and 154). These art tiles were the prima donnas, designed not so much for foot traffic as eye traffic.

Stained glass became one more architectural surface upon which artistic attention could be lavished. The craft of stained glass, mostly dormant for centuries, was suddenly revived. It was spurred by an increase in church building, especially by Anglo-Protestant "high church" sects devoted to rich ritual and display. These churches loosely modeled themselves after the medieval parish churches of Europe, especially those in the English countryside, where the crafts of stonework, ironwork, fresco painting, wood carving and stained glass were enshrined. The same architects and artists who undertook ecclesiastical work were active as domestic designers. So, wealthy parishioners commissioned stained glass for their homes, then artisans and manufacturers began producing stained glass that could be bought readymade through an architect or even by catalog.

Americans were truly innovative in the field of stained glass, as artisans and as marketers. The two geniuses in the field, recognized around the world, were Americans: John La Farge and Louis Comfort Tiffany. They did not try to use stained glass to imitate painting, as was the prevailing mode. Instead, they used glass for its own sake, originating new effects in color and light. They, and many other producers, applied the era's design principles to stained glass, relying on the nature of glass to produce flat planes of glowing color. Stained glass, like wallpaper and tiles, was recognized as a special

product of the era: "The great aesthetic wave, which has carried taste and beauty into the adornment of the modern home, has borne colored glass upon its crest."[4]

John La Farge, painter, collector, inventor, put all of his talents to the task of achieving the unique effects of luminous color that are only achievable in glass. He realized that the usual method of stained-glass production (a cartoon was handed to a fabricator) separated designer and maker and invariably weakened the final product. He inserted himself in the process. He went to glass suppliers and chose the imperfect streaked and striated pieces. He experimented by layering different colors of glass and embedding cast-glass "jewels" within larger pieces of glass. He began working with the molten glass, stretching it, rolling it to get corrugated surfaces, pricking it, stamping it with patterns and otherwise manipulating its surfaces. Around 1878, he made a series of related windows on the theme of peonies blowing in the wind, a motif informed by his profound knowledge of Japanese prints and decorative arts. In other windows, La Farge integrated design sources as diverse as Ming painting and medieval stained glass in the watercolors

that served as working models for his windows. He sourced glass directly from glassmakers and worked with a team of master craftsmen to execute his designs.

Simultaneously, Tiffany was innovating. Like La Farge, Tiffany had worked as a painter; he had traveled and looked at much art. All of this informed his artistic sense. In 1879, Tiffany created a window for his apartment showing a still life of eggplants, the curvature of the vegetables suggested by different tones of purple. He was particularly adept at using glass to suggest illusionistic effects and abstract patterns simultaneously; water ripples could be inferred from the corrugations of glass surfaces or drapery could be implied by the swirls of different colors in glass. By 1881, both Tiffany and La Farge had patented methods of making "opalescent" glass, a milky white opaque glass that contained flashing hints of color in its depths, like fire opals.

The two pushed the field forward. Both all but abandoned painting on glass. Both worked with furnaces to produce ever more novel effects in glass color, opacity and texture. Their work in domestic settings focused on secular themes, taken from the Orient and from nature, and

4 "Costly Tints in Glass"; quoted in Metropolitan Museum of Art, *In Pursuit of Beauty*, 177.

Mantelpieces for Charles W. Chandler, an illustration from *American Architect and Building News,* March 15, 1879, later hand colored by an unknown artist. During the Aesthetic era, mantelpieces were showcases of architectural detail, incorporating wood, tile, metalwork and more. These designs came from the office of James P. Sims, a Philadelphia architect. Both designs are apparently by the young Wilson Eyre (see his signature, lower right), who became an important interpreter of the Queen Anne in domestic architecture. The mantel design at left, with its tiles showing nursery tales and aquatic motifs, would have been suitable for a child's room, while the larger mantel at right was suitable for a parlor.

employed a rich vocabulary of historical ornamental motifs. Each was kept busy by a roster of very rich clients, who sometimes had work from both artists in their houses.

By the mid-1880s, there was a large field of stained-glass producers in America. Charles Booth, already strongly aligned to Christopher Dresser's rigid geometric and abstract botanical forms, came to work in the United States from Liverpool by 1875. In 1876 and 1878, Booth published two books and started a journal that showed and described his designs (the influence of these on the nascent graphic design field has not yet been traced). He also produced windows that celebrated his weird, flattened plant forms. Daniel Cottier, the retailer, had begun his career in Glasgow as a color-boy (i.e., an assistant to a painter) and as a glass stainer. By 1873, from his shop in New York, he advertised his services as an upholsterer, cabinetmaker and stained-glass maker. His designs, featuring Pre-Raphaelite women, were decidedly secular. La Farge continued as a stained-glass producer, but his pace slackened after his interior decorating firm disbanded in the mid-1880s. By then, Tiffany's large stained-glass workshop was producing secular and ecclesiastical windows, and Tiffany sometimes collaborated with the leading painters of the day on the preliminary drawings for windows, whose execution he supervised. At several glasshouses, he supervised the making of the glass for his windows, and in 1893 he inaugurated his own glass factory. Tiffany, La Farge, Booth and Cottier were the most well-known among a large number of artisans making stained glass; many more advertised directly to artistic patrons in magazines. They supplied transom lights, large panels for stairwells and other architectural settings, and they worked for private clients or developers. In 1884, at the height of the artistic era, some two thousand people were employed in New York City in the design and manufacture of stained-glass windows.

Besides wallpaper, tiles and stained glass, the visual effects of interiors were accomplished through a myriad of architectural detail. Mass manufacture of decorative woodwork, known as millwork, was made possible by power machines that lathed, scroll sawed, carved and otherwise manipulated raw wood. With machines, the size and shape of spindles, brackets,

fretwork and moldings were infinitely variable and infinitely replicable. Wood components were used decoratively in transoms, banisters, ceiling beams, dado paneling and elsewhere. Ads for wood fancywork were directed towards builders, of course, but were also found in the pages of pattern books and decorating magazines aimed at consumers. Using catalogs from manufactures like the National Wood Manufacturing Company, builders or homeowners could compose wood "carpets" of prefabricated parquet tiles. One could buy a whole floor, or simply lay borders or center ornaments. Miscellaneous bits of hardware were advertised to the consumer: solid leather decorative nails, etched-glass panels, tooled leather, marble hearths and flooring panels. The homeowner could work with an architect, interior designer or a carpenter in choosing and siting such details. J. L. Mott Iron Works, an important manufacturer of cast-iron storefronts and stoves, made porcelain-lined bathroom fixtures, some with artistic bands of enameled decoration. Its ads show bathtubs, toilets and sinks set into wood-paneled enclosures ornamented with tiles. Architectural detail culminated in natural focal points, such as fireplaces, stair railings and front doors. These were often extravaganzas of wood, glass, metal and tile.

Metal was a fertile medium for the expression of artistic ideas in architectural detail. Brass, bronze, copper, cast and wrought iron were all used and used in combination with one another. These metals could be plated with other metals or given chemical coatings that produced patinas of many shades and textures. To the standard vocabulary of conventionalized flowers, birds and historic motifs, designers added a set of abstracted motifs, such as flanges, knobs, angled feet and arms, sunbursts, twisted cord moldings and more. These forms, based on solid geometrical shapes, were especially suited to the casting and stamping processes used in production of sheet metals. The metal-making firms were concentrated in certain locales, especially New York City, Newark, New Jersey, and in a band of towns across central Connecticut, extending from Waterbury to Hartford. British imports from a long-established metalworking industry centered in Birmingham competed strongly with American products. Many makers used many different metals and made all sorts of architectural objects, but there was some specialization.

Metal was a suitable material for much architectural trim: hot-air gratings, curtain rods, fireplace frames, grates and fenders. Decorative elements, such as plaques, bosses and moldings, were fabricated from sheet metal and applied

Ornamenting Architecture Now

Monsoon Mambo, mosaic panel designed by Robert Kushner, installed in the restaurant Tabla, New York City, 1998. Modern, upscale restaurants highlight fine architectural detail, just as they did in the Aesthetic era. This mosaic ornaments a stair landing in Tabla, a nouvelle-cuisine, Indian fusion restaurant in New York City. The panel, over eight feet tall, is composed of pieces of marble, glass, mirror, abalone shell, mother-of-pearl, amethyst, topaz, garnet and lapis lazuli. In the 1970s, Robert Kushner was among a group of painters that critics dubbed New York's Pattern and Decoration movement. Now, his interest in patterning, rich color and sumptuous surfaces is seen in mosaics and other decorative arts as well as paintings. This mosaic is an apt visual accompaniment to the exotic food. (Photo: Adam Reich; courtesy of Robert Kushner.)

to wood or plaster. High-end decorators put their own designs into production at their workshops; an 1876 article on Pottier and Stymus describes a department for that purpose. A few important American artists designed firebacks. Elihu Vedder designed a set that was produced for a few months in 1881–82 by J. and J. G. Low Art Tile Works. An active hardware industry turned out all manner of solid hardware necessary for a functioning house, such as locks, doorknobs, hinge plates and doorplates; the Nashua Lock Company (of Nashua, New Hampshire) and the American Ring Company (of Waterbury, Connecticut) were especially productive. Cast-iron stoves began to exhibit Aesthetic movement motifs and have inset art tiles. The lighting fixtures of the Aesthetic era, designed and redesigned in response to the evolving and still-unreliable technologies of oil, gas and electricity, became major artistic statements. Leading producers were Mitchell, Vance and Company and Manhattan Brass Company in New York City, but these firms were simply the tip of the American iceberg. These chandeliers became showcases for all the different metals, patinas and artistic motifs, but brass predominated. Often other materials were incorporated into the shades and reflectors of large chandeliers so that a pleasing contrast of metal, glass and ceramics would result.

The Aesthetic era encouraged the brilliant melding of architectural shell and interior fittings. Many such *gesamptkunstwerks* are documented (albeit in black and white) in George William Sheldon's *Artistic Houses*, the lavish photo album of interiors (see image on page 40). The names of the most prominent tastemakers who created these interiors have already surfaced: the firm of Herter Brothers, Louis Comfort Tiffany and his collaborators in Associated Artists, John La Farge's work as a designer and organizer of other artists, and Stanford White's role as the designer of the fittings of his houses.

top: Doorplates, by an unknown maker, perhaps English, ca 1875. These brass doorplates protected the wood surrounding the doorknob and keyhole from scratches. They are ornamented with sunflowers, an emblem of the Aesthetic movement. The doorplates were not marked by the maker but have the monogram of the homeowner, "RD," suggesting they were a private commission. (Courtesy of Associated Artists, LLC, Southport, CT. Photo: John Cessna.)

bottom: Gasolier, by Mitchell, Vance and Company, New York City, with ceramic elements by Longwy Faience Company, Longwy, France, ca 1880. Mitchell, Vance and Company was among America's most productive manufacturers of metal furnishings and fixtures. This fixture is cast brass with silver plating, and although it is now fitted for electricity, and has period replacement shades, its original keys to open the gas cocks remain in place. Mitchell, Vance and Company, like many of the other "art brass" makers, incorporated ceramics into their designs, and here the distinctive bright blue ground of the Longwy ceramics contrasts vividly with the silver. The ceramics are used ingeniously: at the center of the fixture is a square tea tray; above it is a sugar bowl; and below the tray hangs the bowl's lid, used as a pendant. The four cylinders could be candlesticks. (Courtesy of Associated Artists, LLC, Southport, CT. Photo: John Cessna.)

Front door of the Samuel Tilton House, Newport, RI, designed by McKim, Mead and White, completed 1882. This house, an early commission for the young architectural firm of McKim, Mead and White, incorporates an astonishing variety of inventive architectural detail in a modestly sized house. Visible in this photo of the vestibule is the front door, composed of blocks of pine cut to expose the end grain, decorated with classical carved rosettes and abstract hammered brass hardware. The window uses bottle bottoms set in a field of red glass surrounded by frosted bricks of clear glass. The interior detailing of the Tilton House draws upon diverse sources: American colonial architecture (part of Newport's heritage), the new Queen Anne style, Japanese woodwork, Jacobean wood carving and even the nascent abstract Art Nouveau. (Photo: © 2005 Jonathan Wallen.)

Herter Brothers produced smooth, polished interiors in elegant historical styles (see image on page 41). For example, in 1884 the firm completed a house for W. D Washburn, then governor of Minnesota. The drawing room was a "light Louis IV style," with silk-covered walls and furniture that matched the paneling in rosewood with brass inlay. In contrast, Louis C. Tiffany & Associated Artists was better known for successfully merging the work of its individualistic contributors (see images on pages 40 and 50): Colman might incorporate Japanese sword guards in the fireplace tiling, Wheeler could invent magical embroideries, and Lockwood de Forest's carved teak panels and moldings were inventively integrated into wall screens and furniture. Although Stanford White became the consummate neo-colonial detailer for the firm McKim, Mead and White, in the 1870s and 1880s his interiors were eclectic and ahistorical. He invented columns sheathed in fishscale carving, superimposed a giant classic paterae on an Oriental basket-weave lattice, arranged brass tacks into sunburst patterns and salvaged

panels from Breton bedbox to panel and inglenook (see image on page 143). Tiffany's most stellar work on his own as an interior designer was arguably the Henry O. and Louisine Havemeyer house in New York City. Completed 1890–91, it was resplendent with glass and stone mosaics on floors, windows and furniture and a spectacular hanging glass staircase. A few architectural elements survive, including a fire screen of amethyst glass rods and gold filigree; an overmantel with two preening peacocks rendered in glass tiles of gilt, iridescent blue and green and mother-of-pearl; and huge glass "jewels" of green and opal glass. It was like living in a jewel box. In these masterpieces of interior design, materials are combined in sumptuous, surprising ways. The luminosity and color of glass, the reflectiveness of metal, the intricacy of carving—these materials play up their own innate characteristics to achieve lyrical effects. All these architectural effects demonstrate the era's slogan, "art for art's sake," on the grandest scale.

ART FURNITURE

The artistic homeowner, proud of the solid yet handsome walls of her house and the fine architectural detail to be seen everywhere, naturally turned her attention to furniture. "The expectant householder now casts about to see if it be not possible to buy chairs that are beautiful as well as comfortable, and to procure tables and sideboards that will mean something, as well as hold plate."[5] In the Aesthetic era, furniture became artful as well as useful, and households were beautified with the addition of "art furniture." Not all furniture of the late nineteenth-century was art furniture. Whole parlor suites in respectable Renaissance, Baroque or the "heavy classic" styles (as writer Harriet Spofford termed them) were made throughout the artistic era.[6] But, the artistic householder recognized that art furniture was something new and sought it out. Art furniture seemed to operate outside the canons of historic styles, yet it used elements of those historic precedents. There were styles within the broader category of art furniture, and these will be described, but rigid labeling defeats the purpose. Art furniture is characterized by certain motifs, mostly ahistoric: a stark contrast of solid areas and voids, the breaking up of flat planes into smaller units, a tendency to embellish, a variety of sumptuous materials used in combination. The aim of art furniture was to transcend style in order to achieve aesthetic effect.

Art furniture first appeared in England but spread more rapidly than wildfire. Designs traveled across the Atlantic and were modified so quickly and so drastically that laying claim for origins can be pointless. For practical reasons, imported furniture did not often serve as models (Clarence Cook noted that Daniel Cottier sold only American-made furniture since he had found that English furniture warped in the American climate) so the transfer of designs

Furniture Designs, by Edward Dewson and S. N. Small, as published in *American Architect and Building News,* January 3, 1880, later hand colored by an unknown artist. This illustration shows that all sorts of furniture could be designed in the new Aesthetic movement style, including cabinets, bookcases, mantels and bedroom sets.

-- --
[5] "Concerning Furniture"; quoted in Metropolitan Museum of Art, *In Pursuit of Beauty,* 143.
[6] Spofford. *Art Decoration Applied to Furniture,* 154.

probably happened by way of printed sources. Whether unconsciously or deliberately (or bits of both), in the process of moving from a two-dimensional drawing to a three-dimensional piece of furniture, modifications inevitably crept in. For example, scholars trace the adaptation of a particular small side table design by E. W. Godwin for William Watt, a London furniture maker, which was copied liberally in illustrations by Agnes and Rhoda Garrett, British writers and Clarence Cook. According to Godwin, even before publication by the Garretts and Cook, his original design had already been transformed into a travesty of its former self by American and British commercial manufacturers. These makers could and did claim this design as their own, since Godwin could and would disown it. All this took less than ten years, from about 1867 to about 1877. And, this is an easy case; the evolution of this table is unusually well documented. The attribution of much art furniture is still a minefield. True, many pieces are marked, or their maker is known because a firm provenance to a documented client and manufacturer can be traced. But much high-quality art furniture is undocumented. And, the full output of well-known manufacturers is uncertain. Curators, dealers and collectors are still working to match extant pieces of art furniture to makers and makers to furniture.

The first manifestation of art furniture was known as Eastlake or Modern Gothic. Like Stick Style architecture (that was known in its own day as Eastlake or Modern Gothic), this furniture strayed far from its rugged medieval models. Arguably, American Modern Gothic furniture evolved from mid-century developments of the Gothic style in British architecture. These developments included Charles Barry's Houses of Parliament (which, down to the inkpots, were decorated and furnished by August Welby Northmore Pugin); Anglican and Roman Catholic churches (which were usually sympathetically and sumptuously furnished) by a host of committed Gothicist architects; the flamboyant color and idiosyncratic antiquarianism of William Burges (who began the astonishing Cardiff Castle by 1868); and the most craftsmanly manifestations of the domestic Gothic by the Pre-Raphaelites and the firm Morris, Marshall, Faulkner and Company (the Red House was first in a long line of fully furnished medievalizing houses). Pugin's, Burges's and Morris's medieval furniture and domestic goods were on view in the 1862 London exhibit.

The pieces that grabbed the most attention featured elaborately painted surfaces, often with medieval narratives from Chaucer, Aesop's fables or fairy tales.

A more muscular, less precious version of the medieval was practiced by Bruce Talbert, who had trained as an architect with George Edmund Street. In 1867, already a practicing industrial designer in Britain, Talbert published *Gothic Forms Applied to Furniture, Metalwork and Decoration for Domestic Purposes* at roughly the same time that Charles Locke Eastlake began publishing his series of essays that were soon republished as *The House Beautiful*. The two designers advocated "honest" construction with obvious joinery, simple finishes and straightforward adaptations of medieval motifs. Talbert's designs, more developed and published with measurements and other details, showed furniture in modern medieval-style interiors. These quickly proved themselves to be a visual resource for designers and their patrons. In his short career, Talbert was amazingly prolific, publishing regularly in books and magazines and designing furniture, tiles, metalwork, carpets and other textiles. In 1881, the year of Talbert's death, a New Yorker brought out *Fashionable Furniture*, a selection of unpublished Talbert designs; the title indicates his continued popularity in America.

By the time of the Philadelphia Centennial, the Modern Gothic style was in full flower in the booths of a number of American firms, especially Kimbel & Cabus (from New York

Sideboard, probably by Kimbel & Cabus, New York City, ca 1880. This cabinet is an extravaganza of Modern Gothic furniture, with its ebonized frame, coved top filled with tooled leather, hand-painted tile, and brass and copper hardware. Even with all these elements, it provides plenty of space for the display of objets d'art. Although not marked, the cabinet relates directly to furniture pictured in a surviving photographic album from New York City cabinetmakers Kimbel & Cabus. (Courtesy of Associated Artists, LLC, Southport, CT. Photo: John Cessna.)

above, left: Chair, by an unknown maker, probably New York City, ca 1880. This chair is typical of the high quality, unmarked art furniture made during the Aesthetic era. It probably would have been called Anglo Japanese, for the ebonized frame with its fretwork back. The openwork carving makes the chair attractive from both sides and makes it suitable for a placing in the middle of a parlor. (Collection of Sarah Eigen, New York City.)

above, center: Cabinet, by Herter Brothers, New York City, ca 1875. This cabinet is a virtuoso expression of the Aesthetic movement. It was made by Herter Brothers, and is probably the design of Christian Herter. The formidable stance of the blocky cabinet is lightened by the delicate saber legs, the fretwork at the base, the spindled rails at the gallery and the tiny lotus flower balls trimming the backsplash. Dozens of kinds of woods are used in the marquetry. From the scene depicted on the center panel (paired storks standing on either side of an urn) to the checkerboard blocks integrated into the legs, the motifs used become progressively more abstract. The cabinet offers a complex feast for the eye. (High Museum of Art, Atlanta, GA; Virginia Carroll Crawford Collection, 1981.1000.51.)

above, right: Wicker chair, by Heywood Brothers, Gardner, MA, ca 1880–90. Wicker, lightweight and malleable, can be molded into the ornate forms favored in the artistic era. This chair was made by Heywood Brothers, one of the country's largest makers of wicker furniture and accessories. (Courtesy Southampton Antiques, Southampton, Massachusetts.)

City) and Mitchell & Rammelsburg (from Cincinnati). Oak, chestnut and ebonized wood predominated in massive case furniture. Doors were often hung off distinctive metal-strap hinges, finished in either bright brass or dull nickel plating. The pieces showed off squat columns, angular braces and shelf brackets, as well as a full range of medieval decorative motifs such as trefoils, quatrefoils, dogtooth carving and crockets (see image on the left on page 26). Some pieces had architectonic hoods that towered over the rest of the piece. Particularly mature versions of the Modern Gothic were originated by Frank Furness, the Philadelphia architect, working with cabinetmaker Daniel Pabst, and by Isaac Scott, whose solid buttress-and-tile ornamented furniture of the 1870s can still be seen in the Chicago home of John Jacob and Frances Glessner.

Some art furniture took an entirely different tack. In 1867, E. W. Godwin described his experiences furnishing his London lodgings, which he wished to be modest but artistic: "When I came to the furniture, I found that hardly anything could be bought ready made that was at all suitable to the requirements of the case. I therefore set to work and designed a lot of furniture, and, with a desire for economy, directed it to be made of deal, and to be ebonized. There were no mouldings, no ornamental metalwork, no carving. Such effect as I wanted I endeavored to gain, as in economical building, by the mere grouping of solid and void, and by a more or less broken outline."[7]

A series of extraordinary tables, chairs, cabinets, stands and other forms resulted. The sideboard is perhaps Godwin's

-- -- -- -- -- -- -- -- -- -- -- -- -- -- -- -- -- -- -- --
[7] Godwin, "My Chambers and What I Did to Them, Chapter 1: A. D. 1867," 5; quoted in Kinchen and Stirton, *Is Mr. Ruskin Living Too Long?* 195.

most famous design, the one that rung in a new phase of art furniture, the "Anglo Japanese." Godwin, like many of his contemporaries, deeply admired Japanese domestic architecture, which emphasized planes framed by black lines. So, too, was his sideboard, which was a set of cubes and rectangular solids set upon stands, trimmed with neat metal handles, hinges and drawer fronts covered with Japanese paper. The sideboard is a minimalist grouping of solids and voids. It is a spooky predecessor, by two generations, of Gerrit Reitveld's de Stijl furniture. Godwin's designs, like Talbert's, were known through illustrated publications that included his furniture in room settings (see image on page 50).

"Anglo Japanese" is a malleable term used in the 1880s that describes not only Godwin's designs, but a style that appeared on silver and other decorative arts. Generally, Anglo Japanese furniture is delicate, composed of straight lines, and is usually ebonized. It is characterized by asymmetry, with a careful balance of solids and voids. Often, but not always, overt Japanese motifs are seen: butterflies, fans, fretwork and decorative devices like the stylized Imperial mon. Fashionable by the late 1870s, Anglo Japanese furniture was lauded and much illustrated by the household art writers, especially by Clarence Cook in *The House Beautiful*. Some makers are now identified with the style. A. and H. Lejambre of Philadelphia made a series of graceful tables with brass-toed saber legs and inlaid Orientalist motifs. Much of Herter Brothers output can be classified as Anglo Japanese. Alexandre Sandier, a designer at Herter's, collaborating with Christian Herter, developed the firm's Anglo Japanese cabinetry and interiors. Their designs were executed by German immigrants who had learned woodworking in the Old World. Herter Brother's Anglo Japanese is characterized by rectilinear form greatly ornamented by galleries of spool turnings, drops, finials and, most of all, exquisitely crafted marquetry featuring conventionalized, Orientalized flora and fauna. These Herter Brothers Anglo Japanese cabinets, designed by a Frenchman, executed largely by German workers, in a firm managed by a well-traveled German immigrant, display a vocabulary of Oriental, Greek, Jacobean and outright abstract motifs. Fittingly, they demonstrate the multicultural character of American decorative arts at the end of the nineteenth century.

The Anglo Japanese style stimulated, or responded to, a taste for simple, light pieces. That same taste was met by all sorts of furniture: some old, some that reconstituted old forms and some entirely new. American vernacular furniture, especially Windsor chairs and ladder-backed, rush-bottomed armchairs, were collected and used in sitting rooms. Recognizing the market, Shaker communities stepped up production of their rockers and other items; sometimes these were upholstered in fashionable fabrics. The Thonet Brothers, originators of the famous bentwood café furniture, did a lively business in America. Their chairs were considered especially suitable for dining rooms because they could be cleaned so easily. Wicker furniture was not confined to the porch; its portability made it suitable for parlors where furniture was regrouped as often as conversational situations suggested, but it was also used for lounges and armchairs. Bamboo couches, tables, chairs and other items were imported in large numbers and also made in the United States. In this sort of furniture, bamboo (or, faux bamboo) often formed the frame, seats were caned, and light wood panels or even Japanese prints were set in as ornament. Morris, Marshall, Faulkner and Company sold several sorts of small rush-seated ebonized chairs with spindles. The lyre-backed model was named after the painter Dante Gabriel Rossetti, several models with lathe-turned spindles in the back were known as Sussex chairs, but in America all of them were known collectively as Morris chairs; many American makers made variants. George Hunzinger's ingenious and surprisingly elegant furniture looked as though it had been pieced together from a box of machine parts, and he devised a number of lightweight stationary and folding chairs, including some with a patented type of textile-covered woven wire. And, the art-brass manufacturers branched out from hardware and lighting fixtures to make furniture. Small side tables, pedestals, magazine racks, hanging shelves, mirrors and lamps were made of metal, often augmented by panels of tile, cloth or glass. All this light furniture achieved many aims: simplicity, portability, exoticism and informality.

Some argue that the culmination of art furniture was the Queen Anne style. This was yet another malleable term for a varied style that drew primarily on the lighter phases of eighteenth-century design but also from other eras. As was true for Queen Anne architecture, many argued that the term was a misnomer, but it still had wide currency. The Queen Anne was characterized by elegance and restraint, and as household art manual writer Harriet Spofford put it, the style "makes none of the pretension of the Gothic, and none of the wearisome iteration of the common Classic." It depended on rectangular, upright, boxy forms, and it was solid and compact. The surface of Queen Anne cabinetry is

left: Oil lamp, by the Charles Parker Company, Meriden, CT, ca 1885. Silver-plated flowers are applied to the brass body of this oil lamp. The lamp is representative of "art brass," which mixes brass and other metals like zinc, copper and silver-plated base metals. Any of these metals could receive a patina that would further enliven the surface. The Charles Parker Company published ads in the mid-1880s showing lamps quite similar to this one. (Collection of Richard Reutlinger. Photo: Douglas Sandberg.)

center: Fire screen, by an unknown maker, ca 1875. This fire screen, lightweight and serviceable, retains its original needlework, a rare survival. It is typical of the kind of needlework made at home by artistic ladies, but there is no record that any members of the family that owned this screen were needleworkers. Instead, the furniture maker probably contracted a small, professional workshop for its production. A similar screen, with a different needlework scene, is in the collection of the Newark Museum. (Maymont Foundation, Richmond, VA.)

right: Side chair, designed by Lockwood de Forest, from woodwork made by Misri workers, Ahmedabad, India, ca 1880s. In 1881, American Lockwood de Forest established a workshop in India to revive the carved teak woodwork of the Misri caste. Working with the native carvers and businessmen, de Forest developed a catalog of components that were worked into furniture and architectural fittings. He also worked with Indian craftspeople to develop pierced and carved brass architectural elements. These were sold in America first through Tiffany's short-lived Associated Artists firm and later through de Forest's own decorating firm. Also an avid antiquities collector and an entrepreneur, de Forest imported old brasses, painted Kashmiri furniture, tile, ceramics, jewelry and fabrics back to America. (Collection of José Arias—Martin Cohen.)

invariably broken up into rectangular units, some solid, some open, some visible through glass doors, each treated as an opportunity for differing ornamentation. An amazing variety of decorative treatments could alight in these spaces: tiles, textiles, lacquer panels, stained glass, stamped metal, painted panels—the list goes on. Niches were fenced by spindled railings or covered by beveled glass, making them ideal for the display of objets d'art. The Queen Anne proved ideal for incidental furniture forms, such as plant stands, easels, stools and fire screens. Spofford said it best: "The Queen Anne style, then, may be summed up as possessing the remarkable simplicity and quietness of old work, together with great picturesqueness and some quaintness."[8]

Writers of the era spoke of the "mixed Queen Anne" style and, indeed, many examples were exceedingly mixed. The visual impact of Cincinnati art-carved furniture depends on its extraordinary carved panels, stretchers and other elements; these are usually fitted into a Queen Anne frame (see the top image on page 44). There was an exotic strain within the Queen Anne, which encompassed the low-relief carving and massive forms of furniture designed by Louis Comfort Tiffany, and the furniture from the Misri-caste staffed workshops of Lockwood de Forest and the Moorish arches and fretwork from many manufacturers. Small gilt tables and chairs with dainty upholstery were produced by

-- -- -- -- -- -- -- -- -- -- -- -- -- -- -- --
[8] Spofford, *Art Decoration Applied to Furniture,* 157.

George Hunzinger and other firms as well. After the death of Christian Herter in 1883, the firm evolved and produced furniture with more classical and Renaissance motifs, very freely adapted. In the 1880s, the firm designed a large cabinet with open, rounded sides and life-like caryatids, an erudite exercise that drew upon numerous classical models. They produced it in two versions: in satinwood, with shallow relief Italianate grotesque masks, as well as in gilt, with inset Limoges plaques and ivory inlay. Throughout Queen Anne furniture, American Colonial decorative motifs were adopted frequently, lifted from as far back as the Jacobean sunflowers of Hadley chests and as far forward as the Federal flower baskets of Samuel McIntire (see image on the left on page 29). The mixed Queen Anne was indeed versatile.

The art furniture of the late nineteenth century forms a close parallel to the modern art furniture of today. The same descriptors apply: exquisite craftsmanship, free adaptation of historical motifs, abstract patterning, bold color. The most famous of modern art furniture makers is probably Wendel Castle. Trained as a sculptor, Castle's furniture is playful and organic. He emphasizes the surface qualities of wood, sometimes using it in trompe l'oiel fashion, at other times using chemicals to invent alligatored finishes. He formed a school for wood craftsmanship that has proved to be a germinator of other art furniture makers. Gary Knox Bennett is known for witty, wacky desks, sideboard, lamps and chairs. He uses fine wood, gold and silver plating along with unconventional materials, like ColorCore (a stacked laminate) and coffee cans. His *Boston Kneehole Desk*, designed for the Boston Museum of Fine Arts' "New American Furniture Exhibition" in 1986, is a reaction to a circa 1760 kneehole bureau table in the museum's collection. Bennett's desk is essentially the same form, but made of Formica, aluminum, rosewood, antique bronze and a base of formed brick. There is a larger, younger group of expert furniture makers, but space limitations preclude listing more: Kim MacConnel, who paints expressionistically on vinyl and wood furniture (see image on page 10); Jay Stanger, who constructs furniture from planes of steel, anodized aluminum, tropical woods and dyed veneers; and Christopher Cantwell, who orchestrates dozens, even hundreds of woods in furniture that carries narrative connotations.

COLOR, SPARKLE, PATTERN AND STORY: OBJECTS AND ARTWORK

Even after a house was built and outfitted architecturally, and furniture was added to its rooms, there was more to be done. Windows were swathed with draperies, shelves were laden with objets d'art and walls were adorned with works of art. Many of these furnishings were more beautiful than functional. And, that was precisely the point. As Thorstein Veblen so brilliantly and bitingly critiqued, the bourgeois American house could be designed purely to proclaim status. Gleaming furniture with luxurious upholstery, a display case filled with rare china—these could be tokens of the tribal warfare of conspicuous consumption. But beautiful household furnishings were also a private, family matter. Household furnishings that were meant only for display—"for pretty," as the stolid

Art Furniture Again
He's Playing with Blocks Again, table by Christopher Cantwell, Oakhurst, California, 2004. Modern art furniture is characterized by expert cabinetry and a delight in materials. Brazilian rosewood, cocobolo, wenge and walnut are the main woods used in Cantwell's table, but at least one hundred other types of wood are also used, plus abalone shell! Cantwell's enjoyment of furniture making is evident—thus the title of the piece. The extravagance and finesse of the cabinetry seen here compares to the work of the finest Aesthetic movement cabinetmakers. (Photo credit: Keith Seamans; courtesy of Christopher Cantwell.)

housewife was likely to say—were the very objects that were the most artistic, the most consciously aestheticized. And these objects were placed in a house less to impress visitors than to beautify family life. The purely aesthetic qualities of showy objects—rich color, sensuous texture, curvaceous form—were the qualities that attracted homeowners to own and display these objects. Objects with superior aesthetic qualities elevated all who came in contact with them. By having artistic objects in the home, the household was improved. To outsiders, showy objects could boast of status, but for the family that lived in an artistic household, beautiful objects ennobled everyday existence.

The stars of several constellations aligned to make ceramics of the artistic era outstanding. Training was readily available for amateurs in schools as well as for professionals on the shop floor. There was an experimental outlook in glaze technology, and a can-do attitude about kiln mechanics and firing. New museums exhibited historic and modern ceramics, and these items could be seen regularly at loan shows and mechanics fairs; a few factories, notably Rookwood, formed collections of historic pottery. This meant that access to models from all over the globe, and all eras, had never been greater. All these factors resulted in a huge range of ceramics, produced by amateurs, small shops and large industrial factories. All budgets were met; anyone of moderate means could ornament a bric-a-brac shelf with a piece of artistic pottery.

Hundreds of ceramics factories were active in America during the artistic era and hundreds of British and European factories imported their ceramics to America. On both sides of the Atlantic, many different styles of ceramics came out of the same factory, and the bigger manufacturers sold both expensive and inexpensive ceramics. The flourishing British ceramics industry trained many who made their way to America, where they worked in small and large settings. So much was made in America and made elsewhere but collected and used in America that only the highlights of artistic ceramics can be discussed here.

The history of Western ceramics was a wellspring for many makers. Ancient Greek terra-cotta, painted and unpainted, ceramics were much admired in the Western world; they were the models for Galloway and Graff, a Philadelphia firm, perhaps the most distinctive of the many firms that worked directly after Hellenistic forms. They made klyixes and kraters and painted vases with black silhouetted figures in the style of Attic vessels. Utilitarian techniques and forms, like sgraffito and beer mugs, were updated and adopted by many makers. For example, Laura Fry made naturalistic renderings of animals and flowers for Rookwood. Detailed motifs, sometimes whole narrative scenes, were painted and/or transfer-printed onto plaques, vases and other display ware. Well-known designers worked for major companies: Christopher Dresser's geometric conventionalizing appeared on Wedgwood jardinières; J. Moyr Smith's romantic medieval themes appeared on Minton plates; the Japonisme of Albert Dammouse appeared on fine Sèvres porcelain. And, imitations of these appeared in the products of countless factories. Artists who were comfortable with carving and modeling translated those skills to very high-relief ceramics on plain, low-fired earthenware. Among them were Isaac Scott (an architect/furniture maker) working at Chelsea Keramic Art Works and Agnes Pitman (a wood carver) working at Rookwood.

Much small-scale production centered around the technical and aesthetic challenges of painting under the glaze. Marie Louise McLaughlin, who in 1877 authored a best-selling manual for china painting over the glaze, became intrigued with the displays of French ceramics she had seen at the Philadelphia Centennial. Not knowing any better, she attempted to imitate the "barbotine" technique of underglaze painting by using mineral paints with wet clay slip applied to a wet clay body (the French makers used fired clay slip on a dry body). She met with some success. With other ladies in her native Cincinnati she formed the Pottery Club. They proceeded to develop the technique of underglaze painting, along with many other techniques, such as overglaze painting, carving and overlaying of figural forms. Another Cincinnatian, Maria Longworth Nichols, was invited to join the Pottery Club, but apparently her invitation never arrived. Nichols felt snubbed, and she and McLaughlin became rivals. The two ladies and many of their friends threw, molded and decorated their vessels in backyard studios and rented rooms at the city's numerous small commercial kilns— the town became a hotbed of ceramics production. They tried to fire their wares in these small kilns, not always successfully. By 1880 Nichols founded her own pottery, Rookwood, the same year that McLaughlin published her second ceramics book, *Pottery Decoration Under the Glaze*. Rookwood eventually hired talented ceramics painters, including Albert Valentien and Kataro Shirayamadani, and business manager William Watts Taylor, and grew as an innovative and profitable business. The first decade of Rookwood's production centered on underglaze decoration, works that today count as masterpieces of the Aesthetic movement.

left: Pilgrim flask, by Chelsea Keramic Art Works, Chelsea, MA, 1875–80. The exhibitions of Haviland pottery from Limoges, France, at the Philadelphia Centennial showcased under-the-glaze painting, and they stimulated many American ceramicists to try the same technique. On this flask, part of Chelsea Keramic Art Work's "Bourg-la-Reine" line, the flowers and foliage are painted over a ground glaze, and then a clear glaze is applied over all. This is known as a pilgrim jug because its flattened shape and its handles, through which a rope could be strung, made this type of flask convenient for pilgrims to carry as they traveled. (Courtesy of Associated Artists, LLC, Southport, CT. Photo: John Cessna.)

right: Pitcher, cup and set, by Worcester Royal Porcelain Company, Stoke-on-Trent, England, ca 1880. The Worcester Royal Porcelain Company mastered a large repertoire of complex porcelain glazes and forms, all derived from a comprehensive knowledge of world ceramics. The decoration on this set loosely imitates a type of Japanese ceramics known as Satsuma. Here, motifs that signify Japan are sprinkled across the surface of drinking cup, vase and tray. Worcester Royal produced a variety of wares in this pattern. (Collection of the author. Photo: Thies Wulf and Egon Zippel.)

Ceramicists elsewhere specialized in underglaze technique, especially Charles Volkmar in New York City and Chelsea Keramic Art Works in Chelsea, Massachusetts. All painted with glazes in a stylized fashion, in an aesthetic dominated by Oriental, asymmetric compositions and rich, earthy colors. These makers used all sorts of innovative decorative techniques: small forms like frogs and flowers were added to the body; glazes were applied with an atomizer (something like an airbrush); leaves or other vegetation were pressed into a wet clay body, leaving a delicate impression; the body could be deeply carved; or painted decoration could be overlayed with see-through decoration (see bottom image on page 44).

Non-Western ceramics were powerful models. John Bennett in New York City and Théodore Deck in Paris adapted classic Persian motifs in underglaze painting. William De Morgan in Chelsea, England, imitated Hispano-Moresque lusterware. In Massachusetts, Hugh Robertson of Chelsea Keramic Art Works devoted some years to replicating certain renowned Chinese glazes, such as celadon, peach bloom and *sang de boeuf*, on simple, classical Oriental forms. The influence of China's and Japan's pottery and porcelain was felt everywhere. High-end British makers, especially Worcester Royal, dominated the market. Worcester adopted several Orientalist modes, including crisply painted blue-and-white ware, the gaily colored and gilded look of Satsuma and the adaptation of Oriental motifs in the restricted but sumptuous palettes of metallic tones so popular in the Aesthetic era (see top left image on page 28). The elegant British Orientalism was matched in America by Edward Lycett of the Faience Manufacturing

Artistry in Ceramics

Teapot, by Ralph Bacerra, Los Angeles, CA, 2005. Some modern ceramicists are using intricate and ornate patterning, reminiscent of Aesthetic movement ceramics. Ralph Bacerra works in the demanding medium of intricately glazed and patterned porcelain. A single piece requires many firings. The patterning on this teapot relates loosely to Japanese Imari and Satsuma ceramics, but other influences can be seen: the psychedelic volumetric mazes of M. C. Escher and the orchids and other exotic plants Bacerra raises. The form of the striding teapot is Bacerra's innovation. (Photo courtesy of Garth Clark Gallery; photographer: Mark Freeman.)

Company in Greenpoint, Brooklyn, and by Ott and Brewer in Trenton, New Jersey. The major British factories, with their large staffs and extensive machinery, seemed to make a sport of imitating other materials. The enameling of Mughal India, the damascening of Middle Eastern weaponry, Japanese lacquerware—all were realistically imitated in porcelain.

The modern era has sustained a flourishing art ceramics scene, one portion of which is highly decorative and sensuous. This segment of art ceramics rejects the austere studio pottery tradition of the 1940s and 1950s, and the rugged, monumental hand-built earthenware of the 1960s. One of the leaders has been Adrian Saxe, who makes gilded and colorful vessels sometimes bedecked with flotsam, such as fishing lures, and Betty Woodman, who makes still lifes of large vessels with gestural glazing. Bennett Bean uses layers of colorful tapes on the exterior of his bowls, which have brilliantly gilded interiors. A large number of Americans are painting on ceramics. Cindy Kolodziejki's enigmatic images together tell a story, but since they are on opposites of a vessel, they cannot be seen together. Many ceramicists use the *pique assiette* technique, in which broken bits of salvaged china set into clay are used as bits of mosaic for decorative and narrative effects. Some work in the demanding technique of porcelain, including Ralph Bacerra whose intricately decorated vessels recall the virtuosity of Worcester Royal porcelains.

Glassmakers were not as prodigiously productive and innovative as ceramicists in the artistic era, but some notable showpieces of art glass were made. Americans and European glassmakers used old techniques in new ways and made innovations in the chemistry of glass and the industrial production of glass. Unlike ceramics, glass cannot be made at home, so all art glass was made in a commercial setting; this inherently violated the era's love of handcraftmaship. Nonetheless, artful effects were achieved. Techniques that yielded figurative motifs were used. Enamels were painted on the exterior and interior of vessels, and everything from winsome Pre-Raphaelite ladies to abstracted patterns of jewels were depicted. Molds for pressed glass were cut with Japanesque palm fronds and abstract shapes à la Christopher Dresser. Thomas Webb and Sons of Stourbridge, England, was the most productive of the many factories that made cameo glass, in which a top layer is cut away to reveal a different color layer below. Other techniques yielded abstract forms, with emphasis placed on the purely aesthetic form of transparent, opaque and patterned glass. Many sorts of Venetian techniques, like *latticino* and *millefiori* that twist, cut, embed and otherwise manipulate canes of different colors of glass, were practiced elsewhere. Several American firms perfected overshot glass (also known as craquelle, or frosted) in which red-hot glass is plunged into cold water, and then immediately reheated; the result is glass that resembles cracked ice. These techniques were the building blocks of art glass.

Distinct types of art glass appeared, were named and became collected by artistic households. American companies invented trade names for their patented styles: Amberina (by New England Glass Company of

East Cambridge, Massachusetts, and after 1888, Toledo, Ohio), which is a transparent glass with different clear red tones, especially rubies and ambers; Royal Flemish (by Mount Washington Glass Company of South Boston and New Bedford, Massachusetts), which evoked stained glass or *plique-a-jour* enamels through lines of raised gilding and rich colors; Spangled (by Hobbs, Brockunier and Company of Wheeling, West Virginia), which sparkled with bits of embedded mica or other reflective minerals; Burmese (by Mount Washington Glass Company, New Bedford, Massachusetts), which was an opaque glass shading from lemon yellow to a light rosy pink. Mostly, these companies produced baluster-form vases destined for the display shelf, though there was some use of historical and exotic forms, like long-necked Persian water bottles. Some art glass was worked into furniture, especially screens to set in front of a window or the fire to catch light.

There was a large trade in imported British, French and Bohemian glass in aesthetic forms, but Venetian glass was the most avidly sought. The glass-making island of Murano exported expertly blown and lamp-worked pieces that capitalized on historic forms and went way beyond them. The virtuoso products of Salviati and many smaller companies pack all glass history into fanciful forms; dragons and sea monsters twine themselves around gold-flecked, rainbow-threaded beakers. Beginning around 1893, Louis Comfort Tiffany began making blown glass for the first time, and around the turn of the century he began fabricating stained-glass lamps. His famous iridescent Favrile glass, the nacreous and pimpled surface texture of his Cypriote glass, the Lava vases that look like just-hardened, still-cooling lava fields, the flowers and insects that glow on the lamp shades—all these might be considered the last gasp of the Aesthetic movement or the first glimpses of the Art Nouveau.

The modern art-glass scene is active and aestheticized. The giant in the field is Dale Chihuly. Trained with Harvey Littleton, who revived studio-glass production in America, Chihuly has been a larger-than-life figure who directs glass-blowing teams while wearing an eye patch (the result of a motorbike accident). He is a master technician and a great colorist, and he uses his organic blown forms as sculptures that often suggest marine forms. He has hung massive chandeliers over the canals in Venice and made glass floats for rivers in Japan. Toots Zynsky, a cofounder of the Pilchuck School and the UrbanGlass studio in New York, is famous for free-form pots made up of thousands of brightly colored glass threads. Richard Marquis uses traditional Venetian techniques in unorthodox and witty forms. For example, he used the hot-slab construction method for a candy-striped dust pan. Dante Marioni groups his opaque colored glass vessels with their lyrical, linear handles to make patterns. In these works, glassmakers use abstract glass forms to suggest other ideas.

Clarence Cook, reveling in the quality of fabrics available to the average homeowner, commented, "There has not been for a hundred years and over, such a time as ours for the beauty and excellence of the stuffs that are used in household decoration. Any one who will go into Herter's or Cottier's and look over their plushes, silks, serges and all the nameless materials that are being made nowadays in England, France and Austria, will easily see enough

Folding screen, by an unknown maker, probably American, 1885. This handsome screen, with its abstract, colorful patterns, was probably made in New York City, the center for high-end stained-glass making during the Aesthetic era. The glass is fitted into a wood frame, and the lower register is made of pierced and painted brass panels. This screen stylistically relates to one in the collection of the Metropolitan Museum of Art in New York City. The screen would have formed a sculptural element in an artistic parlor, filtering and coloring light. (Courtesy of Associated Artists, LLC, Southport, CT. Photo: John Cessna.)

Modern Art Glass

Soft Form, Kelp (Dictyoneuropsis), by Kait Rhodes, Seattle, WA, 2005. American art glass is undergoing a renaissance as a generation of skilled, imaginative craftspeople are reviving old techniques and inventing new ones. This sculpture is composed of hollow canes of glass, wired together to make a form suggesting kelp. At sixty-two inches high, the sculpture is scaled like the kelp Rhodes sees when she scuba dives in the Puget Sound. The sculpture suggests a natural form but also plays with our assumptions about the rigid, brittle qualities of glass. (Photo: Roger Schreiber; courtesy of Kait Rhodes.)

in half an hour to justify my remark."[8] Industry revolutionized fabric weaving and ornamentation. Threads formerly spun in a day now took an hour, and an hour's worth of hand-weaving was now turned out on a power loom in minutes. Now, fine fabrics were much more widely available. Plentiful fabrics and trims as well as advances in the springs used for upholstery enabled upholsterers to achieve effects never before witnessed in the parlor. The different planes of a chair could each be treated with different fabric, and each fabric could be applied in a different manner; the seat and back of a chair could be covered in buttoned silk damask, the depth of each emphasized by being covered in darker-colored, pleated plush side panels. Only a small segment of overall textile production could be termed, unequivocally, artistic, but, used imaginatively, even plain textiles could contribute to an artistic effect.

Repeating the practice in other industries, top designers worked for major textile mills, but factories also had their own designers who remained anonymous. William Morris, again, was a leading light. His chintzes and woven woolens, like his wallpapers, featured flat patterning with botanical motifs. And, Morris's textiles, like his wallpapers, were ubiquitous in the artistic home. Christopher Dresser and Bruce Talbert also designed for the major English mills that exported large quantities of furnishing fabrics to America. Oriental silks— plain and embroidered, new and antique—were sold through the thousands of Japanese novelty stores peppered across America. They were used as upholstery and even wall coverings (see image on the right on page 29); Samuel Colman used a large collection of Japanese silks to cover the ceiling and walls of Henry Havemeyer's library. Cheney Brothers of Manchester, Connecticut, employed Candace Wheeler to design a number of silks, linens and cottons. Many look very modern, including a design of carp swimming among large bubbles, printed either as white on denim, or orange on blue silk. Portieres, the large curtains hung in doorways, became blank slates for artistic expression. The best designers in the major decorating companies, like Associated

-- --
[8] Cook, *The House Beautiful,* 139.

facing, left: Side chair, probably made in New York, with original upholstery, 1880–85. Clarence Cook commended the high-end New York shops for the wonderful "stuffs" they carried—fabrics from around the world, old and new. This chair is rare, since it retains its original upholstery. The chair was probably made in New York City. It uses the new technology of springs to achieve its shape. The origin of the upholstery fabrics are unknown, but probably both imported and domestic material was used. The seat and back are covered in embroidered silk, the side panels are two shades of velvet, and the trim is a system of fringed netting, drop tassels, gimp and passementerie. A complex color scheme of brown, red, olive and orange is maintained throughout all the fabric and trim. (High Museum of Art, Atlanta, GA; Virginia Carroll Crawford Collection, 1984.117.)

facing, right: Portiere panel for the John Sloane House, New York City, designed by Herter Brothers, manufactured in France, ca 1882. This portiere panel showcases the luxurious fabrics and expert workmanship typical of the era, especially of Herter Brothers designs. The panel, composed of silk damask, velour and many types of embroidery, was fabricated in France. The apricot-colored fabric with the pattern of dragonflies and water lilies was designed by Christian Herter, who had it made in several colors and used it in other commissions as upholstery and as drapery. (Brooklyn Museum 41.980.83; gift of Mr. and Mrs. William E. S. Griswold in memory of her father, John Sloane.)

Artists and Herter Brothers, integrated the design of portieres into the design of the room. Typically, the dado-field-frieze divisions of the room would be paralleled in the horizontal bands of the portiere, each composed of different fabric, each treated separately. A group of expert needleworkers, including Mary Tillinghast and Maria Oakey Dewing of New York City, supplied embroidered, appliquéd and otherwise ornamented textiles, usually on commission to decorators, for costly metropolitan houses. The wealthy could also buy William Morris's hand-knotted wool rugs, woven of vegetable-dyed yarns; these were called Hammersmith carpets, after the location of the workshop. Imported Middle Eastern carpets, now avidly collected, were only a little less expensive than they are today.

Interestingly, there is a new generation of needleworkers. They use old stitches and invent new ones, incorporate beads and bricolage into their stitchery, all in very modern motifs and compositions. Not surprisingly, they are mostly women: examples by Missy Stevens and Renie Breskin Adams are important.

Painting and sculpture, which served no functional purpose at all, were the top dogs among the showpieces of the artistic house. Following the exuberance and bravado of Hudson River School landscape paintings and the heroic marble statuary of mid-century, there was a turn towards a more introspective, more introverted viewpoint among painters and sculptors. A stylish portrait by John Singer Sargent, a melancholy landscape by Alexander Helwig Wyant, an academic genre scene by a French or English painter, a bronze animal figural group by Antoine Louis Barye—these were the stars of the show. One painter, Charles Caryl Coleman, specialized in still lifes that celebrated the sort of artistic objects that connoisseurs sought: imported Venetian glass, antique textiles, Persian tiles, Italian maiolica pottery. But very few people could buy such a treat. Patrons of only moderate means could, however, own paintings and sculpture by less well-known artists or copies after famous ones. Very high-quality engravings after the old masters and the modern masters were made by Timothy Cole and sold worldwide. Casts of certain classical and Renaissance statuary, such as

Needleworking Revived
Queen of the Ocean, needlework piece by Missy Stevens, 2002. Stevens is part of a needlework revival that is occurring among professional artists and amateur craftspeople who are mostly women. This needlework piece incorporates silk, cotton, rayon and metallic threads, glass beads, seed pearls and more in many kinds of stitches. A mermaid swims in a seascape embroidered on the back of a kimono. Although the narrative is mysterious and charming, the intricacy and subtlety of the stitchery is the real topic of the piece. (Collection of the author. Photo: Thies Wulf and Egon Zippel.)

the Venus de Milo or Luca della Robbia's charming choir boys in song were a tasteful accompaniment to any decor. And, Prang's color lithographs after more popular paintings, as well as framed copies of the color supplements from magazines, were the scenery of many, many artistic rooms.

FAMILY FURNISHINGS

Artistic things were used everyday in the artful household. The tableware of the era, the furnishings of bedrooms and nurseries—these were also the domain of the Aesthetic movement. The commitment to the artistic life was evident with these private family objects.

The combination of the lowered costs of ceramic production and new artistic graphic design revolutionized the American mealtime; everyone could afford some artistic tableware. The era's genius for flat patterning, so evident in trade cards, wallpaper and textiles, was also evident in the designs devised for ceramics. Transfer printing made it happen. In this process, an image is drawn on an engraving plate, a colored ceramic glaze is applied to the plate, a paper print is pulled from the plate, this print is rubbed onto a ceramic surface and then the ceramic is fired. Thus, any image that can be drawn can be printed onto china. Multiple colors can be printed, gilding applied or touches of color added. But, it was much cheaper to begin and end with an elegant one-color design. Following the now-familiar pattern, well-known designers, like Walter Crane and Christopher Dresser, worked for ceramics manufacturers. Motifs were cribbed from books as diverse as Charles Booth's designs for stained glass and Japanese prints. Different but related designs were applied to the various components of a dinner service, so that the soup bowls might show a Japanese fan, the bread plates might show a lacquer box, but both would have the same diagonal band of abstract patterning marching across the surface. Hundreds of factories in Staffordshire, England, had already mastered transfer printing, and it was applied to inexpensive earthenware, sturdy stonewares and fine porcelains. In England, to comply with copyright law, designs were registered (making dating easy for modern collectors) and sometimes named (creating a demand for a particular pattern in the nineteenth century and now). Excellent examples by Spode, Wedgwood, Minton and the smaller factories are still common in garage sales and on eBay. Staffordshire could have supplied the world with artistic transfer-printed tableware all by itself, but American, French, Scandinavian and German factories put up stiff competition.

Majolica was also inexpensive and attractive. The majolica used on the table in the artistic era is one type of ceramic labeled with this term (maiolica was first made in central Italy in the Renaissance, and the term was used across Europe for brightly colored, tin-glazed earthenware). Late-nineteenth-century majolica is heavily modeled and covered with thick glazes in deep, saturated colors. One inspiration for artistic majolica was the clever trompe l'oeil of sixteenth-century-ceramicist Bernard

Still Life with Peach Blossoms, oil painting by Charles Caryl Coleman, 1877. In the 1880s, Coleman produced a number of still-life paintings depicting the sort of items that were avidly collected and lovingly displayed in artistic homes. Here, peach blossoms sit in a Venetian vase on a Turkish carpet, against a background of a brocade hanging. The frame was designed by Colman; it incorporates Italian Renaissance motifs. The painting is a view into an artistic parlor and would itself have been displayed in an artistic parlor. Coleman's self-referential still-life paintings seem to encapsulate the Aesthetic movement love of looking. (Private Collection; photo courtesy of Berry-Hill Galleries.)

Transferware plates, by various English manufacturers. (left to right) 1) Luncheon plate, by an unknown maker, design registered 22 October 1883, in the "Congo" pattern. 2) Dinner plate, probably manufactured by Keeling & Co., Dale Hall Works, Burslem, Staffordshire, ca 1890, in the "Fan Davenport" pattern. 3) Luncheon plate, manufactured by Minton's, Ltd., design registered 12 June 1878, showing a scene from Shakespeare's play *Cymbeline*, designed by J. Moyr Smith. 4) Dinner plate, probably manufactured by James Beech, Swan Bank Works, Tunstall, Staffordshire, 1877–89, in the "Saigon" pattern. 5) Bread plate, manufactured by Minton's, Ltd., designed by J. Moyr Smith in 1873, showing a scene from Shakespeare's play *The Tempest,* designed by J. Moyr Smith. All these plates were made in England between 1873 and about 1890. The transfer-printing technique, which appears on all the plates, was mastered by the British ceramics industry centered in Staffordshire. This technique made mass production of complex Aesthetic movement motifs easy and inexpensive. The plates sold at various price points. The plate at upper right in the "Saigon" pattern is of heavy earthenware and printed in only one color; it would have been relatively inexpensive. The plate in the center is stoneware, much thinner and more complex in its form, and was printed in three colors; it would have been the most expensive plate of this group. A catalog of artistic designs is seen here, from the clichéd (Japanese fans, cherry blossoms, storks) to the more innovative (the two Shakespearean designs by J. Moyr Smith for Minton). (Collection of the author. Photo: Thies Wulf and Egon Zippel.)

Pallisy, who made marvelous beastiaries of ceramic snakes, frogs and fish wiggling across platters. Artistic era majolica similarly manifested fanciful forms, such as an asparagus basket in the form of a bundle of asparagus or a plate formed as the blossom of a sunflower. The colors of majolica—apple green, hot pink, mottled brown, turquoise blue—were a contrast to the neutral bodies of transfer-printed services. Minton produced, literally, boat loads of majolica for the world market, and there were also prolific American makers like E. & W. Bennett of Baltimore and Griffen Smith and Company of Phoenixville, Pennsylvania.

The American silver industry as a whole grew fivefold between 1869 and 1899, spurred largely by the production of tableware. Many forces lay at the root of this expansion. A tariff in 1842 on imported silver fostered the growth of the American silver industry. America found silver on its own soil (the rich Comstock Lode was discovered in 1859) and American companies mined it elsewhere, especially Mexico and Peru. All this made silver much cheaper. Dining, tea time and other social rituals grew more elaborate during the Victorian era, and silver serviced these rituals. Silver was an investment; it declared wealth. No wonder that Americans chose to purchase silver tableware. Between 1871 and 1879, Henry Jewitt Ferber, president of Universal Life Insurance Company and his wife Elvira Irwine commissioned a 740-piece dinner service from Gorham. Their example is extreme, but it illustrates the general trend toward the production of ever-more specialized pieces of flatware and hollowware for particular foods and special ways of serving. Many Americans, like the Ferbers, added to their silver over time.

Technological advances changed not only the quantity of silver produced during the artistic era but also the quality. Hollowware could be spun up out of the flat sheet by a mechanized process, not raised by hand. Steam power made molding and extruding silver easy. Innumerable processes were devised for stamping patterns into components. Lathes turned polishers. Electroplating further reduced the cost of silver. The process uses an electrical current to separate the elements of a metallic solution so that one component, usually silver, can be deposited upon another metal that is dipped into the solution. Electroplating was accomplished

first on a mass scale in the 1840s by Elkington, Mason and Company in Birmingham, England, and quickly adopted by American makers. By the time the artistic era began, American silver makers had mastered dozens of techniques for manipulating gold, silver and base metals. The description of Tiffany and Company's goods in the catalog of the American exhibitors at the 1878 Paris Exposition Universelle hints at the myriad technologies used: "Repousse work of high quality. Encrusted work. Chromatic decoration of silver. Damascened work of Steel, Gold, Silver, and Copper. Hammered Silver decorated with alloys of various metals and their patinas. Mixed or laminated metals, consisting of Gold, Silver, Copper, and their alloys."[9] Tiffany won the grand prize for artwork in silver, upstaging British, French and Danish competition. America became a global producer in the silver tableware market.

Artistic silver tableware was surely a delight to see and use. A block of ice cream could be cut with a silver hatchet. Ice water could be poured from a pitcher rimmed with icicles. As the guests at a dinner party each buttered their bread, the flock of butterflies that had alighted, one on each silver butter pat, would be revealed. A Christmas table could be

set with party favors: "toys," like thimbles, match safes, pill boxes. The variety and novelty still astonishes. Some American companies were leaders in the production of artistic tablewares: Gorham Manufacturing Company of Providence, Rhode Island; John Vansant of Philadelphia; Whiting Manufacturing Company, George W. Shiebler, Tiffany and Company, all of New York City. Tiffany and Company also acted as the country's leading retailer of foreign silver and objets d'art, and all the firms had large New York City showrooms.

Artistic silver was made in many styles, and very often incorporated other metals, enameling and even jewels. The Moorish (also known as the Saracenic or Byzantine) style was favored for long-necked Turkish coffee pots and often used some form of the interlacing arabesques common in Arabic design. The Russian style was more amorphous, but might include niello work, engraved or enameled floral decoration derived from Russian folk art, and a distinctive type of trompe l'oeil imitating draped textiles. All firms worked in all styles, but certain items became identified with one firm: Edward C. Moore designed coffee services with Moorish strapwork for Tiffany and Company, Gorham devised a rich

-- --

[9] Pickering, *Paris Universal Exposition 1878*, 109; quoted in Venable, *Silver in America*, 112.

ruby red patinated copper set off by silver and brass insets; Shiebler applied Greek heads onto a ground of hammered silver stamped with tiny bugs (see image on page 11 and the top right image on page 27). Tiffany and Company won their prize at the 1878 Exposition Universelle with Japanese-style silver, and their version of Japonesque was imitated around the world. Some pieces were mainly silver, but copper and iron were also used as grounds, and specific Japanese metalworking techniques were replicated, especially *mokume*, an alloy of iron, brass and copper that produces a mottled effect. The firm's designers excelled in engraved and modeled versions of the sorts of objects seen in Japanese prints: irises, carp, bamboo stalks, ladies in kimonos, all rendered naturalistically. Tiffany and Company's Japonesque silver was very sophisticated; it came from a close study of Japanese metalwork and a canny eye for upscale taste.

Bedroom furniture and furnishings were made in the same style as furnishings for the public rooms of the house—but they were usually less elaborate and thus less expensive. Bedroom furnishings were, however, no less artistic. An ornamental pattern might be pressed into the wood, rather than carved, or less fretwork or fewer inset tiles might be used. Bedrooms, nurseries and upstairs sitting rooms often had wall-to-wall carpeting. This was manufactured in wide strips on power-driven looms. In an artistic house, a carpet with a flat pattern, rather than an illusionistic one, would have been the norm. The motifs found on Middle Eastern rugs were adopted, as were the sorts of abstracted botanical patterns and geometric figures found throughout artistic graphic design. Machine-woven carpets, known as American Smyrna, suggested Persian rugs. Or, smaller rugs might be used in conjunction with matting, imported very cheaply from Asia. A wide variety of relatively inexpensive cottons and wools were woven and printed with artistic patterns; these were suitable for upholstery, pillow covers and curtains. Some specialty bedroom silver, such as mirrors, hair brushes and whatnot trays, adorned dresser tops. Nurseries could be hung with wallpaper that depicted fairy tales, Kate Greenaway children or any number of children's patterns. Artistic furnishings were invited into bedrooms, nurseries and private parlors, where they could make life cozy and beautiful.

THE ARTISTIC LOOK

Now we can envision Mrs. Kenner's house. She probably lived on a new suburban street near Chicago, only recently transformed from a cornfield into a neighborhood. She and her husband chose a wooden Queen Anne–style house, painted buff, terra-cotta and sage green. She prized her artistic wallpaper, and the art glass in the transom that she had ordered specially from New York City. Her mahogany sideboard had several pieces of very good ceramics, some of them antique. She set a lovely table with a gaily patterned Staffordshire dinner service, each piece slightly different. The mantel in the bedroom had tiles she had painted herself, replacing some rather bland ones from England. In all, the house was filled with delightful episodes of color, pattern and light. It was cozy and a joy for the family.

Consciously or unconsciously, Mrs. Kenner picked the house and the furnishings that celebrated certain visual qualities. She knew that the most satisfying things were those that had no sham parts—no veneers, no illusions of three-dimensions when there were only two. She adhered to the canons of "honest" architecture and furnishing articulated by Ruskin, Eastlake and Morris. But, it was acceptable to ornament the structural and make the structural ornamental. The turnings on the railings of her front porch were painted in contrasting tones. She admired how the leg of a Herter cabinet could be articulated from top to bottom: from the griffen-head finials, through the checkerboard marquetry in the body of the cabinet, down to the saber feet (see middle image on page 100). She saw how such detailing both connected and disjointed the composition of the cabinet, and she was drawn towards this complex system of design.

Aesthetic movement architecture and art objects tended toward the abstract. A house was envisioned as a set of volumes to be pushed together or juxtaposed, a set of building blocks. Rooms were not regular, finite units, but a series of fluid spaces opening off the wide stair hall or closed off from it by pocket doors. The facade of a house or the front of a sideboard was conceived as a set of solids and voids: a clapboard wall pierced by a deep porch or paneled door fronts flanking a niche. Flat planes were broken into units: a wall became dado, field and frieze; a dinner plate was segmented into patterned borders and panels.

Even while Aesthetic movement objects tended towards abstraction and simplification, they accumulated textural variety. A facade was made of brick, stucco and many patterns of shingle. A sideboard was constructed of dark wood and shiny hardware, laden with sparkling glass and richly colored ceramics. An artistic chair had an unbroken plane of smooth satin, next to a tufted satin seat, next to deep fringing. A successful Aesthetic movement object seemed to say, "More is better, more is more."

Mrs. Kenner's house, and every Aesthetic movement object in it, was full of visual surprise and delight. Ceramics amaze by resembling carved ivory, cloisonné or lacquer. The sunflower appears in a thousand guises: naturalistically cast in a brass doorplate (see the top image on page 96) or carved in wood as it was in seventeenth-century pilgrim furniture (see image on left on page 29) or stitched into a fire screen (see image on page 102). The form of pillars, balusters and pediments are borrowed from historical precedents but utterly transcend them (see top image on page 85). Light is managed, masterfully. Light glints off mica specks in wallpaper, light passes through stained glass and becomes colored, light glints off the brass table in a dark corner. Everywhere pattern and color combine and recombine. The back of a chair or an embroidered portiere offers unexpected asymmetries. Artwork suggests a story but does not tell it outright. Aesthetic movement furnishings are intriguing. Mrs. Kenner furnished her house to give herself and her family a visual treat as they lived their days. Now we know what Mrs. Kenner's house *looked* like.

NOTES ON SOURCES

American Aesthetic movement decorative arts are masterfully surveyed in the exhibition catalog from the Metropolitan Museum of Art, *In Pursuit of Beauty*. The chapters on surface ornament, furniture, stained glass, ceramics, glass, metalwork and architecture were especially helpful. Another exhibition catalog *The Quest for Unity*, published by the Detroit Institute of Arts, is also helpful, although it discusses art that cannot be considered part of the Aesthetic movement.

The book that first made sense of American vernacular Aesthetic movement architecture was Scully, *The Shingle Style and the Stick Style*. A city with a concentration of Aesthetic movement architecture is described by Yarnall in *Newport Through Its Architecture*. The early Aesthetic movement phase of the firm is described and pictured in *The Houses of McKim, Mead and White*, by White. The development of middle class housing is described in Clark, *The American Family Home, 1800–1960*, and Reiff, *Houses from Books*.

Many monographs on specific artists and firms were consulted; these books are listed in the bibliography. I found the following books especially helpful:

Lynn, *Wallpaper in America: From the Seventeenth Century to World War I*.

Johnson, *Louis Comfort Tiffany: Artist for the Ages*. This book has several interesting essays, especially "Tiffany's Contemporaries: The Evolution of the American Interior Decorator," by Gray.

Karlson, *American Art Tile, 1876–1941*.

Howe, et al, *Herter Brothers*.

D'Ambrosio, *A Brass Menagerie*.

Peck and Irish, *Candace Wheeler*.

Venable, *Silver in America*.

Living in the Artful Home

 Mrs. Kenner had high hopes. Last year, she had heard a moving speech by the principal of the Presbyterian School for Orphan Girls, and she had promised herself that she would do something to help. She devised a scheme: host some ladies at her home who could, in the course of an afternoon, make something that would benefit the school! It could be a pink luncheon, and she could invite ladies who had a good eye for needlework and other dainty things for the house. She resolved to do it. She planned a menu and a project for the ladies to do and set a date. She prepared her invitations: a scrap of pink satin, with pinked edges, on which she lettered the particulars in silver ink. "Bring your needles and your threads; we will ply them for the orphan girls." She sent out the invitations in pink envelopes.

As she organized her luncheon, Mrs. Kenner consciously embraced a tenet of the Aesthetic movement—to live artistically. She was determined to create a special episode for herself and her guests, and she saw no reason that charity and beauty should not come together in the service of the orphanage. The creation of beauty, for the enjoyment of the process and the result, would distinguish the luncheon as an artistic event, different from the ordinary charity luncheon.

Mrs. Kenner decided to make herself a dress for the occasion. It would have a high neck, ornamented with lace, a series of gathers along the dropped waist, and a sash that tied loosely at her hips. She bought the correct yardage of a dove gray wool crepe with a tiny mauve stripe, along with some mauve silk for the sash. Last winter, she had made some lengths of lace tatting, with a scallop pattern, and this would form the collar and some bands along the sleeves. Using her new sewing machine, Mrs. Kenner finished the dress in two days, with no interruption to her regular housework. She tried it on, without her corset. She thought the effect was simple, elegant and not too daring. She could wear the dress at home for years to come.

ARTISTIC DRESS

Ladies' artistic dress of the late nineteenth century was the product of two unlikely allies: beauty and health. Almost as soon as billowing skirts and nipped waists came into style at mid-century, there were those who warned against the fashion. Doctors voiced concern that the tight corsets used to achieve those small waists compressed internal organs and enforced an unnatural posture. Elizabeth Cady Stanton, Amelia Bloomer and other prominent representatives of the nascent feminist movement decried corsets and crinolines as symbols of women's enslavement to fashion and the home. (Somewhat reluctantly, Bloomer became an advocate of ankle-length pantaloons that could be worn for exercise and day dress; these were named after her and became a symbol of a feminism many found too strident.) And many everyday housewives noted the difficulties of such dressing. There were inconveniences (not being able to sit at ease in a hoop skirt or having the boning of a corset snap) and downright hazards (tripping on stairs, being unable to run after a toddler headed for trouble or having a skirt catch on fire while one was cooking on an open hearth).

The dress reform movement sought to make women's clothing more healthful and practical. In Britain, one furrow of dress reform was plowed by the Pre-Raphaelite circle. Dante Gabrielle Rosetti favored a particular type of gaunt, thick-tressed beauty, and he clothed these models in gowns based loosely on medieval styles: flowing robes of richly colored and patterned fabrics. The models wore the gowns out of the studio and entered the small but intense Pre-Raphaelite world as artists, wives and lovers. Jane Burden married William Morris and became an embroiderer (and the lover of Rossetti), and Elizabeth Siddal married Rossetti, wrote poetry and committed suicide after a stillbirth. Paintings by Rossetti and Edward Burne-Jones and their circle popularized the Pre-Raphaelite type of beauty, while the Pre-Raphaelite ladies made the style of dress popular. The silhouette was long, lean and unfettered (at least on these lithe ladies). Conceived to please the eye, Pre-Raphaelite gowns also satisfied doctors. Beauty and health were thus served by aesthetes and dress reformers even before the Aesthetic movement flourished in America.

By the 1880s, when Mrs. Kenner got dressed in Chicago, there were many variants within the rubric of artistic dress. These stood apart from the common house dress and conventional street wear; both could be attractive and serviceable. Artistic dress, however, made a bolder fashion statement. One of the most avant-garde styles, the Mother Hubbard, was a gown that pulled on over the head and hung straight down from a prominent yolk. It usually had ornamental details, such as a ruff at the neck or puffed shoulders and sleeves that tapered to the wrist. It was akin to our granny-gown nightgowns and, indeed, for late nineteenth-century women, the Mother Hubbard evoked the image of New England grandmothers. Kate Greenaway's children and mothers wore variants on Mother Hubbards in their pastoral, sentimentalized settings. There were many variations upon the "wrapper," essentially a loosely fitted dressing gown that wrapped or buttoned up the front. Mother Hubbards and wrappers were at-home wear, especially suitable for maternity, the sickroom and childcare, but

Portrait of the Artist's Wife, oil painting by Edwin Howland Blashfield, 1889. Evangeline Wilbour Blashfield wears an artistic evening gown, probably of silk damask. Details of the dress relate to her own biography. The ancient coin sleeve clasp alludes to her father's profession as an Egyptologist, while her loose-fitting, uncorsetted silhouette relates to her mother's interest in dress reform. Evangeline herself was a writer, and she moved in artistic circles in Paris and New York. (Private Collection; photo courtesy of William Varieka Fine Arts, Newport, RI.)

the more elaborate versions were appropriate when receiving intimate friends. One particularly artful and popular wrapper was a kimono. It could be an authentic kimono, a Western-made variant or a type of Japanese-made quilted gown made for export.

The tea gown was one step up in formality. It was fitted at the waist and always had an important ornamental element, be it a set of ruffles, a contrasting overskirt or elaborate trimmings. Tea gowns straddled the public/private line; always appropriate for the hostess, they could also be worn by her guests. Street dresses, the most public and most conventional clothing of the late nineteenth century, entailed a corseted waist, often a bustle, layers of petticoats, a skirt and often a coat, all in rather somber colors and patterns. Although they telegraphed a lady's wealth, status and taste, street dresses usually did not reveal her artistic side. Evening gowns, on the other hand, were opportunities for artistry, if the wearer was so inclined. A vast array of silhouettes, ranges of décolleté and palettes were acceptable, as the portraiture of the era shows; the lady expressed her own taste and artistry in her wardrobe.

Artistic dresses evoked a large but not infinite set of motifs and sources. Designers drew upon medieval court costume and their conception of peasant wear, Elizabethan formal dresses, Regency gowns and Japanese kimonos. Certain details recur: the Watteau back that extended into a train, the stand-up lace or ruffled collar, wide sleeves, the dropped waist defined by a loose sash or a high Empire waist. The colors of wallpapers, upholstery and wall paint were also popular colors for clothing: sage green, dove gray, brick red, mauve or watered yellow. All sorts of fabrics were used, from worsted to calico to silk. Patterned fabrics in various colors were combined. Very often careful handwork, like embroidery or appliqué, was the highlight of the dress. Great attention was paid to the way that draperies laid and how light played among the folds. Aesthetic dresses were a part of an artistic toilet that included jewelry, fresh flowers and, when a woman was going out, a hat.

Whether or not one's dress was artistic hovered around a question: to corset or not to corset. In our day, corsets are part of an edgy subculture of in-your-face sexuality; when we see corsets (on Madonna, in her younger days, or on transvestites), we know we are seeing a woman (or man) we wouldn't bring home to meet mama. But, the meaning of the corset in the late nineteenth century was more subtle. The corset created a silhouette that communicated femininity *and* propriety. The corset, often augmented by the bustle, created a womanly waist, pushed up the bust, encouraged straight posture and discouraged strenuous activity. To emphasize these traits a lady need only lace her corset ever tighter. A corseted figure was feminine, with leisure enough to engage in society. Even though corsets brought a level of discomfort, women willingly wore them; they created desirable silhouettes (today, ladies wear Manolo Blahnik pumps for the same reason). The corset defined a respectable public figure. At home, away from men and the public eye, a woman could be uncorseted. Whether or not one wore a corset at home was a matter of preference, not propriety. Artistic dress, which tolerated many sorts of silhouettes, often dispensed with the corset. Artistic dress was therefore especially appropriate as at-home attire, whether in one's own home or the home of another lady. Artistic dress—loose, flowing, unorthodox and creative—was a natural flowering of the at-home culture of the late nineteenth century.

Floral pin, by George W. Shiebler, New York City; earrings, by an unknown maker, probably English, ca 1880; locket, by an unknown maker, probably American, ca 1885. These three pieces are typical of the sort of artistic jewelry worn by upper middle class women during the artistic era. (Collection of the author. Photo: Thies Wolf and Egon Zippel.)

Artistic dress could be controversial. It could look too much like lingerie, even for at-home wear. And, when it was worn on the street, the lady could be considered a streetwalker—in 1884, after arresting one Lizzie Brait, a prostitute who wore a Mother Hubbard outdoors, the Louisville police were ordered to suppress suggestive costumes. Or, artistic dress could be silly; *too* utterly utter. Sleeves that attained too high a puff at the shoulder, poke bonnets that were too deep, an over-large sunflower worn at the waist—any of these would attract ridicule. Magazines carried stories and cartoons contrasting the sensible country girl and her languid, affected, fashionably dressed cousin from the city. If artistic dress became a time-consuming distraction from duty, it was condemned.

Advisors helped ladies avoid these pitfalls and fashion their own artistic dress. There was a vast literature of dressing manuals, advice columns and fashion magazines. Some portion of this literature advocated imaginative artistic dress. Oscar Wilde himself (unconventional dresser par excellence) urged women to think for themselves: "I do not know of greater heroism than that which opposes the conventionalities of dress."[1] Mrs. H. R. Haweis, author of the popular *The Art of Dress*, cautioned against excessive ornamentation: "Any part of dress, like any part of architecture, which has not *raison d'etre* and does not belong to the rest . . . is ungraceful."[2] Shades of William Morris! He was using much the same language to explain excellence in home furnishings. Fashion-advice literature advocated imagination tempered by appropriateness for the occasion and not too great of a show of wealth.

If it did not overstep its territorial and temporal boundaries, artistic dress was a legitimate concern of an artistic woman. "To dress well is to make a picture of one's self. Such a result then must be reached by the means an artist uses."[3] Specifics followed. Ladies were urged to look to nature's color schemes when dressing. For example, use pink sparingly against blue, rather than vice versa, just as rosebuds stand out against a blue sky. The natural extension of artistic at-home dressing was, of course, to dress to match your interior. Some felt this was carrying things too far but plenty of respected critics cautioned that a lady's costume should not clash with her parlor. In the end, one journalist asked, "Why should we get angry with languishing ladies . . . who sit in the rosy twilight of a deftly darkened room, clad in a tinted costume of duly adjusted hue? . . . They are assisting the artist who colored and gilded the walls and hung the draperies and composed the assemble of the drawing-room."[4] Of course, often that artist was the homemaker herself.

Sensitive novelists made artistic dress one component of an interior and used the whole to portray their character's persona. In Edith Wharton's *Age of Innocence,* the heroine, Madame Ellen Olenska, is a New Yorker returned to her native city after a failed marriage to a Russian count. Her clothing is chic, but her patched-together parlor, filled with exquisite but obscure European objets d'art, is a touching reflection of her perilous social standing. Charmian Maybough, the superficial artist but sincere friend in William Dean Howells' *The Coast of Bohemia,* has a studio that is all trappings and no substance—but here she self-consciously uncorsets! And, in Harold Frederic's *The Damnation of Theron Ware,* a young minister is overwhelmed by the redheaded Celia, who has decorated her private music room/studio in hues of

Trade card for Broadhead Worsted Mills, Jamestown, NY, 1880s. A little story is being enacted on this trade card—a lady uses her artistic dressing mirror to try on her gown (perhaps a new one) and practice a gracious greeting. The innovative color scheme and historicist detailing of the neckline mark this as a moderately artistic tea gown, especially suitable for afternoon receptions. The lady is, however, wearing a bustle and a corset, which gives her figure a measure of propriety and formality. (Collection of the author.)

[1] O'Brien, *Oscar Wilde in Canada*, 156.
[2] Haweis, *The Art of Dress*, 19; quoted in Blanchard, *Oscar Wilde's America*, 143.
[3] Steele and Adams, *Beauty of Form and Grace of Vesture*, 158.
[4] "The Aesthetic Craze"; quoted in Blanchard, *Oscar Wilde's America*, 143.

Gooseberries and Foliage, preparatory drawing for a china painting, by unknown artist, probably American, 1880. The gilt rim around the image suggests that this was a design for the decoration of a plate. China painters and other craftspeople often tried out their ideas on paper first. Here, the artist made an under-drawing of ink and added color with gouache and watercolor. This drawing is typical of the excellent draftsmanship achieved by amateurs in the late nineteenth century. (Collection of the author.)

amber, straw and blue to match her complexion. He misunderstands her offer of artistic companionship as a seduction; she rejects him altogether as unbearably crude.

Artistic dress was a way to explore the space between domesticity and bohemia. If you believe that metaphors reflect reality, as linguists tell us, the conflation of women, their dress and their homes is telling. Some women collapsed the space between domesticity and bohemia by wearing artistic clothing at home—living and breathing their artistic statement as they wore their clothes. Mrs. Kenner did that, as she donned her uncorseted artistic dress and prepared for her party.

ARTISTIC HANDWORK

On the day of her luncheon, Mrs. Kenner set the table with napkins she had embroidered, each with a different flower. At the center of her large dining table, Mrs. Kenner made a centerpiece of the materials for the work to be done during her party: fabric scraps, thread, yarns, bits of lace, stamping patterns, buttons, little jars of paint and tiny brushes, even tiny artificial roses. Of course, all shades of pink predominated among all these materials, ranging from lightest rose to deepest magenta. Each lady would choose a piece of fabric and the materials to decorate it. They would spend an hour or two embroidering, painting or trimming their patch. Even the ladies who claimed that they could not sew could certainly tack a rose on or glue lace neatly around the edges. The ladies were to make a crazy quilt, with a pink theme—appropriate for a girl's orphanage. The quilt would be auctioned off at the orphanage's annual bazaar. It would be the star attraction.

Mrs. Kenner knew her guests could make the better part of a quilt in an afternoon; many ladies had the skills. Artistic homemakers produced an astonishing variety of homemade or assembled-at-home objects. Janet Ruutz-Rees, author of *Home Decoration,* noted that her manual restricted itself to "work which can be undertaken *in* the home *for* the home" (her emphasis).[5] The manual describes needlework; painting on silk, velvet and wood; leatherworking and wood carving. Many other crafts were practiced in the home: knitting, crocheting, rug hooking, ceramics, photography, wood burning, arranging dried flowers. The end product of these efforts, be it an embroidered tablecloth or a decorated plate, might be functional. But the enjoyment experienced while making the object and the enjoyment experienced when it was admired were just as tangible.

The artistic era encouraged a general "ferment of the human brain in designing something new and strange," according to an author of an 1884 essay on homemade crafts.[6] The verb expresses the quiet, unceasing energy of women as they devised their own artful objects. In the process, they were helped by the chapters on the principles of two-dimensional design that could be found in many household art manuals. There were lessons on color theory, balance, asymmetry and form. Few household art craft manuals undertook a thorough course of drawing instruction but many offered examples of how plant forms could be conventionalized to become regularized but recognizable items. Many manuals assumed basic competency in drawing, especially the ability to produce a recognizable outline drawing.

Some projects began with a drawing pencil, paint brush or lump of clay, and the lady

[5] Ruutz-Rees, *Home Decoration*, 6.
[6] *Household Conveniences*, 141; quoted in Blanchard, *Oscar Wilde's America*, 96.

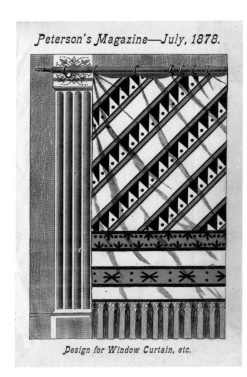

Peterson's Magazine—July, 1878.

Design for Window Curtain, etc.

carried onward from these raw materials to some functional object, such as a handkerchief or a cup. More often, household art began with store-bought objects, from picture frames to coal scuttles. Manufactured items could be improved in thousands of ways. A picture could be added if, as the magazines noted, "the lady can paint at all." Some projects incorporated some aspect of a pattern. Using stamping patterns (stencils commonly made of perforated parchment), ladies could transfer a motif to an object. Vast libraries of motifs were available and suitable for a wide range of techniques on many media. So, a stamping pattern for a dogwood blossom might be embroidered on a tablecloth, painted on a window pane or carved onto a magazine rack. Some projects involved adhering to a set of precise instructions. More often designs were freely transferred from advice books or the magazines to the homemaker's own imagination; she had wide scope in her choice of materials, techniques and ornaments. In fact, ladies were urged to use their imaginations and trust their design instincts. After all, as Clarence Cook pointed out, "Any lady who can trim her own hat can trust herself to lay bands of harmonious color across the ground-work of her curtains."[7]

The quality of some amateur work was very close to professional work, especially in certain craft fields. Amateurs made very fine embroidery, ceramics, wood carving and painted textiles. A national exhibition of American pottery and porcelain held in Philadelphia grouped pieces from amateurs and commercial makers indiscriminately. (Unfortunately, neither understood the principles of decorative design, the reviewer thought!) Mrs. Oliver Wendell Holmes Jr. (wife of the supreme court justice and daughter-in-law of the poet and writer)

COPYRIGHTED BY   W.J MORGAN & CO CLEVELAND O

DECORATE YOUR HOME WITH A "WHITE" SEWING MACHINE

top: Design for Window Curtain, etc., a supplement published with *Peterson's Magazine* for July of 1878. This design, with its distinctive dog-tooth running at a forty-five-degree angle and its newly fashionable ring clasps, is very closely related to a design for curtains by Charles Locke Eastlake, which appeared in his *Hints on Household Taste.* The first edition of this book was published in 1868 in England, but the fourth revised edition of 1878, which had many more illustrations, found a huge American audience. This illustration from *Peterson's Magazine* was published at the time that Eastlake's fourth edition appeared in America. The illustration adds color, an elaborate border and fringe to Eastlake's design, suggesting possibilities for its readers, who could use the design as a basis for their own home-made curtains.

bottom: Trade card for White Sewing Machines, ca 1880s. This card advises, "Decorate Your Home with A 'White' Sewing Machine," hoping to convince potential buyers that the sewing machine was a great aid in making furnishings. The items seen (the fire screen, the footstool, the portieres and the lambrequin) could have been partially machine sewn and partially hand sewn. (Collection of the author.)

-- --
[7] Cook, *The House Beautiful,* 137.

Vase, by an unknown maker, probably Cincinnati, 1884. This vase poses a mystery. It is signed "Mate C. Bristol 1884," but the maker apparently is not recorded in the literature on art pottery. Searches under various interpretations of the name have been fruitless. (Is "Mate" a nickname for Matilda? Martha? Matt? Is "Bristol" the residence of the potter, not the last name?) This is surprising. It is unusual to find such a large vase—it is almost twenty-one inches tall—without an easily decipherable mark and straightforward history. The maker of the vase may have been a talented amateur, with access to a large kiln. Or, the maker may have been a professional ceramicist employed by a commercial pottery, who could have made this vase on his or her own time, for sale or for pleasure. We can be sure this is not a normal commercial production; if it had been, it would have the mark of the factory. The vase is hand-thrown and carved earthenware, with applied lion-head handles, enamel and gilt decoration. These techniques were used in Cincinnati in the Aesthetic era. The deep carving seen on this vase was widely practiced in Cincinnati in the early 1880s; carving in clay was a common first step in the city for the training of woodcarvers. Although this vase lacks the Rookwood mark, the shape of the vase is related to one recorded in the so-called Rookwood shape book for 1882. The works of amateurs, notably the members of the Cincinnati Pottery Club, were often fired in the commercial potteries of the city, including, for a time, Rookwood. There were several small, short-lived commercial potteries in Cincinnati at this time, notably the Cincinnati Art Pottery Company; professionals worked there and probably the firm fired work for amateurs. There were also many other pottery centers in America and England where such a vase could have been made by an amateur or a professional working solo. The vase is a brilliant reminder of how many expert ceramists are unrecorded and how fluid the line was between amateur and professional during the Aesthetic movement. (Courtesy of Associated Artists, LLC, Southport, CT. Photo: John Cessna.)

produced needlework panels with extraordinarily realistic effects, such as grasses waving in the wind. Her work was featured in the national press, and Candace Wheeler reported that her designs were the basis for the Madison Square Theatre curtain by Tiffany and Wheeler. In fact, the distinction between an amateur and a professional could become fuzzy, as ladies sold their works in select venues, such as the showrooms of the Society of Decorative Art. Few amateurs attained the proficiency or productivity necessary to make their products known far beyond their household walls. But some did, and only the fact that they did not need to sell their works distinguished these amateurs from the professionals.

The most popular field of at-home art production revolved around textiles, especially needlework and all its allied techniques. Artistic households sewed. Textile production, the province of ladies since Penelope wove and unwove her loom threads, was a common household task well before the artistic era. The heavy lifting of textile production—spinning, dying and weaving—was taken over by industry during the course of the nineteenth century. The home sewing machine and the factory production of some garments further lessened the load of at-home textile production. By the artistic era, the focus shifted to the creation and application of embellishments to textiles—embroidery, lace, the addition of trims and even the direct application of paint and dyes. These activities occurred over and above the common (inartistic) chores of darning socks and monogramming napkins and knitting mittens. It was a rare artistic household that did not lavish attention on its table linens, sofa pillows, portieres and tidies (small patches of fabric that protected the upholstery of headrests and armrests, which were so often askew that they were rarely tidy). In the Aesthetic era, it seems that all flat surfaces were covered with a cloth that showcased handwork.

Needlecrafts had always been widely practiced in America, but this era added artistry and imagination to the mix. Needlework was a wide, wide field, practiced at varying levels of competency. Beginners could purchase kits, complete with all materials and instructions; kits with William Morris botanical patterns and Morris crewel threads were available in America in the 1880s. For those with even less time and fortitude, already-embroidered patches could be purchased and appliquéd to fabric. Very commonly women purchased plain items and then added their own designs, either by hand, or by transferring a stamping pattern. So, a plain

Photo of an unidentified woman, probably American, ca 1880s. The penciled inscription on this photo, "Aunt Annie Blackman," identifies the subject, who probably made or ornamented most of the textiles seen in her parlor. The piano stool cover was crocheted or tatted, the pillow behind Aunt Blackman shows a tatted cover, the tidy on the armrest of the chair is an example of whitework, and the triangle of cloth hanging from the shelf is cutwork. Probably the only textile in the room that was store bought is the cover on the top of the upright piano: a fringed, woven figured silk. (Collection of the author.)

gray linen table cover could be embroidered with outline scroll patterns, and further jazzed up with red and yellow berries. Even if she had only the simplest skill level, a lady could assemble the appliqués and stamped patterns that came in a kit into her own imaginative design.

The Aesthetic era encouraged very sophisticated needlework. Constance Cary Harrison's *Woman's Handiwork in Modern Homes,* one of the most thorough in this field, describes and diagrams dozens of techniques, references examples in museum collections and even provides depictions of needleworked fabrics to be seen in old master paintings. Countless types of embroidery stitches were executed with a needle, using a variety of threads, from very fine silk to thick yarns. The term "needlework" also encompassed techniques executed with a needle, such as tatting (a kind of lace or edging made with a shuttle); drawnwork, also known as cutwork (pulling warp threads out of an area of completed cloth, and then gathering the remaining woof threads with decorative stitches); and trapunto (a quilting technique involving stuffing some sections to achieve decorative effects). Macramé, which used cords of flax and linen, was applied as fringe. By the 1890s, "whitework" became a popular adornment to clothing and household linen; the term was used to describe white-on-white decorative effects, executed especially in embroidery and drawnwork. Knitting and crocheting, common household skills, could be adapted to the production of tatting,

left: Pillow, probably American, ca 1880s. This pillow is probably home-made. It shows off the kind of elaborate needlework that better amateurs mastered. The flowers are stumpwork, which achieves a three-dimensional effect by embroidering over wadding; several different types of embroidery stitches are also seen. (Collection of Brian Coleman. Photo: Linda Svendsen.)

right: My Crazy Dream, a quilt by Mary M. Hernandred Ricard, 1877–1912. This is an especially elaborate crazy quilt, made over a thirty-year period. Using an underlying symmetrical structure, Ricard has embroidered and appliquéd a dizzying array of scenes and stitches onto silk taffeta. Many standard Aesthetic movement motifs are seen: fans, a peacock, a bunch of sunflowers. Unconventional motifs are also seen: "Mr Erl King" carrying off a struggling child; Ricard's own photo, rendered on cloth and appliquéd on as a patch. The center scene may be a school, with Mary and her lamb in front. (International Quilt Study Center, University of Nebraska-Lincoln, 1997.007.0541.)

lacework and whitework. In this era, all these skills were mastered and aestheticized. Pockets of high refinement and skill produced exquisite needlework: crewel embroidery was revived by the Deerfield Society of Blue and White as they painstakingly reproduced seventeenth- and eighteenth-century American colonial samplers; stumpwork (another Elizabethan technique) that achieved three-dimensional effects with yarn was found on sofa pillows; and, especially in New York and Boston, ladies made "art needlework" that achieved painterly effects with thread on the panels of screens.

Mrs. Kenner capitalized on an aesthetic fad: crazy quilts. The crazy quilt sprung up, flourished and faded in the Aesthetic era; it was a quintessential product of the American Aesthetic movement. Its lifecycle was well charted by magazines of the 1880s, which illustrated the new style, trumpeted its popularity and then described its fall from favor. The sources of crazy quilts are various: a centuries-old Japanese patchwork technique known as *kirihame*; the "cracked ice" look of some glazed Oriental pottery and contemporary art glass; and, not least, the prevailing urge towards asymmetry. Strictly speaking, a crazy quilt often was not a quilt, for it might not have a batting layer or be quilted; it was simply a patchwork of irregularly shaped scraps of cloth. The dark jewel tones of the era predominated, and, although cotton could be used, more often silk and velvet were employed. Crazy quilts showcased embroidery techniques, elaborate bits of lace, buttons, ribbons and other notions. Fashionable Aesthetic motifs made their way onto crazy quilts; Japanese fans, sunflowers and children in Kate Greenaway costumes can be seen on many a crazy quilt. A crazy quilt was not a ragtag remnant; it was a showcase of taste and creativity, and it was displayed proudly.

There is a resurgence of quilting today, and the craft is still feminine. Although quilting never died out, it lost vigor because sewing skills declined and so many quilters repeated old patterns. The tide turned with

Quilting Today

Fireworks, a quilt by Terrie Hancock Mangat, 1989. Mangat is representative of the newest generation of quilters, who are reviving the craft with expert needlework and imaginative compositions. This quilt shows fireworks exploding against a background that suggests a field of kites. Mangat used a calico ground and onto it stitched and painted her motifs. (International Quilt Study Center, University of Nebraska-Lincoln 2000.005.0001.)

the counterculture movements of the 1960s and the bicentennial, and the stature of the feminine crafts grew. More artisans turned to quilting and to a myriad of needlework and textile techniques. A small group of self-consciously feminist artists of the 1970s, including Miriam Schapiro, Judy Chicago and Radke Donnell, decided to work in a decorative mode and a feminine idiom, against the prevailing male-dominated minimalist grain. Schapiro fabricated collages (which she termed "femmage"), made from lace, rickrack, buttons and fabric scrap; Chicago organized ceramics and needlework collectives that made pieces on feminine themes, like childbirth; and Donnell began quilting in a brand new style. There are now many prominent quilters working within the conventions of historic quilt motifs, often embellishing these motifs, subverting them or abandoning them altogether. Now, "art quilts," distinguished from other quilts by their innovative designs, appear in the juried competitive biannual exhibition Quilt National in Athens, Ohio; are featured in the quarterly *Quilt Digest*; and are sold in art galleries.

Today's readers will find it surprising to learn how often ladies made ceramics at home. Constance Cary Harrison drew a charming picture: "In the boudoir or morning-room, where of old the Penelope's web of worsted-work was wont to languish, may now be found, *tête-à tête* with the graceful basket of soft-hued crewels, a little table bearing an equipage of tools and tubes and brushes, with perhaps, a half finished vase of ivory-tinted ware, over which the fair artist sits for hours, blending, stippling sketching, outlining, with ever increasing absorption."[8]

As Harrison suggests, the most common form of at-home ceramics production was china painting. One household art manual recommended that ladies paint directly on the inexpensive Chinese-made jars for imported ginger and other preserves, or even glue crepe paper scraps with Oriental figures onto these jars. Most ladies, however, aimed for greater permanence. Porcelain blanks (glazed but otherwise undecorated white porcelain) were widely available in many types of household wares, from teacups to vases. The amateur could use a pattern found in a magazine; it often included step-by-step instruction, from the first color to "lay in" to the last touches of gilding. Or, she could adapt a pattern or make up her own design. The finished piece could be sent off to be fired; there was a network of commercial kilns that accepted the work of amateurs. A smaller, but not inconsiderable, number of ladies made the bodies of their ceramics. Hand building and throwing were both common. Some substantial number even fired their own pieces in their home

-- -- -- -- -- -- -- -- -- -- -- -- -- -- -- -- -- -- --
[8] Harrison, *Woman's Handiwork in Modern Homes*, 99.

kilns. These pieces were fired by charcoal, natural gas or even gasoline, and advertisements for them include signed testimonials from amateurs. Making and decorating ceramics was the basis for clubs across America. Hundreds of hand-painted ceramics survive today.

The craft of wood carving flourished in the late nineteenth century, after it was jumpstarted in Cincinnati in the mid-1870s (see top image on page 44). During its long life, the Cincinnati carving style stressed naturalistic floral and vegetal motifs, while outside of Cincinnati, the influence of Ruskinian naturalism lessened, and historical motifs and other styles were found. The craft was explained by many manuals, gouging tools were sold through the magazines, and decorative patterns suitable for wood carving were published nationally. Wood carving was done at home on manageable pieces of seasoned wood, using gouges of various sizes. Ladies turned out finished plaques, hollowware and architectural elements; many pieces became components of furniture.

Basic skills in drawing, sewing, ceramics or woodwork were not even required to create many ingenious home-crafted objects. A whimsical fire screen could be made from half a dozen Japanese fans stuck pinwheel fashion into a disk of wood mounted on a stand. The images from greeting cards and trade cards became the raw material for découpage, or "decalcomania" as it was otherwise known. Greeting cards could be pasted above a picture rail to become a frieze, or tacked to a screen placed at a convalescent child's bedside, where the images became the jumping-off place for stories. Baskets could be interwoven with ribbons or grasses. Buttons, upholstery tacks, brass rings, strips of leather—all these could become ornaments to be tacked to textiles and rigid surfaces. A simple lamp table could be covered, head to feet, in a stamped olive green velveteen, attached by decorative tacks and further ornamented with needleworked appliqués; the only tools needed for this piece of fashionable furniture were a small hammer and a glue brush. Often, several techniques were combined and elaborated into multimedia craft extravaganzas. For example, a screen "transparency" could be made of designs painted or embroidered onto thin muslin, mounted in a thin ebony frame, and put in front of window to catch and color the light. Special paints could be applied to all sorts of surfaces: textiles, mirror, glass and wood. Ingenious projects could be made out of almost anything.

Whole classes of artistic furnishings often had at least some element of at-home craftsmanship. Practical, ephemeral items were very, very often made at home, but very, very few survive. Ladies made wastepaper receptacles from peach baskets, pen wipers from old flannels and a plethora of wall-mounted or tabletop holders (wall pockets, catchall boxes and so on). Large-scale screens for corners and doorways, small-scale screens for the fire or tabletop— screens appeared all over an artistic house. While the frames for screens were usually purchased or bought cheaply from a carpenter, the panels were often homemade. Japanese paper, printed cottons, rush matting—these and many other relatively inexpensive materials formed the panels. The panels could be embellished in any way, and then glued or sewn onto the frame. Some ladies made objects that hid unfashionable or decrepit architectural features; renters could thus assert some measure of control over the architecture they inhabited. Lambrequins, a kind of fitted mantelpiece drapery, were the solution to hide the old-fashioned marble mantels of mid-century. Lambrequins became showcases for household artistry; they were beaded, embroidered, studded and otherwise designed to the hilt. At the very least, a Japanese umbrella could be hung from the ceiling and even festooned with seasonal foliage,

Jug, manufactured by Haviland, decorated by an unidentified maker, 1887. This jug was manufactured as an undecorated "blank" by Haviland, a French firm with a large export business to America. The undecorated blank would have been sold to an amateur, who painted it by hand. The autumn leaves surround an artfully rendered monogram, probably the initials of the decorator, who dated the piece 1887. (Collection of Sarah Eigen, New York City.)

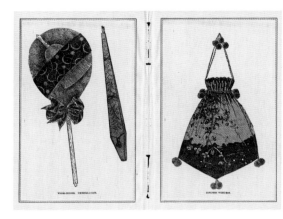

Wisk-Holder, Umbrella-Case and Japanese Work Bag, a supplement for *Peterson's Magazine* for July 1887. The Aesthetic era fostered all sorts of handmade craft objects. This illustration shows three items that could be made at home, and it also gives directions. The band holding the wisk broom is to be embroidered in bronze tinsel thread; the exact dimensions for the umbrella case are given and the material for the work bag—Japanese crepe paper and a silk lining—are described.

thus brightening and scenting a room while hiding cracks in the ceiling. The materials for these projects could be found in the network of Japanese import stores, stationery shops, and yard-goods and notion stores that covered the country; even tiny villages had small department stores that supplied these things (see images on pages 76 and 77).

Flipping through the pages of *Peterson's Magazine* for 1887, where the screen for the convalescent child was described, and then turning immediately to the November/December 2005 issue of *ReadyMade* magazine, any reader is struck by the similarities. *ReadyMade* (subtitle: *Instructions for Everyday Life*) offers all sorts of artful, ingenious projects. Make your own Andy Warhol–style family portraits by running old snapshots through a Xerox machine, enlarge them by many multiples, put four images together in a grid formation, color them with bright acrylic paint and mount them on canvas. Make keepsake boxes by hollowing out textbooks you've found at yard sales (instructions included). *Creative Home* magazine offers more ambitious projects, like stenciling an armoire and pillows for the nearby couch. And Marian McEvoy, formerly the editor of *Elle Decor* and *House Beautiful*, has given that up to proselytize a new craft she calls Glue Gun Decor (also the title of her book on the topic). She glues intricate patterns of household objects (buttons, shells and so on) onto any sort of household furniture or fixtures. Her book features lamp shades, arm chairs, mantelpieces, doors and much, much more. Decorative realms are opening to homeowners as they take advantage of the new technologies for transferring imagery onto various modern finishing surfaces. Anne Sorin, a fashion designer, realized that her favorite chintz patterns could be blown up (or reduced) in scale and printed onto wallpaper and the laminates used for her kitchen cabinets. The urge to make something—anything—creative is alive and well.

Not everyone thought that all these examples of household artisanship were a good thing. Editors included biting asides on flimsy homemade parlor furnishings, and

Modern Handicraft

Forest Princess Bedroom, decorated by Marian McEvoy, ca 1998–present. The decoration of this room is composed of pinecones, acorns, wheat shafts, thistles, seeds, pods and other bits of vegetation, all glued directly onto the wall or the furnishings. McEvoy, author of a how-to book, *Glue Gun Decor,* created this room in her own home. (Photo from *Glue Gun Decor,* by Marian McEvoy, © Chris Kendall 2004; courtesy of Stewart, Tabori & Chang, 2005.)

more than one cartoon lampooned a bedraggled lady fleeing an exploding kiln. It was the excesses of household craft production that prompted satire. For the most part, commentators (many of them, after all, lived in ornamented homes) admired the effort. "There is a sweet charm, a special tenderness experienced, and purity of love infused in a household where the ladies and the girls lend a hand in adding to the home beautifying by their own industry."[9] Making home furnishings, like wearing artistic dress in the home, was a way of putting one's self into the home.

ARTFUL DINING

The ladies arrived promptly for Mrs. Kenner's luncheon and assembled in her parlor. They all wondered what they could accomplish for the orphanage in only one afternoon. When the question could not be put aside any longer, the doors to the dining room were opened and the centerpiece was revealed. The ladies sat down to the table where pink could be seen on almost every bit of china. The first course was a bowl of cream of tomato soup; the second course was a salmon salad. While they ate, Mrs. Kenner explained the project, and the ladies planned which materials from the centerpiece they would claim to decorate their patch. Although it was unorthodox not to proceed directly to dessert, the ladies were glad to rise and circulate, as the table was brushed, and choose their materials. They sat back at the table to work; sip coffee, tea and pink lemonade; nibble cookies with pink icing; and, of course, talk.

Mrs. Kenner's pink luncheon was one instance of artful dining. Formal dining, the age-old practice of social codification and bonding, entered a new phase in the artistic era. An artful meal satisfied all the senses: sight—the colors and forms of everything on the table were carefully considered; smell and taste—the scent and the flavor of the food and flowers were melded; touch—the feel of good silverware and fine table linen were enjoyed; hearing—the good meal stimulated good conversation. There were few new practices, but rather just an elaboration and differentiation of old ways. Artful dining was less ritualistic, less conventional than formal meals had formerly been. Artful dining was a well-orchestrated feast.

Certain forms prevailed in artful dining. At night, gas lighting was banished in favor of oil lamps, or the still more popular candlelight. Hostesses had a hard time resisting the urge to use candle shades because candlelight became even more flattering when it was cream or pink toned. The shades, however, so often wilted into the flame and caused a commotion that in *The Coast of Bohemia,* one dinner

guest excuses a late arrival by noting, "The candles haven't begun to burn their shades yet; so you are still early."[10] Fresh flowers could be arranged in any choice piece of pottery or glass, instead of the standard vase or epergne. Some etiquette was abandoned: the china need not match, a cream soup might appear in a bullion cup (especially if the cup was pretty), and the hostess might dress the salad herself so that the maid could remain in the kitchen (out of earshot). More often, meals might be served with less formality, alfresco or as a buffet. Ethnic foods might appear on the table, especially if the members of the household had traveled. Welsh rarebit in its chafing dish, a symbol of the kitchen-less bohemian life of artists, was popular. Above all, the ruling convention of artistic dining was its insistence upon unconventionality.

Artistic meals were heightened by the custom of dining *à la Russe,* the system of serving each course separately, on its own plate. Dining in courses became newly fashionable, made possible by servants and French chefs. Chefs and their employers could show off their taste—literally. Edith Wharton describes the dinner of a prosperous lawyer, who dined "deliberately and deeply": "After a velvety oyster soup came shad and cucumbers, then a young broiled turkey with corn fritters, followed by a canvasback with currant jelly and a celery mayonnaise."[11] Each course in such a meal required its own set of plates. "The changes are kaleidoscopic and bewildering. You take your soup in Sevres, your entrees in England, and so on, till you come to fruit and coffee, in China and Japan. It is like a 'voyage around the world in eighty'—minutes."[12] Because meals were divided into small courses, tableware manufacturers produced specialized pieces that bore appropriate decoration: fish servers would be etched with scales, silver nutpicks were crowned with acorns, and plates for the poultry course would be hand painted with different sorts of game birds. Dinners *à la Russe* gave collectors the opportunity to show off their treasures with each course; having unmatched china could be a sign of a highly developed collection.

Much effort was poured out on centerpieces and other ornaments for the table for dinner parties. Often, one or two colors became the motif, with everything harmonizing. A centerpiece could be assembled from many layered components: flowers, set in a bowl, set on top of a tablecloth. Flowers, fruit, greenery and fabrics were the most common components. A beveled mirror was a common base layer, and its reflectiveness suggested a pond upon which any sort of decorative item could be set afloat. Magazines explained

[9] "Exceedingly Pretty Curtains," 94.
[10] Howells, *The Coast of Bohemia,* 72.
[11] Wharton, *The Age of Innocence,* 98.
[12] Harrison, *Woman's Handiwork in Modern Homes,* 222.

Tea set, manufactured by Josiah Wedgwood & Sons, England, design registered April 24, 1879. The formidable custom of the formal social call was often enacted over a cup of tea. Tea services for two were known as tête-à-tête sets (literally, "head-to-head"), and they signified an intimate chat over a cup of tea. This one has a Japanese flavor, with fan motifs and faux-twig handles, but it was made by an English firm. It is made of thin porcelain, with enamel, gilt and silver glazes. (Collection of the author. Photo: Thies Wolf and Egon Zippel.)

how to form floral arrangements upon a base of damp sand piles, set into a simple wooden box. Some part of the dessert, such as bonbons, little cakes, tangerines or crystallized ginger could be set out, like jewels, studding the table.

Artistic dining often centered around a theme, and the theme was often based on a color and the season. A dinner for spring could involve a piece of yellow Chinese silk embroidery as centerpiece, topped by a bowl of "Old Blue" (an antique blue-and-white china punchbowl) mounded with fresh, young, yellow jonquils. Yellow food, in all shades, from vichyssoise to saffron rice to a roast chicken would be served. At a June dinner, the dessert could be baskets of new strawberries, passed around on a very old Chinese blue-and-white china platter. Entertainments with a pink theme, like Mrs. Kenner's luncheon, were common; infinite variations on the theme were described in the magazines. Themed dining could be built around favorite china or a recently completed piece of needlework. The point of themed dining was a display of imagination.

That evening, as their husbands came home from the city, Mrs. Kenner's guests all reported that the pink luncheon came off as a delightful and most artistic event. They admired the care she had taken with the details: from the invitation, to the centerpiece, to the pink cookies. Many ladies had learned new stitches. The quilt would certainly be lovely, once assembled in all its pink glory. The whole afternoon was "of a piece," held together by the theme. It was this attention to aesthetic detail that set her luncheon apart from other luncheons, and made it artistic.

ARTFUL ENTERTAINMENTS

Emma Churchman Hewitt, author of *Queen of Home,* noted that parties used to be more standardized, consisting of a dance and a supper; everyone knew what to expect and how to behave. But in the artistic era, things were different: "Entertaining one's friends

Calling card case, unknown manufacturer, probably American, ca 1890s. This card case was used by Vida Harrison as she made her calls in Lincoln, Nebraska, in the 1890s. Harrison was the aunt of the current owner. (Collection of Richard Reutlinger. Photo by Douglas Sandberg.)

One of the most common sorts of entertainments in the artistic era was a "kettledrum," a tea party usually held in the afternoon. This was a consciously Anglomaniac variation upon the late-eighteenth-century fashion for parties where tea was served from a large tea urn, a custom well known by this generation of novel readers. Ketteldrums were attended by ladies and men of all ages. These occasions offered everyone the opportunity to mix and chat. Some hostesses held their kettledrums at regular intervals, establishing a sort of salon. Constance Cary Harrison described the ritual: spread the tea cloth, an exemplar of artistic needlework; gather the choice china because nothing was as sweet as "the draught of Chinese nectar sipped by a collector in the sight of her china-loving friends, from a fragile cup of which she knows no duplicate!"; bring out the heirloom silver teapot; gather quaint and delicate chairs around a tea table, preferably "immortal Chippendale"; and permit the wood fire to sink into embers but stoke the spirit lamp under the kettledrum water boiler—"this will complete the spell lingering around that enchanted spot—the five o'clock tea table."[14]

The fun multiplied in the evening during the artistic era. Musicales, charades, costume parties, fortune-telling, the performance of *tableaux vivante* (a human still life enacting a historical episode, a famous painting or the like)—all were popular. None of these forms of homemade entertainment was new, per se, but each was given an artistic twist with a new informality and a new exoticism: tableaux vivante might enact scenes from Japanese fables, or a reproduce a medieval altarpiece. Masquerades were an opportunity to dress up, artistically and imaginatively. Masquerade costumes need not be extravagant, and instructions for them appear in magazines: to become "Night," drape yourself in midnight blue cloth spangled with gold foil stars, and, to become "Morning," don a white dress flecked with silver stars at the hem, wear a silver foil crescent in your hair and carry a nosegay of budding flowers. The masquerade was a welcome moment of unconventionality: "Here is Queen Elizabeth talking to a page! There is Napoleon dancing with Bo-Peep! Across yonder—who *is* that? Why, Old Mother Goose herself, and in her wake Simple Simon and Bobby Shafto . . . Prince and Peasant, queen and page, Ethiopia and Europa, all meeting and mingling in one common throng! All distinction of rank and brain forgotten!"[15] Acting, in service to the common fund of entertainment, gave people an opportunity to let down their hair.

seems to consist of selecting first, something for them to do, and then providing the means whereby they may do it."[13] Mrs. Kenner followed this strategy to the letter; her entertainment was the making of the quilt. The whole event was highly orchestrated, and her guests enjoyed the artful artificiality. Artful entertainments were wonderfully and aesthetically staged.

The long-established custom of paying social calls was made artistic through special equipage. For a generation or two in the major urban centers, social ties had been established and maintained by making calls. An elaborate etiquette governed who made the first call upon whom, when the return call should be made, and the relaxing of the rules as subsequent visits occurred and friendships were formed. Many ladies kept "at home" mornings so that their friends and acquaintances could find them ready for visitors. The call consisted of a brief chat of twenty minutes or so, just enough time for a cup of tea. If no one was at home, the caller left his or her card. The event was an opportunity to exchange news and gossip, but, more important, it was a chance to enact the rituals of social status, family ties and friendship. The edges of this rigid hierarchy could be softened with a graceful tea set or an artful calling card case.

[13] Hewitt, *Queen of Home*, 321.
[14] Harrison, *Woman's Handiwork in Modern Homes*, 214–15.
[15] Hewitt, *Queen of Home*, 333.

left: Photo of a young woman dressed for a *tableau vivante,* probably by Alice Gerson Chase, ca 1898. This photo probably commemorates the numerous tableaux vivantes that were performed at the art colony of Shinnecock Hills, where William Merritt Chase lived and taught summer painting classes. Chase had a collection of antique costumes that his sitters wore, and these were used in the performances. This unidentified woman playfully poses behind a huge frame for the photographer, who was probably Chase's wife, Alice Gerson Chase. The sitter is dressed as an infanta from a Velázques painting, a topic that Chase painted. (William Merritt Chase Archives, the Parrish Art Museum, Southampton, NY.)

below: Moment Musicale, oil painting by Charles Frederic Ulrich, 1883. Ulrich's painting shows an impromptu concert; the woman has paused in her task of arranging flowers to perform at the piano. Music was as much a part of an artistic household as the collection of vases arrayed along the top of the piano. (The Fine Arts Museums of San Francisco; gift of Mr. and Mrs. John D. Rockefeller 3rd, 1979.7.99.)

Music, that very old parlor entertainment, remained as popular as ever during the artistic era. Music was performed for guests but also comprised the evening's entertainment for the family. Men and ladies, boys and girls played instruments and sang. The piano and violin were common, but so were instruments with bohemian overtones: guitars, banjos, harps, accordions, harmonicas, mandolins and zithers. "Musicales," on the other hand, were more formal performances that showcased guests and family, usually in the parlor (see image on page 21). There was often a written program listing the several pieces. Readings, tableaux and other performances could be included. The program could be highbrow (with Chopin, Beethoven or Mendelssohn headlining), uplifting (hymns and patriotic songs) or just plain fun (popular songs, maybe even a trio performing "Three Little Maids Are We" from Gilbert and Sullivan's *Mikado*). The polite audience would not talk during the performance, saving conversation for the refreshments, which were always served.

Just as there were themed dinners, there were themed parties. A party could be formed around a soap bubble–blowing contest or a taffy pull. The hostess who gave the "bag party," described in an 1891 magazine article, proved to be a real artistic workhorse. The invitations each depicted a pretty cloth bag, hand painted. By a clever raffle, each guest received a handmade bag, of the handsomest materials and greatest variety: bags made of Japanese crepe, India silk, brocade, ornamented in some way with tasseled drawstrings, buttons, embroidery or fringe. The artistic party had a theme or a purpose and it was artful and contrived.

There are contemporary advocates for artful entertaining. The reigning diva on the topic is, of course, Martha Stewart. Her empire encompasses a fleet of magazines, several TV shows, several online shops, a Web site packed with tips and links to the rest of the empire. The topic of entertaining appears everywhere. Her precise, even fussy style is much parodied. But, Martha is not the only game in town. Books on elegant dining and party giving are plentiful. DIY, a cable channel with an affiliated Web site that archives its programming, is devoted to Do-It-Yourself projects, including entertaining. DIY covers all sorts of celebrations for rites of passage, explains modern etiquette on dining and entertainments and provides ideas and instructions for themed parties (a 1980s karaoke party anyone?). CBS produced one season of *Wickedly Perfect*, a reality show that placed two teams in a posh Georgian estate "somewhere in New

England." The teams competed to produce the most imaginative and elegant meals, craft projects and entertainments. The judges eliminated contestants who weren't artful enough. The viewers' hopes and fears for their own parties were certainly played up by catty judges, bizarre menus and the staged drama of booted contestants shedding tears in the limo on the way home.

Raising Artistic Children

As a special treat, Mrs. Kenner's daughter, Clara, and her friend Annie came to the pink luncheon. They had each gotten a dress for the occasion. Clara had a dress with a big pink sash, and Annie wore a pink hair ribbon. Though Clara politely declined the salmon salad, Annie asked for seconds. The two girls were learning to embroider, and they were eager to help. As the afternoon progressed, they circulated among the guests and watched the work. They each took a patch and began their own designs. All worked diligently, and, by the end of the afternoon, there were dozens of completed patches. The quilt would be a success.

Mrs. Kenner, like many other mothers, thought that children ought to have plenty of opportunities to cultivate their artistic talents. The emphasis on aesthetic instruction went far beyond drawing lessons and daily music practice, although those were not neglected. Artistic playthings and a lovely home could cultivate a child's taste. Beauty in everyday life should nourish a child, as much as bread and butter.

Emma Churchman Hewitt's *Queen of Home* encouraged children to learn at play, and, while they were at it, to make something beautiful and useful. Girls should make doll clothes, learn to embroider, knit and crochet and, in general, learn fancy work at the feet of their mothers. But boys, too, should learn an at-home, rainy-day, convalescing sort of hobby. But, she acknowledged that some might object to boys having hobbies: " 'Fancy-work for boys?' growls an irate father. 'Is my son to take his crazy-work when he goes out to tea, and sit around and stitch, stitch, stitch, like all the rest of the lunatics! Ugh!' "[16] But, Hewitt insisted that boys should learn to sew, and, if not that, then scroll saw, mount a specimen for a microscope, make castles from cardboard or make a fully rigged model boat. Robert Shoppell, one of the many who published architectural-pattern books and offered mail-order architecture, also sold cardboard models of his houses. An 1891 ad pictures a young boy gluing together a Queen Anne–style house and the copy notes that this was "more than a toy. It is, in fact, a most practical lesson in Architecture: a perfect scaled

[16] Ibid., 256.

model, so exact that it is useful to builders." Many other pursuits, for boys and girls, could be made artistic: flower gardening, music, clay modeling, painting, drawing, china painting. All these things could be done *with* mother.

There was much emphasis on decorating children's bedrooms and playrooms aesthetically. Walter Crane and Kate Greenaway designs appeared on wallpapers, textiles, clothing, picture books and small-scale ceramics; all these were wildly popular in children's rooms. One little girl, the daughter of a clergyman, received a wonderful surprise when she returned home from a vacation to find that the ladies of the congregation had decorated her room. The ceiling was sky blue, with clouds and swallows painted on it. A motif of daisies and bluets was carried out in wallpaper and carpet. The curtains were a white-on-white design of Swiss muslin figured with daisies with a border woven with a blue ribbon. There was low bamboo furniture, ornamented with blue bows and blue floral cretonne pillows. Best of all, one closet was turned into a multilevel doll's house, with a working gas chandelier. The child confessed that the first night she could not sleep in the fairyland. A child's room should be practical, to accommodate play, but must be beautiful, to stimulate the aesthetic imagination.

These artistic environments were a natural extension of the era's belief in cultural environmentalism. If an adult is influenced by his surroundings, what of the impressionable child? Clarence Cook preached to the parents:

Perhaps it is fanciful; but suppose that one of the Japanese spheres of polished crystal were put within the daily reach of a child, and that he were pleased enough with it to often look at it, and let the eye sink into its pellucid deeps, as from time to time he stopped in his reading of Froissart or King Arthur. Would not the incommunicable purity and light of the toy make a severe test for the heroes and heroines in the boy's mind; and could his eye, cooled in such a bath of dew, get pleasure any more from discordant color or awkward form?[17]

In other words, a simple thing of beauty could form a child's taste, and, moreover, serve as a measuring stick for purity of character. A child's whole life could be bettered by contributing lovely things to a household: "There is no delight like the use of the creative powers of the mind, and if children can really materially add to the beauty of the household in which they live, they materially add to their own happiness, and life is full of interest to them, and a whole world is within their grasp."[18] The knowledge of the importance of refined beauty lasts a lifetime.

"I Had a Little Nut Tree," illustration by Walter Crane from *The Baby's Opera*, London and New York: George Routledge and Sons, nd (ca 1877). Crane illustrated many books of fairy tales and legends. Clarence Cook called these "the most beautiful children's books that were ever made; and indeed they are altogether too good to be confined to the delighting of children." Children and their parents would have sung along to Crane's illustrations in *The Baby's Opera*. Reportedly forty thousand copies of the book were sold. (Photo: Thies Wolf and Egon Zippel.)

-- --

[17] Cook, *The House Beautiful*, 103.
[18] Dewing, *Beauty in the Household*, 149–50.

Nowadays, there are products and pedagogy that specifically aim to instill aesthetic appreciation in children. In the twentieth century, research has revealed much about cognitive processes and the appreciation of beauty, product design and the bio-morphics of growing children, and the value of arts education in teaching creativity. We think we know (or can guess) how to teach taste and beauty to our children. These ideas manifest themselves in all sorts of ways: baby toys are made in high-contrast colors and black and white to stimulate infant senses, three-year-olds learn the Suzuki violin method and children are welcome in museums. Photographer Laurie Simmons and architect Peter Wheelwright collaborated with toy-manufacturer Bozart on a modernist dollhouse accessorized with miniature versions of contemporary art and classic modern furniture. They are not sure if the house is art or commerce, but the parents who have purchased it must have believed in the power of an aesthetically superior toy.

Creating an artistic life was a part of creating the artful home. Prosaic activities, like dressing and eating, could be made artistic. Children could share in the blessings of an artistic life, as they played with toys and learned their lessons. Artful enter-tainments enriched home life and friendships. Beautiful things were made in the artistic home, for the artistic home. The process of creating these things—sewing, painting, knitting, arranging a cen-terpiece, planning a menu, singing to a child—were all part of the artistic life. The philoso-phies of the English esthetes, and of John Ruskin and William Morris, came full circle. Aesthetic movement objects might be "art for art's sake" but the activities that happened in the artistic home could be termed "art for life's sake."

-- -- -- -- -- -- -- -- -- -- -- -- -- -- -- --

NOTES ON SOURCES

On artistic dress see, Gordon, "Woman's Domestic Body," as well as two works by Blanchard: "Boundaries and the Victorian Body," in the *American Historical Review*, and chapters 1 and 4 in her book *Oscar Wilde's America*.

Although it concentrates on wood carving, Howe's *Cincinnati Art-Carved Furniture and Interiors* also covers ceramics and other craft activities in Cincinnati during the Aesthetic era. Much informa-tion on artistic needleworkers can be found in Peck and Irish, *Candace Wheeler*.

The best sources on Aesthetic crafts, dining, child rearing and other aspects of artistic life are the nineteenth-century books quoted in this chapter. These books can be purchased surprisingly cheaply on eBay. An additional source on entertaining is Sherwood, *Home Amusements*, an 1881 guide.

Playing House

Kaleidoscope Doll House, designed by Peter Wheelwright and Laurie Simmons, manufactured by Bozart Toys, ca 2000. The exterior walls of the house, made of transparent polycarbonate material, slide open to allow play. The house includes reproductions of contemporary fur-nishings, like Big Easy, a chair by Ron Arad. The house has an "Art Kit," with reproductions of contem-porary artwork, including a film still by Cindy Sherman. Simmons, a photographer, and Wheelwright, an architect, populated the house with miniature figurines of themselves. (Photo: Laurie Simmons.)

Creating the
Artful Home

After months of careful consideration, Mr. and Mrs. Kenner decided they needed a new place to live. There were many reasons. While their wood-frame house was certainly cozy, it was so plain it could scarcely be distinguished from the others on the block. Mrs. Kenner had never liked her small, dark kitchen, and the two square, perfectly matched, perfectly plain parlors. Clara was now eight years old and Fred had just turned eleven—they needed more room for their hobbies and a separate place for schoolwork. The children needed a place for bicycle riding and other outdoor exercise. To their dismay, Mr. and Mrs. Kenner had watched as their city neighborhood became more and more commercial. The city had long since risen from the ashes of the Great Fire of 1871, but this transformation was gobbling up the old residential neighborhoods. The two- and three-story houses on the large avenue near their street were now all stores, with small workshops and offices on the upper floors. A stable full of draft horses for the carting firms had just appeared on their corner. They surely needed a new home.

Mrs. Kenner began the hunt. Many of the new neighborhoods just outside the city were now accessible since a trolley line had just opened that terminated near Mr. Kenner's office, and it connected to three omnibus lines. Or, there were the apartment buildings going up across the street from the vast new park on the shores of Lake Michigan. There were many options. She poured over the newspaper ads, reading every line of description and studying the pictures; some even had floor plans. She made appointments at some of the new apartment buildings in the new residential neighborhoods springing up on the outskirts of downtown Chicago and along Lake Michigan. On a fine spring day, while the children were at school, she took the trolley out to Rogers Park to look at houses. The next week, she took two more trolley trips. After every excursion, she sat down with Mr. Kenner and told him her impressions of the homes. They considered building their own house; their neighbors had had good luck with Mr. Schumer, a carpenter turned builder. Mrs. Kenner bought several books full of house plans, and she spent spring and summer evenings pouring over them. They proved useful because they sharpened her thinking. Soon, in conversations with friends, the Kenners were describing and debating the merits and demerits of macadamized roads, plumbing in tall buildings, and brick versus wood construction. Mr. Kenner spoke admiringly of Mrs. Kenner's knowledge of the neighborhoods and which types of homes were available in each place; and, of course, Mrs. Kenner knew the needs of their own family. Increasingly, Mr. Kenner put the matter of the new house in Mrs. Kenner's hands; in the end, she would have to make the decision.

BRICK DWELLINGS OF MODERATE COST.

FIRST FLOOR PLAN.   SECOND FLOOR PLAN.

FINDING THE ARTISTIC HOUSE

Thousands of families like the Kenners fueled a homebuilding boom in the late nineteenth century, and all of them were looking for their own special home. Often, women, as the primary homemakers, took the lead in choosing housing for their families. Like Mrs. Kenner, they spoke of practical considerations: respectable neighborhoods, fresh air, clean streets, the calming effect of trees. And, many articulated the desire for something more. A commentator wrote in 1898, "A knowledge of architecture is more important to the people of this time than of any preceding age, because the individual counts for more. Who among us builds a home, who would not give it an artistic touch if he could?"[1] But, how did different Americans go about finding their own artistic homes and putting their own individual artistic touches on them?

Some Americans looked in the cities. By the 1880s, fireproof steel-frame construction, improvements in elevators and the development of reliable electrical service made apartment living desirable. Large, well-staffed multistory apartment buildings opened in the major cities. To be successful, they had to overcome the stigma of tenements and boarding houses, the only kind of multifamily urban housing that had been available. The apartment houses offered all sorts of architectural perks. For example, each many-bedroom apartment in the Berkshire in New York City had its own complement of decorative detailing, such as paneled ceilings, fireplaces with inglenooks, many bedrooms, a full kitchen and separate servants' quarters.

The urban row house, an old architectural form, was enlivened during the Aesthetic movement. Stone, brick and even wood row houses in the Queen Anne, Richardson Romanesque and related artistic modes were erected. Their architectural flourishes (turrets, bay windows, gables and purely decorative niches and panels) made them distinctive in the streetscape. Architects designed floor plans that had new spatial variety. Residential neighborhoods grew up around these apartment houses and row houses that were divorced from commercial/entertainment districts and certainly from slums.

It was in the suburbs, however, that the largest range of artistic housing was found. The industrialization of the city core, rapid expansion of public transit networks and cheap land far outside the city all encouraged the development of suburbs full of freestanding middle class homes. While it was possible to buy a newly built but old-fashioned house in an Italianate, Second Empire or Beaux-Arts classical style, or a plain, vernacular foursquare, it was not easy. Most new housing built after the Centennial proudly wore what the Palliser Brothers termed the new National Style. The suburbs filled up with houses that could be termed Eastlake, Modern Gothic, Queen Anne, Tudor, and Early English, or styles that were even less easily named. They came in all sizes: cottages, solid family houses, mansions. No matter the size or the style, all signaled artistic taste.

Owners customized their houses, even ones built by developers or ordered out of pattern books. They could make architectural changes, adding a south-facing porch or eliminating a fireplace. Owners were invited to specify ornament, from hall tiling to the pattern of cast-iron crest railing on the roofline. The facades of Aesthetic movement houses—the public face they presented—were exuberantly colored. The homeowner could choose where on the house to place color and the means by which to express color. Even masonry houses could be colored. Brick houses need not be brick red, and brownstone houses need not be solely brown; homeowners could specify tones from pale beige through the oranges and reds, to the deep browns. Often, gables, chimney tops, and otherwise ornamented walls were highlighted by an inset plaque or panels; these were always highly colored and could bear a personal motif, like a

facing: Brick Dwellings of Moderate Cost, a supplement to Scientific American, Architects and Builders Edition, June 1891. Row houses populated urban areas during the Aesthetic era. They were erected by builders and sold or rented as individual units to homeowners. The homes in this row, in a combination Queen Anne and Richardson Romanesque style, would have housed middle class families.

---

[1] Gibson, "Architecture and the People." 21.

monogram, symbol or the house's name. Wood houses offered endless possibilities for color and for the expression of personal color preferences. With the help of examples from color supplements in magazines, color catalogs from paint companies and the examples of their neighbors, homeowners worked out highly elaborate painting schemes. The rows of Queen Anne, Shingle Style and Free Classic houses that lined the new suburban streets all came from the same family, but each was different, each playing its own variation on the theme.

The wealthiest Americans built their own houses; these were the most innovative and deftly realized houses of the era—in short, the most artistic. Architect-designed, one-off houses were built in all settings: on urban lots, within urban rows, on suburban plots, in estates. In the design process, clients and architect worked together to determine how needs and desires could be met with architectural form. The final design would reflect both the input of the clients and the talent of the architect. While some houses of the era surely reflect the artistry of the architect much more than the taste of the clients, the best houses seem to be a happy marriage of both. Many houses achieved architectural excellence and functioned well for modern life (see the images on pages 82 and 85). These houses became tastemakers. The variety of room arrangements, the way materials were handled, the design of decorative details—architect-designed houses were set out in the landscape like a smorgasbord from which others could nibble. The homes of wealthy tastemakers were occasionally copied wholesale, but, far more often, bits and pieces were adapted or adopted by builders and pattern-book house authors, so their influence is subtle but profound. During the Aesthetic movement, the

artistry of high-end houses diffused quickly through the housing stock.

FINDING THE ARTISTIC HOUSE TODAY

In modern America, it is difficult to build an artistic house. The housing industry stacks the deck against innovation and individuality, much less artistry. Developers and buyers, in unthinking collusion, believe that only houses in a limited range of styles and configurations are possible. To achieve economies of scale, developers buy materials in bulk and recycle old designs. The result is the same old housing. Buyers believe that an uncommon house is not a good investment, and perhaps buyers prefer the old-shoe comfort of familiar houses, even dull ones. A mobile population does not want to invest financial or psychic energy in developing an artistic house that they may soon leave. A big budget is no guarantee of artistry; witness the McMansion, which is large and well-appointed. However, it rehashes style thoughtlessly and is as prepackaged as its namesake, the Big Mac.

There are those who have fought the general current of monotony to create their own artful homes. An army of renovators and rehabilitators is at work in America. A few restore ramshackle Queen Anne houses or much-subdivided apartments to their pristine 1880s appearance, down to the hardware, the linoleum and the plumbing fixtures. This requires extraordinary time and money and few attempt it. More renovate by respecting the architectural shell of the Aesthetic movement home but update it with modern touches. So, painted ladies are repainted in authentic 1880s colors and sprout double-height great rooms that are well-planned and executed with craftsmanly care (see image on page 139). Then and now, the well heeled can work with architects to achieve an artful home. Modernism is the prevailing mode, but it is usually a modernism mellowed by the use of the many textures of wood, stone, tile and glass as well as color. Modernism is also the prevailing mode for the increasingly popular prefab houses, which, paradoxically, are not sterile or doctrinaire. Some customization is possible, but more significant, prefab houses are so nonconformist they constitute an artistic choice. Houses of "new traditionalist" and "new Victorian" design are now common enough to have earned their own stylistic label. These reformulate some of the leitmotifs of Aesthetic movement architecture, such as shingled facades, turrets, wide porches and stained-glass windows. It is by these routes, some straightforward and some less obvious, that artistic houses are being built in America today.

Artful Modernism

Jon and Susan Huberman House, Rancho Santa Fe, CA, Doug Austin, architect, completed 2004. Some modern artful houses have elements that parallel and update features of Aesthetic movement houses. The Huberman home has an irregular fan-shaped floor plan. It maximizes views across a hilly landscape to a lake. It has door-sized windows that open to the outdoors, and many different materials are used in the construction, including glass, quartzite and copper. (Photo: Brady Architectural Photography.)

facing: "Design 16, Twin Cottages Painted with Harrison's 'Town and Country' Ready Mixed Paints," from *Practical Illustrations of Various Combinations of Harrison's 'Town and Country' Ready Mixed Paints*, ca 1885. Suburban Aesthetic movement homes could be customized through architectural style and through color. This is one plate from a portfolio produced by the Harrison Brothers Paint Company of Philadelphia to sell their line of "Town and Country" paints. The portfolio includes illustrations of suburban buildings: a train station, a library, many houses. Each building is shown in several different paint schemes. The back of each illustration gives the paint colors required to execute the scheme. Many of the buildings, like this two-family cottage, were designed by Hazelhurst & Huckel, well-known architects who often worked in a Queen Anne mode. (Photo: Smithsonian Institution Libraries, Washington, DC; photographer: Matt Flynn.)

BETTER LIVING THROUGH ARCHITECTURE

By the end of the summer, Mrs. Kenner had found their house, a small Queen Anne in a new suburb. She had never seen an apartment that would suit her family, and she was relieved to have found a completed house, rather than having to put herself in the hands of a builder, who might not understand everything she wanted. The house was on a brand new street that had recently been a cornfield but was now newly planted with oak saplings and lined with sidewalks. It stood on a fourth-acre lot, rather closer to the street than the back alley. It was a very handsome house, with clapboard at the first story, shingles at the second, and stucco and half-timbers in the attic gables. There was a porch at the front of the house that could be a lovely summer sitting room and another at the back, off the kitchen, a good place to do light housework. There was a large bay window on the first floor, which faced a sunny patch of lawn, and a two-story turret on the other side of the house, with a peaked roof. Although the house was essentially a rectangle, with its long side facing the street, it appeared more varied. Instead of the old-fashioned double parlor, there was one large room off the hall. The hall itself was intriguing since it had a fireplace next to the wide staircase. The dining room was small but received the morning sun. The kitchen was large enough to accommodate two rocking chairs in one corner. Mr. and Mrs. Kenner would share the large bedroom, leaving the two smaller bedrooms for the children. There was also a tiny room right above the front door that offered possibilities. Right now it would be room for the hired girl, but it could also be used as nursery, should another baby come, or as bedroom for Mr. Kenner's mother, who often visited for a month or more. Or, perhaps someday soon, as a studio for painting or drawing, work in clay or any other work that caught the interest of her family. Mrs. Kenner realized that their old house had hemmed her in; its spaces were so small, regular and unchangeable. This house was quite different from their old one and would suggest new ways of living.

As Mrs. Kenner realized, the architecture of Aesthetic movement houses offered a break from constricting conventions. Maria Oakey Dewing, in *Beauty in the Household*, encouraged innovative ways of housekeeping: "It will be only when we believe it quite unnecessary to emulate our neighbors, and wholly interesting to make our own little plan of life complete in itself and true to its laws, that we shall attain the ease and beauty that make an atmosphere in which the mind and heart may expand, instead of wearing themselves smaller and smaller against the friction of sordid striving."[2] And in *The House Beautiful*, Clarence Cook told the story of newlyweds who rented a whole town house, but used only one floor of it, letting out the rest to tenants. Their experiment ended when relatives, who could not endure the bohemian arrangement, bought them a brownstone. A real-life, influential example of unconventional housekeeping was set by Richard Watson Gilder, the new editor of *Scribner's Monthly* and his wife Helena de Kay, a painter. In 1874, as newlyweds, they set up housekeeping in a converted hayloft in a mews in New York City. They lived in this "studio," as they called it, until 1882, entertaining the New York art and literary world; their house was an influential example of unconventional housekeeping. The Kenners also made some unconventional choices: they would have no formal parlor, but would use the big room downstairs as a living room, supplemented by other sitting areas in the hall and on the porches. In summer, they would live partially outdoors. The kitchen rocking chairs would form a little sitting room. There would not be separate bedrooms for the couple. They would leave one room open for possibilities. The new house would foster new ways of living.

LIVING ROOMS, NOT PARLORS

In perhaps their biggest break with the old rules, the Kenners had no parlor. They followed the pattern of many other artistic families, who rejected the usual arrangement of a parlor and a sitting room. This generation remembered the parlor of their youth as a grim room that was usually off limits, full of the family's costliest, showiest things. Here were enacted solemn rituals: funerals, weddings, Sunday prayer, catechisms and visits from people who were not really friends. Here was where the preacher sat when making a condolence call, here was where the older sister's beau was ushered, here was where mother chatted awkwardly with the new couple from church and here was where father listened to the insurance salesman. In *Villas and Cottages*, the architect Calvert Vaux ridiculed the old-fashioned parlors as "a sort of quarantine in which to put each plague of a visitor that calls; and one almost expects to see the lady of the house walk in with a bottle of camphor in her hand, to prevent infection, she seems to have such a fear that any one should step within the bounds of her every-day home life."[3] The little-used parlor embodied all the formality and insincerity and wastefulness that the artistic homeowner hoped to rise above.

Instead, artistic families had living rooms. In *The House Beautiful*, Clarence Cook's chapter on living rooms opened emphatically: "I use the word 'Living-Room' instead of 'Parlor,' because I am not intending to have anything to say about parlors."[4] He, and many other household art writers concurred that few American families had the kind of social obligations that necessitated a parlor, so, "happily, the notion that such a room is absolutely

Hall at Shinnecock, pastel by William Merritt Chase, 1892. During the Aesthetic era, artistic families rejected the separation between formal parlor and family sitting room. They combined the rooms to make a living room, which became the central gathering space. This pastel shows the central living hall in Chase's own summer home, a Shingle Style house near the art colony and summer school where he taught. The cottage was an "off the book" work by McKim, Mead and White; Stanford White, a friend of Chase's, was probably the principal designer. The two entrances to the house were at either end of this central hall, which served as the living room for the family. In this house, art and life are one: the children are examining a book of Japanese prints, Mrs. Chase poses for her husband (who can be seen in the mirror of the large cabinet) and the vases are filled with branches from the Shinnecock Hills bayberry bush, which Chase often painted. (Terra Foundation for American Art, Chicago / Art Resource, NY.)

[2] Dewing, *Beauty in the Household*, 6.
[3] Vaux, *Villages and Cottages*, 95–97.
[4] Cook, *The House Beautiful*, 45.
[5] Ibid.

necessary to every respectable family is no longer so prevalent."[5] Like the sitting room of old, the living room would be the center of family life, a space for socializing, for cordial informality. But, the living room would also usurp the functions of the parlor, and its furnishings. Older hierarchies, made visible by the parlor/sitting room divide, were disintegrating. The presence of a living room suggested that all who entered could interrelate as equals and as individuals, on their own terms.

The Kenners' new house had another expression of the new informality—a hallway that was as much living space as passageway. The front doors of Queen Anne houses and even the new apartments opened into a wide, open area that often had a stairway, fireplace, inglenook and perhaps some furniture. The public rooms opened off this hall area, usually through wide doorways that could be opened or closed with pocket doors or portieres. Thus, the hall could be shut off and become the boundary across which unwelcome visitors or drafts could not pass, or the hall could be opened to become a fluid connector between all the other rooms. In winter, with an inviting fire and a few pieces of furniture, it could be another living space; in summer, with the front door open, it could be a dim, cool, breezy living space.

The Kenners' house also had several special nooks. There was a seat built into the base of the stairs, next to the fireplace. The turret formed two interesting, half-round alcoves, one in the dining room, and one above it in the big bedroom. Such unexpected spaces were a hallmark of Aesthetic movement houses. Inglenooks, window seats, wide porch steps, balconies—all broke the regularity of the standard house based on the rectangle or square. These nooks were extras, gifts of inviting space that were ready for colonization.

In Aesthetic movement houses, some spaces served dual purposes or converted to other uses. The living room quite naturally could be the family library and study. But, if bookcases were built into a wall, the dining room might also become the library. An alcove off the bedroom would serve well as a study or writing room. A corner of the living room could house a sofa that converted to a bed for a convalescent or an unexpected guest. Many architects and writers addressed the problems inherent in tiny urban row houses, some only sixteen feet wide. The solution was an untraditional front stair hall/living room that could be entered directly from the street, abolishing the former warren of rooms on the first floor, including the narrow, dark hall with its staircase. The Kenners' house, like other suburban houses, had space enough for an expansive hall/living room. In fact, Mrs. Kenner realized that when the doors to the dining room and living room were left open, the hall would form part of a large suite perfect for parties. Mrs. Kenner and other artistic families valued flexible spaces.

Living Halls and Great Rooms

Great room in the home of Charlie Shepard and Wendy Swallow, Fauquier County, VA, Alan Dynerman, architect of the renovations, completed 1996. The living hall, a space derived from medieval manor halls, was reinvented during the Aesthetic movement to foster artful living. Our own era has reinvented the living hall as the great room, which still fosters artful living. The great room seen here was created when an unsympathetic 1950s addition to a century-old farmhouse was demolished and constructed anew, becoming the main gathering space of the house. (Photo by Bruce Buck.)

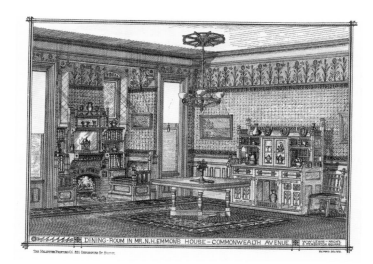

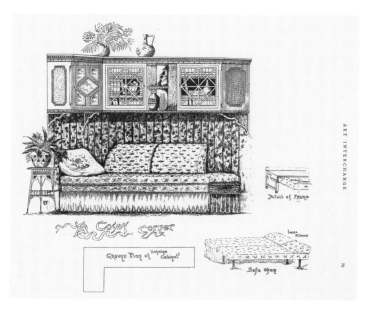

top: *Dining-Room in Mr. N. H. Emmon's House,* a hand-colored engraving probably from *American Architect and Building News,* ca 1878. The alcoves, turrets and bay windows of Aesthetic movement houses often yielded extra nooks that could become special spaces and give rooms dual functions. Here, a dining room has gained an inglenook, furnished with benches and bookcases, to make a small, cozy library.

bottom: "A Cosey Corner," from the *Art Interchange* 26, no. 2 (January 17, 1891), 29. This magazine illustration shows how to construct a corner with a hanging cabinet full of display space and a sofa that pulled out to become a double bed.

FULFILLING ARCHITECTURAL POTENTIAL

Mrs. Kenner knew that the new house would need some adjustments and refinements, but she had worked out exactly what was to be done. She would bisect the hall by adding a transom panel midway down it. Then, the back half of the hall, with the fireplace and the cozy inglenook seat, would be demarked as another living room. She would also hang portieres from this transom; they could be closed to make the back of the hall more private and less drafty. The hall would be a lovely place for Clara to read on cold winter evenings, but could still host games of ring toss on rainy days. The west-facing bay window formed an alcove in the living room; here Mrs. Kenner would build a three-sided window seat. When a screen was set up in front of the alcove, a little room-within-the-room would be formed. She would plant a maple tree outside of the bay window—in summer it would shade the alcove, and in the winter it would make beautiful patterns of shadow on the snow. She would start a fund to buy stained glass for the upper panels of the dining room bay that faced east and borders of stained glass for the staircase window that faced north. But right now she could find a carpenter to make wire screen panels to enclose part of the front porch, so it could be used on summer evenings.

As Mrs. Kenner realized, it was only after their home was built and bought that families could begin their own artistic modifications. The architectural shell was a merely the starting point; it was ready for slight embellishment or radical restructuring. Household art writers sympathized with the owner of an architecturally imperfect home. In her *Principles of Home Decoration,* Candace Wheeler called typical builder's houses, "accidental homes," and stated that "malformations and uglinesses" could be easily corrected by "various small surgical operations."[6] These operations might include a strategically placed room divider, wallpaper that seemed to raise a ceiling, an arrangement of curtains that filtered glaring sunlight. "Houses are very often intractable things to deal with, badly built or ill-arranged, with little of architectural merit, either in design or execution, and yet the love of beauty, the striving to make the best of what is unavoidable, will convert a desert-like structure of mere brick and mortar into a bower of elegance and prettiness." So said Janet Ruutz-Reese, in her household art manual, adding that it all could be done "without any great outreaching or expense."[7] With ingenuity and perseverance, homeowners worked to make their architecture artful.

LIGHTING THE ARTISTIC HOME

Hourly, daily and seasonally, artistic homeowners controlled the most fickle influence on architecture—light. For practical and aesthetic reasons, Victorians preferred much lower lighting levels than we do (pampered as we are by cheap, reliable electrical light). The pre-Victorian home (especially the American rural home) had been designed as a refuge from the outdoors; stout walls and small windows made the home warm, dim and secure. The people who lived during the Aesthetic era were the first generation whose lives were not entirely ruled by the sun and the seasons. Their days were extended by large plate-glass windows, nighttime lamplight and central heating. Nonetheless, traditional lighting patterns remained part of the collective psyche. By regulating natural and artificial light, homeowners achieved appropriate light levels. With stained glass, a drawn curtain or a well-placed candle sconce, a homeowner could establish artistic light tonalities and patterns, making radical visual alterations to the architecture.

Artistic homeowners often modified architecture by modifying the natural light from the windows. Some began with the windows themselves. The upper pane of the large double- or triple-hung windows was often bordered by small panes of glass, or divided into a checker-

"Staircase Hall, decorated with the 'Birge Velours,' " designed and manufactured by M. H. Birge & Sons, Buffalo, NY, a color supplement to the *Decorator and Furnisher* 5, no. 3 (December 1884), opp 91. The light from a stained-glass window would cast colored patterns on the walls, which often were already patterned with wallpaper. This ad shows a full suite of "Birge Velours" hung in a stair hall with its large stained-glass window.

board of small panes; this sort of window was so ubiquitous in the era that it is called a Queen Anne sash. These little panes could be clear, filled with bull's-eyes, colored glass, etched glass or painted glass (see image on page 142). These Queen Anne sashes broke up the light and cast patterned shadows. Clear, leaded-glass windows, also popular, produced a similar effect. Stained glass also filled all or part of windows, greatly altering the light, coloring it and diminishing it. The warm colors (yellows to reds) cast warm, lively tones, while the cool colors (greens to purples) cast cool, somber tones; these tonal schemes could dominate and totally alter a space. Stained glass could also mask an unwanted view into an alley or the gaze from a neighboring house. For those who could not afford stained glass, the household art magazines had many designs for individuals who wished to paint their windows to resemble stained glass. Mrs. Kenner's plan for stained glass in her east-facing dining room would give her family magical colored light at breakfast. Her plan for a border of stained glass in the window at the stair landing would allow plenty of light to flood the hallway along with bands of lovely colored light.

There were many other devices for moderating light flow at the windows. The most popular were shutters; Venetian blinds; roller shades; and so-called glass curtains, which were made of a thin,

[6] Wheeler, *Principles of Home Decoration*, 23–24.
[7] Ruutz-Rees, *Home Decoration*, 5.

"Window Gardening," from *How to Make Home Happy* (Philadelphia: Hubbard Brothers, ca 1885). A bay window houses a healthy set of plants, including ivy twining around the window frames and outlining the bay. Here, stained glass and plants are used to moderate light, instead of curtains or shades.

light-transmitting fabric like muslin, lace or thin cotton. If the glass curtains were made of a colored or patterned fabric, the light flowing through would be colored or patterned. In fact, during the artistic era, there was a fashion for glass curtains made of Indian muslin printed with delicate patterns. Sometimes glass curtains covered the whole window, but if there were ornamental panes in the upper portion of the window, the glass curtains would usually be mounted below it, and a complex situation of cast light would result (see image on page 50). Heavier curtains were mounted directly in front of the blinds or glass curtains, giving the windows two layers of light control. Thus, blinds, curtains, shutters and shades could be drawn in various ways to admit or restrict light. Curtains were closed at night, to limit drafts and also to prevent the "fish bowl effect" of views into the house at night. In addition to the curtaining systems, many artistic families used horticultural devices for light moderation. These included ivy or other twining plants trained to grow up and around windows, shelves of potted plants in windows and low, spreading trees and shrubs planted just outside windows.

Artificial light illuminated the house at night. The lighting options available varied by region and income level; but public gas and electrical-generating facilities were more commonly found in wealthy metropolitan households. The era's most common lighting technologies are now rare; today's chandeliers are never fitted with gas light and few of us have spent an evening by kerosene lamp. We have lost much understanding of the quality of artificial light in the artistic era, but some things are known. The age-old, warm, flattering effect of candlelight was popular in the Aesthetic

era, but the flickering light of candles was unsuitable for reading or handwork and candles were expensive. Similarly, firelight was lovely and warm but not sufficient as a room's sole source of light. Gas light, which was available both through municipal generators and, in wealthier households, through private generators, was supplied throughout houses by pipes in the wall. The pipes fed central fixtures, wall sconces and even free-standing lamps, albeit ones with very limited mobility—they were tethered by a gas tube to the central fixture. Although reasonably plentiful, the light from gas fixtures was bluish, somewhat smelly, and generally thought harsh. In the artistic era, oil was probably the most common light source. Kerosene and related petroleum derivatives burned in clear glass chimneys in fixed or mobile lamps. Kerosene gave an even, yellowish light, which could be modified by shades. Glass, paper and fabric shades could be painted, embroidered and otherwise decorated to give an infinite variety of colored light. Shades could also be pierced or fringed, so that the light would cast patterned shadows.

In 1882 in New York City, Thomas Alva Edison opened the first permanent central electric-light power plant in the world, but electrical service was not widely available in America until after the Aesthetic era. At first, a few wealthy urbanites installed electrical systems in their homes, even though service was unreliable and only small wattages could be generated. As soon as electricity was available, many households installed combination fixtures, with gas jets and light bulbs on the same chandelier (in case the electricity failed). Lamps with candles and oil wells also remained common. And, most households used several light sources simultaneously, often in the same room. So, a living room could have a large floor oil lamp near the lounge, candles on the mantelpiece and gas sconces. Center hanging fixtures were common, especially in dining rooms, and gas or oil sconces lit halls. "Student lamps," solidly built oil lamps, gave concentrated light for table tops. Nighttime illumination was a big change from the daytime, when

Inglenook in the Isaac Bell House, Newport, RI, McKim, Mead and White, completed 1883. This inglenook is part of the central living hall of the Isaac Bell House, an early commission of McKim, Mead and White. The firm's eccentric anti-quarianism is expressed in the Delft tiles that form the fire surround and in the chestnut paneling, which is comprised of sixteen panels sal-vaged from nineteenth-century Breton folk furniture. Elements of armoires and box beds from the Morbihan district of Brittany have been reconfigured in a highly pic-turesque assemblage. The inglenook simultaneously separates and connects spaces: we see through the box bed opening to the staircase; through the window to the outdoors; and, if we turned around, into all the other rooms on the first floor. Even the architectural details transmit light and can be seen through: the firelight would shine through the glass blocks below the mantel, and light would reflect from the copper sheeting behind the dowelled openings of the paneling. (Photo: John Corbett; courtesy of the Preservation Society of Newport County.)

comparatively more light entered a room from the side, through the window. At night, lamps made pools of light throughout the room and the location of the pools could be varied if lamps were moved. Lamps gave much less light than the sun and cast deeper shadows that varied if the lamps were moved or the flame flickered. All this could be manipulated and managed for artistic effect.

DIVIDING SPACES

Mrs. Kenner's hall transom was one of many devices used to segment space within rooms. With the help of a local carpenter, she could purchase a length of spindled railing that would form the nucleus of the transom, and then it could be further carved, painted or otherwise embellished. A transom with openings, like spindles or carvings, would allow for light and air circulation. Mrs. Kenner would design and execute portieres that would hang from a rod below the transom, fur-ther dividing the space. The transom would demark the front half of the hall as a foyer and the back half, with the fireplace, as a sitting area. When the portieres were drawn, the two rooms would be quite distinct. Other architectural devices to divide space, some fixed and some moveable, were ubiquitous: portieres, pocket-doors, full- or half-height bookshelves used as room dividers and waist-high half walls. With these dividers, room size and shape became more malleable.

Screens, ubiquitous during the Aesthetic movement, also segmented space. They could divide a large parlor into a number of social centers, or with the addi-tion of a few pieces of furniture, transform a window recess into a sunny boudoir. Edward Dewson, an architect, felt that a screen placed near a fireplace suggested a rosy home: "No pleasanter sentinel could meet our view, inspiring by its pleasing suggestions of mystery, a certain feeling of awe, ere we enter the sacred precinct of the domestic hearth."[8] Depending on how many of their panels were opened and arranged, screens could divide space in any number of ways, and they could be moved around the room (see image on page 107).

Turkish corners, nearly as ubiquitous in the artistic era as screens, suggested a luxuriousness bordering on the decadent. Turkish corners (sometimes also known as cozy corners) were a sort of tent in one corner of the room, constructed out of

-- --
[8] Dewson, "Screens and Their Uses," 15.

draped fabric, and usually furnished with a divan. Nearly always, Oriental or Oriental-themed textiles were used, along with Middle Eastern metalware and even weaponry; the archetypical Turkish corner would have kilims draped from fierce spears, with a Persian carpet on the divan and a brass lantern on the floor.

Mrs. Kenner even devised a way to segment her outdoor spaces. She would install panels of wire screening, from floor to ceiling, on a portion of the front porch, so that it could be used at night as a summer sitting room. These panels could be removed in the winter months, or even replaced with glazed panels, making the porch into a sunroom that could be used for three seasons. Thus, the distinction between indoor and outdoor spaces began to break down—an artful effect.

WALLS, CEILINGS AND FLOORS

The era's urge to fragment extended to the flat planes of walls, ceiling and floor. Often, walls were separated into dado, fill and frieze, each painted, wallpapered or paneled separately. Sometimes, walls had only two portions (dado and fill, or fill and frieze). Or, sometimes the frieze was combined with the border of the ceiling. Floors were covered in wood parquet or ceramic tiles, sometimes in elaborate patterns and borders. Or, floors were covered in patterned wall-to-wall carpet, sometimes with rugs laid over the carpet. Ceilings, too, were rarely left plain; they could be stenciled, treated with textured paint or ornamented with wallpaper medallions. Costlier treatments included plaster coffering or wood beams. The colored or patterned light of stained-glass windows or leaded glass windows would further fragment these already fragmented planes. And, there were optical tricks to change architectural proportions. By painting the ceiling a light color, the ceiling would appear further away and make the room seem bigger; the converse was also true. A deep cornice would lower ceiling height, but a small one would raise it. The aim of these treatments was to emphasize the wall, floor and ceiling as flat planes, to be divided for decorative effect.

All the modification that homeowners undertook presumed that architectural form was mutable. Architecture could be changed for pragmatic reasons or for aesthetic effects; these goals often merged into one accomplishment. The era showed an impulse to segment architecture, to make it permeable, moveable or changeable for the season. A room composed of a set of

top: Trade card for Mauro and Wilson, dealers in wallpaper, window shades, books and stationery, Burlingon, IA, ca 1880s.

bottom: Trade card for G. W. Clarke & Co., dealers in wallpaper and window shades, San Francisco, ca 1880s. These two trade cards show how wallpaper and other patterned, colored treatments for walls and windows could emphasize each surface of the room as flat plane. Each flat surface is further divided into segments—baseboard, fill and frieze, window within wall, or medallion within ceiling. Each room seems infinitely divisible. (Collection of the author.)

facing: Wallpaper manufactured by Robert Graves Company, ca 1880. This wallpaper is printed in tones of copper, silver, gold and pewter on a tan and cream-colored ground. Because of the way the metallic portions of the paper reflect light, they seem to stand away from the ground. This optical trick would have made it seem as though the wall were covered with a metal filigree of many colors. (Photo: Wulf Thies and Egon Zippel.)

two-dimensional planes could be divided and subdivided to emphasize the planarity of walls, ceiling and floor. These divisions could even lower or raise ceilings and move walls, making solid architectural form seem less substantial. The metallic motifs that appeared so often in artistic wallpapers added another element of optical insubstantiality to walls. The motifs printed in metallic colors seemed to stand in front of the rest of the plane of the wall, appearing like a free-standing network.

Volumes within the house could be divided by pocket doors, screens, portieres and transoms. These, too, could be moved at will, or pierced so that they were partially transparent. One could retreat into a Turkish corner or a cozy corner, miniature rooms within rooms. Light could define a space, shadows could erase space and colored and patterned light set space apart, making it magical, mysterious, playful or somber. Like never before, light could be managed. New artificial lighting technologies and newly fashionable complex arrangements of draperies meant the possibilities were many. A house was a set of interconnected volumes and planes, like building blocks, that could be manipulated to fulfill artful potential.

The "Bones" of Artistic Decor

Once Mrs. Kenner was satisfied with her architectural vision for each room, she focused her energies on the decor. She had a scheme for coordinated wallpaper and portieres that would link the hall, living room and dining room. The hall would be papered in a light color; she had seen a light yellow paper with an allover pattern of a trellis printed in copper. The rooms opening off the hall would have darker tones. Since the dining room was flooded by morning sunshine, it would be slate blue and pale yellow. She had seen a wallpaper set by Frederick R. Beck and Company that had a dado with a complex pattern in blue and a fill pattern of delicate blue flowers on a yellow background. Since it got less direct sun, the living room would also be blue and yellow, but more yellow than blue, and lemon yellow at that. Mrs. Kenner was a little embarrassed when she thought about the old parlor, with furniture and drapes with classical motifs, including Doric columns. This new living room would not be so doctrinaire. She would mix some of the old furniture with new things she would buy downtown. And, she would continue her hunts at country auctions and the secondhand shops. She would make two sets of similar portieres. The set for the opening between the living room and the hall would be ochre velvet richly decorated with blue embroidery and perhaps copper spangles. The other set would hang from the transom in the hall—it would be blue wool, with large panels of ochre and yellow embroidery on a buff ground. The bedrooms would be in tones of green—a restful color. Because there was a luxurious bathroom on the second floor, which shared the water heater with the kitchen, there was no need for washstands in the bedrooms. This left room for an easy chair and a desk in each bedroom. Mr. and Mrs. Kenner had been able to pay the builder a bit more to install tiles and basins they preferred—a lovely design of Grecian maidens pouring water. Each room would be different but every room would have something in common with its neighbors.

Even while artistic homeowners dissected the domestic interior by manipulating the architecture, they reconstructed it through decor. Underlying the furniture, carpets and wallpaper was a set of choices that made up the "bones" of decor. Artistic homeowners, consciously and unconsciously, made good bones. They understood that following a set of simple, basic principles that revolved around fitness and taste ensured successful decor. Color formed the skeleton of decor, and it supported the musculature of furnishings. Decor was fleshed out by achieving a high density of stylistically varied furnishings. Wonderful effects were sought but not at the expense of pragmatic solutions. These ideas were the underpinnings of artistic decor.

"There are a few fundamental rules, however, that can not be discarded, for in a well-furnished apartment there must be fitness, appropriateness, proportion, simplicity, harmony and durability."[9] With this pithy statement from her book *How to Furnish a Home*, Ella Church laid down the basic ground rules for choosing decor. Use, function and quality were the necessary conditions for beauty. Know what is useful for your family, whether it be a piano or a magazine rack. Do not choose delicate silk upholstery if young children will use the easy chairs. Understand the scale of the rooms and of the furnishings and fit them together. Consider whether colors, patterns and textures will harmonize.

[9] Church, *How to Furnish a Home*, 7.

Church's words were amplified by other household art writers. Maria Oakey Dewing spoke of elemental aesthetic principles and how they could be put to good effect: "Proportion is the first element of form; line comes next. Most of us have to accept such forms as we find already made in the rooms we furnish; but we may apparently alter the proportion greatly by our arrangement of line and mass."[10] At base, the home-owner must match beauty and utility. "To complete the beauty of the home . . . [requires] even something more than the love of beauty and cultivation of it, and that is a perfect adherence to the law of appropriateness."[11] All these writers must have been inspired by William Morris's watchwords on home decor: "Have in your houses only those things which you know to be useful or believe to be beautiful."[12]

HARMONIES AND SYMPHONIES OF COLOR

The most powerful mechanism for the expression of beauty in the artistic house was color, expressed in single tones, through patterning and in an array of accessories and furnishings. "Although the very existence of a house is a matter of construction, its general interior effect is almost entirely the result of colour treatment and careful and cultivated selection of accessories."[13] As Candace Wheeler stated, color was the backbone of decor. Education in basic color theory was readily available and restated in household art books: every color exists somewhere on a scale between the three primaries of red, yellow and blue, and each can be mixed with the others and modulated by the addition of white and black. Successful color schemes balance tone derived from two colors, such as yellow and blue. Most artistic homeowners moved beyond primary colors into the world of subtle relationships among the secondary colors of oranges, purples and greens and into the tertiary colors, all liberally toned by gray—thus, the era's love of dull, dusky "tender" colors like ashes of roses, puce and "greenery-yallery." Universally, writers advised the same thing: establish a key of color to which all other tints relate. The color key and its related tints should be expressed in patterns and accessories. Flat patterns, not illusionistic ones, convey truthfully the planarity of surfaces, and flat patterning was a foil for complex color schemes. Moreover, flat patterns read as ornament only, rather than as any motifs that could distract from the overall decorative effect. Color and pattern could be expressed in paint (including stenciling and textured paints), wallpaper, paneling, carpets, wood carpets, ceramic tiles, upholstery and window treatments. Usually, room schemes combined many of these elements. Color and patterning

Trade card for A. H. House, dealer in "furniture, bedding and &" Ilion, NY, ca 1880s. This trade card illustrates how color and patterns could be expressed in various household furnishing fabrics: lace curtains, tasseled valance, portiere, seat back, pillow, lambrequin and fire screen.

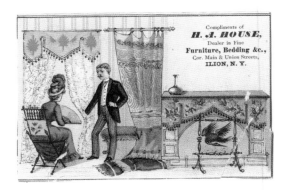

Pattern upon Pattern

Jala bed linens from John Robshaw Textiles, New York City, 2006. These bed linens are produced by an American, John Robshaw, in India, using woodblock printing onto cotton silk and linen. Robshaw produces dozens of patterns, which can be mixed and matched. His fabrics are one among many products that satisfy a growing interest in exotic textiles, rich colors and intricate patterns. (Photo courtesy of John Robshaw.)

-- --
[10] Dewing, *Beauty in the Household*, 41.
[11] Wheeler, *Principles of Home Decoration*, 42.
[12] Boris, *Art and Labor*, 40.
[13] Wheeler, *Principles of Home Decoration*, 34.

The library of the Mark Twain house, Hartford, CT, Edward Tuckerman Potter, architect, completed 1874. The library of Samuel Clemens (better known as Mark Twain) and his wife, Olivia, was the main gathering room for family and guests. In 1881, the Clemenses hired the innovative decorating firm of Louis C. Tiffany & Associated Artists, who designed the blue-and-gold stencil pattern on the walls and ceiling. With a big bay window, the room is well lit by day, and by night the metallic stenciling reflects pinpoints of light for a magical effect. The Clemenses bought the mantelpiece from a castle in Scotland and added the brass hood, inscribed "the ornament of a house is the friends who frequent it." The room reflects the family's love of literature and evenings spent with friends. (Photo: Paul Rocheleau.)

worked in concert on walls, floor and ceiling to make passages in the symphony of decor.

Extraordinarily subtle and complex color and pattern schemes were contrived in the artistic era. Not surprisingly, Candace Wheeler, a writer who was a textile designer, described wondrous color harmonies. She praised a pink-and-silver room for a young girl, with a frieze of deeper pink stenciled with a fountain-like design spraying lacey cream white water; the bed and curtain rods were silver, coordinating with the silver dressing table accessories. Knowing that good decor made for happy people, Wheeler gave special attention to servants' bedrooms. She advised that salmon or rose pink, cream white or spring green be used for bedrooms on the shady side of the house, but that bedrooms on the sunny side should use turquoise, pale blue, or a grayish green, "like the green of a field of rye."[14] Brilliant colors should be balanced by subdued ones. She cited a fawn-colored room that everyone remembered as gay and bright, merely because touches of peacock blue were found in one Chinese jar, in the border of a black tablecloth and on one footstool.

Some tried to accommodate the effects of seasonal and even daily changes of light. In 1886, the magazine *House Painting and Decorating* described the decor for a small reception room that had good light and a high ceiling: use a wallpaper with values of warm gray, paint the ceiling a faint yellow, use a ten-inch frieze of flocked paper of India red bordered top and bottom with three inches of gold, gray, and India red. The woodwork should be painted the darkest gray in the paper. In winter, use a dark gray carpet with red, yellow and olive in the design; in summer, use olive matting, with cotton rugs in dull purple and ecru. Maria Oakey Dewing cautioned her readers to consider the effect of artificial light sources on color: some purples look ugly by gas light, but others gain brilliancy; rich browns look lovely in gas light.

Dewing, who like Wheeler was a working designer, also made persuasive color arguments in her writings. In *Beauty in the Household*, she gives an extraordinarily detailed description of a very small parlor—only twelve by fifteen feet—that is worth citing at length because it demonstrates the sophisticated understanding of color

[14] Ibid., 48.

and pattern among her readers."We can imagine such a parlor . . . the walls of a dark rich orange, a narrow frieze of gold-color, on which the leaves of the horse-chestnut, just turning brown, are painted, with their thorny balls in gold; a ceiling of pale gold-color, with a design of the same chestnut; . . . beneath the narrow frieze a gilt picture rod." She goes on in loving detail. The simple woodwork was brown orange; pictures hung from copper wires; the curtains were brown plush embroidered "in shades of yellow from pale gold to an orange that becomes brown;" the portiere was an orange that was a little lighter than the wall, embroidered in brown and gold, lined with pale greenish blue like a green turquoise, "so that it is difficult to say if it be green or blue"; there was a dark carpet of browns and yellows and a brass grate and andirons. The sofa was upholstered in rich, dark brown sateen, with unmatched cushions: one of greenish turquoise blue, embroidered in brown and cream color and gold; the other gold, embroidered in orange and brown and the green turquoise blue. The mantelpiece was of dark, carved wood with bronze bas-reliefs, or very dark purplish marble—she only regretted that "it would be an Aladdin's dream to make it of dark green malachite." There was an upright piano with painted panels showing figures, and on it sat a low glass dish with yellow or purple pansies or a Satsuma china bowl of yellow roses. There were straw or rattan chairs, painted brown and gilded in parts, with cushions of deep orange or brown sateen and between them sat a little tea table, of yellowish polished woods. On the table was a tea set of silver or silver gilt, red Kaga ware or Satsuma with cream white, orange-gold and green motifs. "This would be a small parlor that the most aesthetic recluse could entertain his one chosen friend or his own little family circle in with perfect content. The effect would be of cozy, somber richness."[15] Indeed, the room was not very costly—its rich effect was achieved with color harmonies.

We can trace a line from Mrs. Kenner's pale yellow and dusty blue harmony through Dewing's orange brown parlor, back to Whistler's blue and yellow dining room. Whistler devised deceptively simple harmonies in his paintings, in his exhibition rooms and in his own homes (see image on page 35). He used the musical terminology of symphonies, harmonies and nocturnes to highlight how color relationships were composed. To carry the musical analogy further, Whistler struck up an orchestra of homeowners, who played out infinite variations on the color symphonies in their own homes. By 1903, in *Principles of Home Decoration*, Candace Wheeler describes this phenomenon as a triumph of artistic questing:

> *Until very recently the relation of colour to the beauty of a house interior was quite unrecognized. If it existed in any degree of perfection, it was an accident, a result of the softening and beautifying effect of time or of harmonious human living. Where it existed, it was felt as a mysterious charm belonging to the home; something which pervaded it, but had no separate being—an attractive ghost which attached itself to certain houses, followed certain people, came by chance and was a mystery which no one understood, but everyone acknowledged. Now we know that this something which distinguished particular rooms and made beautiful particular houses, was a definite result of laws of color accidentally applied.*[16]

Wheeler and Whistler both compared color and music; the principles governing harmonies and discord were analogous in both mediums. The idea prevails in modern color theory.

MORE IS MORE

Dewing's description of the orange brown parlor, a glance at the Kemp house salon (see image on page 40) or the Vanderbilt drawing room (see image on page 41) reveal another principle of aesthetic decor: the conviction that more is more. In these rooms, all surfaces are colored and ornamented, every piece of furniture is composed of many materials, and many, many objects are packed into only a small number of square feet. The craving for a high density of furnishings is a hallmark of artistic taste. As Harriet Spofford noted, "The davenport, the étagère, the corner shelves, all help fill the room and give it the air of occupancy and use and agreeable life. Provided there is space to move about, without knocking over the furniture, there is hardly likely to be too much in the room."[17] Lest you imagine that she is joking, she goes on to state firmly, "There are those who think that to fill a room is to rob it of half its size; but they are mistaken."[18] It is probably the sheer density of aesthetic decor that was most repellent to succeeding generations. Even our eyes, hungering for more than minimalism offers, look at aesthetic decor with a mix of wonder and suspicion. (See image on page 48, for example.) Did they really live like that? Every photograph, illustration and description gives evidence that yes, they did.

---

[15] Dewing, *Beauty in the Household*, 108–114.
[16] Wheeler, *Principles of Home Decoration*, 39.
[17] Spofford, *Art Decoration Applied to Furniture*, 222.
[18] Ibid., 236.

above: Photo of Mr. and Mrs. John T. Green, by Fred L. Yagear, Panama, NY, 1912. Mr. and Mrs. Green sit in their very comfortable living room, which was probably decorated in the 1880s or 1890s. There is a profusion of cushions and upholstery, and many worn spots have been covered, including the carpet under Mr. Green's chair. The room is ornamented with flowers, probably grown by Mrs. Green. This image is from a 1912 card celebrating the couple's sixtieth wedding anniversary; by the time this photo was taken, this was no longer a fashionable room, but it was still artistic and comfortable.

below: Jim's Cottage at Gull Lake, photo by L. L. Joy, Galesburg, MI, ca 1890s. Jim has decorated his simple cabin with the materials at hand: rocking chairs, machine-made lace curtains, a piece of embroidered fabric draped from the mantel, Japanese fans, pages from magazines (probably color supplements), wildflowers in the household china, and some kind of striped bunting on the ceiling. The decor is inexpensive, ingenious and highly artistic.

Our era looks at these interiors and diagnoses horror vacui—fear of vacant spaces. But the artistic homeowner was not afraid of vacant spaces; she was merely bored with them. She turned every corner into a healthy opportunity for expression.

ARTISTIC PRAGMATISM

Underlying all the principles of aesthetic decor was deep-seated pragmatism. Artistic decor was built around what a family owned or could afford. It was about renovating, substituting and making do—but artistically! Simple solutions were best. Household art books were full of clever, attractive tips: color and varnish kitchen floors rather than cover them with oil cloth, which is easily worn. For the glaring red or blue silk used by piano makers to cover the sounding board cavity, substitute bits of antique Chinese silks done up as a shirred curtain. Old (or simply old-fashioned) decor was updated aesthetically. The glaring old white marble mantel should be covered with a lambrequin. A classical cornice molding could be painted in the new fashionable palette. New wallpaper would transform a room. A suite of Rococo Revival furniture might be covered in unmatched yet coordinating upholstery. Above all, the comfort of the family was considered. Father's overstuffed armchair and Mother's beloved rocker could be reupholstered or outfitted with cushions, but they were never abandoned. If the artistic homeowner knew enough about the needs of the family, the requirements of the space and the principles of beauty, wise choices could be made. The lesson was clear—apply taste pragmatically.

When considering the decor for her new living room, Mrs. Kenner was happy to leave her old matched parlor set behind, with all its Doric details. Why, all who sat in that parlor must have felt like Samson, entrapped among the columns tumbling down around them! Many felt the stifling effects of stylistic coherence. "A room where absolute purity of style is insisted upon in every trivial point—window glass, andirons, wall sconces—is like a straitjacket, and its rigidity destroys all the comfort of home, and seems mere affectation."[19] So noted Harriet Spofford. Mrs. Kenner's new room, like other artistic living rooms, would mix furniture and accessories from different eras and regions. Delightful effects could be achieved by juxtaposition, and Constance Cary Harrison described them with delight: "One sees the little Louis XV gilt beauties, their satin seats powdered with embroidered flowers, drawn confidingly up to the arm of a square Puritan 'Cromwell' in oak, severely plain save for its dark cushion in maroon plush. Gilt wicker, flaunting with bows like a bed of poppies confronts the rigid dignity of a Tudor or Eastlake specimen in solid wood, while India teak and Wakefield rattan hob-nob most cordially."[20] Mixing diverse furnishings was pragmatic and practical.

To achieve artistic decor, it was necessary to keep the fundamentals in mind. Choose appropriate, useful things that would serve a definite purpose. Establish a color key as a framework for each room. By all means, mix stylistically unrelated furnishings but work within the elaborated architectural shell. Provide this skeleton with the substantial flesh of furnishings. More is more—achieve a density of furnishings that give sustained visual delight. By following these guidelines, the bones of artistic decor would be vivified.

Artistic Furnishings Artfully Arranged

Finally, Mrs. Kenner was ready to place all the many things she loved. She would put all the books in the living room, the chaise lounge diagonally in front of the fireplace, along with the two upholstered easy chairs and a tea table between them. This would make an interesting space separate from, yet not so distant from, the bay window and its seating. The street side of the room would have Mother's solid dining table, covered with a richly patterned cloth. The room would be a real family study and workroom, and when work was finished, a room for relaxation. It would be the place where the children would do homework, where Mrs. Kenner would sew or do her china painting, and everyone would read. The mantel would be a little museum of china and pottery, including the small Rookwood pot Mrs. Kenner had received as a birthday present last year, the Doulton pitcher, the plates she had painted, the vases thrown and glazed by the ladies of her pottery club and even the misshapen but charming efforts of her children. She had found a new round table for dining room—it would be better for conversation and better proportioned for the room. And, they could use the old dining room chairs around the new round table. Although the dining table could only seat eight people, the house could be rearranged for parties. The big table in the living room could be set for twelve for a holiday meal. Or, when the children were older and wanted to have a dance, they could move the furniture out of the living room. Mrs. Kenner would furnish the mantel in the hall with the brass elephants and

"We met by chance."
No. 62

We Met By Chance, illustration by Francis Lathrop, from Clarence Cook, *The House Beautiful*, 184. Here, a Persian rug, Jacobean chair, Chinese stand, Japanese kakemono and brass sconce have "met by chance" in a corner of the room. Cook included this illustration "to hint at ways of grouping simple objects in a picturesque and yet natural way, so as to get something out of them besides their individual elegance or interestingness."

[19] Ibid., 237.
[20] Harrison, *Woman's Handiwork in Modern Homes,* 190–91.

tigers she had brought back from the exhibition of Indian goods and the art glass vases she had been buying, one by one. In the front half of the hall, she would put that sturdy painted bench she had bought from the German farmer and the two old-fashioned ladder-back chairs. In the back half of the hall, she would put the dainty sofa that looked almost as nice as a Herter piece (but cost only half as much!). She would supplement the kitchen rocking chairs with a pretty painted table so she could take tea while doing housework. In the bay of the master bedroom, she would put her dressing table. Mrs. Kenner would hang their good engravings on the walls leading up the stair, where the engravings would be lit by the big north-facing window. In her mind's eye, she drew pictures of corners of the rooms and whole rooms. She was pleased with what she envisioned.

CONSIDERING COLLECTIONS

Artistic households were populated by collectors, like Mrs. Kenner, whose homes were the showcases for their collections. They were constantly on the lookout for treasures. They took excursions to country auctions, rummaged through dusty junk shops and frequented Oriental import stores (see images on pages 45, 123 and 72). They attended exhibitions and expositions, from prestigious art shows, to mechanics fairs, to ladies' bazaars (see bottom image on page 18 and the image on page 78). The wealthy patronized the elegant antique stores in the big cities, and on their travels abroad, they dirtied their hands in the antiquarian shops. They prized art made at home by skilled hands: painted vases, carved wood and needlework of all sorts (see images on pages 44 and 125). And, serendipitous bits of nature—an exquisite seashell, a wonderfully striated stone—also entered collections.

The choicest items in the collections were called bric-a-brac. These were the small things that simply sat on a table top or in a cabinet, items that were just for show. Many sorts of objects were classed as bric-a-brac: costly objets d'art, amazing curiosities, singularly beautiful bits. Modern productions, like art pottery and glass were bric-a-brac, but so were antiques, like old Spode, Italian lace, carved jade or Delft tiles (to name some popular collectables of the artistic era). Bric-a-brac was beautiful in and of itself, but it also suggested stories and meaning. In 1885, James Jackson Jarves, art critic and collector, stated that bric-a-brac

has become the dainty pet of the finest ladies and gentlemen, whose footsteps a stray rose-leaf might shock.

In their mouths bric-à-brac is the sweetest, most delectable of words, radiating an atmosphere of beauty, bargains, and preciousness of every grade; fragrant with the romance of history, fashion, the caprices of taste, the fortunes of great families, the careers of genius, the joys and vicissitudes of human life and its endless inventions and imaginings in pursuit of its ideals; a compound of archeology, antiquarianism, sentimentalism, wit and fun, with touches of sadness too, but on the whole emitting a delightsome, aesthetic, and artistic aroma.[21]

Above all, bric-a-brac suggested the discernment and poetic sensibilities of the collector.

While the items in a collection were the raw material, furnishing a house was more than a mere matter of conglomeration. Harriet Spofford warned, "One, in short, may be a connoisseur in all sorts of curios, and yet be totally destitute of any faculty of putting them together so as to make the most of their congregated beauty, of the first idea of grouping various articles for the sake of their picturesque charm when united."[22] Many collectors fell into the trap of straining after the bizarre or the fashionable. Dewing condemned the homeowner who spreads "meaningless draperies about, loads the tables with bric-a-brac, covers the walls with Japanese fans, chooses the furniture because it is old, not because it is pretty, and, if there are pictures, prefers faces of hideous old people, in strange, ugly headdresses—all this idea of the picturesque shows not an artistic sense, but an absence of the true capacity of selection, of the distinction between beauty and ugliness, between fitness and unfitness."[23] The key was to establish connections between the objects, so that they almost spoke to each other. Harriet Spofford wrote that "the furniture in any permanently and well-arranged room seems to be living a life of its own; the various pieces consort in friendly relations; and you never descend, on any errand, into such a room at night without being aware of a certain conscious existence on the part of the room, much like that of a tree, and without being suspicious, if you are at all imaginative, of a still more active life behind your back."[24] Special furnishings, the collections and bric-a-brac of a household, took on something of the life and the stories of past and present owners. The taste of the true collector not only reconciled diverse objects but also established harmonious relations between them.

[21] Jarves, "The Pursuit of Bric-à-Brac," *Italian Rambles*, 305–06.
[22] Spofford, *Art Decoration Applied to Furniture*, 231.
[23] Dewing, *Beauty in the Household*, 40–41.
[24] Spofford, *Art Decoration Applied to Furniture*, 234.

Establishing Aesthetic Contrasts

While planning her furnishing with an eye towards comfort, use and picturesque contrast, Mrs. Kenner also kept aesthetic effects firmly in mind. She thought about how furniture could be arranged to create interesting spaces, about where engravings could best be seen, about how light would shine on metal and glass. She planned for pleasing contrasts of mass, texture, color and light. She imagined the experience of looking at a mantel, of how the eye would move around, alighting on various pieces. She

was following the advice of Harriet Spofford who set out some simple axioms. Good composition could be achieved by "arranging the furniture with a view to masses, and then combining the masses themselves with a view to harmony; that is, where heavier objects, such as cabinets or pianos, tables or davenports, and the darker paintings, make a place of deep shadow, that place must be balanced by another having relation to it, and must be relieved by lights—by the bare wall surface, by gilded articles, by marbles, by the delicate window drapery."[25]

Harriet Spofford and Mrs. Kenner understood the basic qualities of each object: form, color, texture and value. They understood how to pose each in relation to the other. By understanding the aesthetic impact of each chair, of each set of curtains, of each cut-glass vase, furnishings could be grouped successfully. It was all a matter of balance.

Telling Stories

The sensitive homeowner grouped furnishings into vignettes that had picturesque and aesthetic appeal. Mrs. Kenner knew that her grouping of brass figures and glass vases on the hall mantel would catch the light from the stair window during the day and the firelight at night. They also told a pleasant little story about collecting. Vignettes were consciously composed still lifes of objects that made pleasing contrasts, that "spoke" to one another and anyone who happened along (see image on page 110). Some vignettes were de rigueur. Portraits of ancestors were placed on easels, and then draped with fabric and garlands. Tall vases stood in the corners of stair landings, holding arrangements of dried flowers and grasses. Hanging wall cabinets were readymade for the display of small objects. Some vignettes were

Japanese bedroom in the home of Richard Reutingler, San Francisco, 2005. This is a room in the home of a contemporary collector of nineteenth-century art. Most (but not all) of the things in the room date from the artistic era, including the six-piece bedroom set, which dates from 1881 and is attributed to Mitchell & Rammelsberg (the dresser, at right, has a monogram and the date September 13, 1881). The wallpapers, which were manufactured in the 1980s by Bradbury and Bradbury, were based on nineteenth-century designs by Christopher Dresser, Bruce Talbert and William Morris, but no pattern is a faithful copy of any period wallpaper. Although this room is a modern creation, the eclecticism of the collections, the density of the furnishings and the rich, subdued palette are all very much in the spirit of the Aesthetic movement and of the collector who assembled the room. (Photo by Douglas Sandberg.)

25 Ibid., 217.

Weary, oil painting by William Merritt Chase, ca 1889. The sitter is weary, perhaps from arranging her collections, which include an Oriental screen, Louis XV chair, Oriental rug, brass brazier and monumental urn. The painting masterfully combines different tones of reds, golds and browns, maximizing the aesthetic effect of each object. (Eleanor S. and C. Thomas May Collection; photography courtesy of Berry-Hill Galleries.)

more contrived. A collector's finds would justify a vignette: a purple piece of antique silk on a tabletop, a vase with the same shade of purple in its intricate painting and a silver teapot to reflect the whole. Or, groupings of functional objects could be made artistic. Clarence Cook illustrated a Chinese plant stand that could make a pretty washstand when it was furnished with a South American water jar and a Russian bowl. Vignettes were sited on practically any flat surface that could hold them: tables, niches, even door lintels. In her book, Constance Cary Harrison included several line drawings of door lintels: one shows two Japanese fans, a miniature parasol and a bunch of cattails tied up with a piece of patterned silk. An infinite number of charming arrangements were possible.

The artistic taste for vignettes culminated in the arrangements for mantels. Mrs. Kenner's living room mantel was a little museum to her life with ceramics—as a collector, as a maker, as a friend of other ceramics makers and as a mother who treasured her children's creations. The various mirrored compartments would show everything in the round. The mantel would provoke merry and earnest conversation and would elicit happy memories. Mrs. Kenner's mantel was, of course, unique, but it would have found peers in other artistic households. Everywhere mantelpieces were focal points. The *Decorator and Furnisher* for July of 1883 devoted a whole article to quotes and illustrations from the leading household

art writers on how to furnish mantels. Harriet Spofford summed it up: "The mantel-piece of the drawing-room is always to be its most elaborated and beautiful point . . . care must be expended upon its scenic capabilities."[26] She went on to say "the mantel is part of the reverence due the chimney, a tribute to the fire upon the hearth, which is the deity of home."[27] The mantel was the heart of the artistic home.

Artistic arrangements did not stay static. To the dismay of the design purists and the delight of the nineteenth-century do-it-yourself writers, homeowners changed things around and embellished. Photographs of ordinary middle class households show that lengths of embroidery or bits of silk often found their way into living rooms; they were draped over the back of a chair or the top of a piano or tied onto the back of a chair as a big bow. Rooms were decorated seasonally or for holidays. The sideboard was the setting for Fourth of July flags, pressed autumn leaves and many a Christmas snow scene of cotton wool and spangles. A well-furnished house was not complete without arrangements of flowers and greenery. Country dwellers used common things from the field and forest, like daisies and moss, while city dwellers had to pay dearly for cut flowers or grow their own in the windows. Everyone was urged to see the artistic in the commonplace. For example, homeowners might use Virginia creeper when it turned red in the fall or lay ferns down in studied arrangements. Flowers and greenery were shown off in containers that were themselves aesthetic objects, from the finest Venetian glass to humble earthenware butter pots. The artistic homeowner achieved subtle color effects by contrasting or comparing the container and contained; gray moss dotted with tiny white flowers was banked in a silver basket or goldenrod competed with its bright brass vase. The crowning achievement of womanhood was a vase of homegrown flowers, artfully arranged (see top image on page 149). Ephemeral furnishings added spice to the artistic household.

Artistic furnishings were valued for their aesthetic effects *and* narrative implications. A bright red jar would be treasured for its color and for its provenance as a votive lamp from a Roman cathedral. Constance Cary Harrison praised the portraits of children that were painted on ceramic tiles by Rosina Emmet, who became a

The Chimney Corner, oil painting by D. Maitland Armstrong, 1878. Armstrong's painting captures the appeal of a well-furnished mantel. There is a choice collection of china and brass, and there is a cheerful fire burning at the grate. The tiles might be rare, old examples from China, Holland or the Middle East—similar tiles were made in all of these places and were collected avidly. Or, the tiles could be new productions in the style of the old. The child reads an illustrated book, perhaps one of Walter Crane's children's books, which were published at this time. (Courtesy of the Preservation Society of Newport County.)

-- --
[26] Ibid., 221.
[27] Ibid., 233.

Decorating Furniture

Revolution, swivel chair designed by Tord Boontje, 2004. The owners of this chair can drape the wool-felt covering in different ways or remove it altogether, in much the same way that late-nineteenth-century homeowners draped and beribboned their furniture. (Photo courtesy of Davies + Starr and Moss.)

well-regarded oil painter. George William Sheldon, author of *Artistic Houses,* singled out a needlework panel designed by the homeowner he was profiling, Mrs. Zerega. Her creative input was as important as the fact that the panel had been executed by august artists John La Farge and Mary Tillinghast. These highly artistic objects were all the more significant because of the stories they told and the sentimental value they held. "Pilgrim" furniture was collected both because of its sturdy form and because of the heritage it proclaimed. The dual value of aesthetics and narrative was true of so many artistic furnishings. The art of furnishing lay in bringing these valuable objects together in pleasing colloquies.

BEAUTY INSPIRES VIRTUE: THE ARTFUL AND MORAL HOME

Soon after they moved in, Mrs. Kenner saw that the new house would be a powerful force for good in the life of her family. The first breakfast in the sunny dining room set the tone. Mr. Kenner discussed the news from the paper with less consternation than usual, and the children seemed happier to go off to school. The hired girl was very pleased with her room that had spring green walls and a pink-and-green bedspread. The children did their schoolwork together quietly at the living room table. The whole family enjoyed the fires at night in the living room, with light flickering on the pots on the mantel, the polished woodwork and the spangles on the portiere. When Mr. Kenner turned in at the gate, he walked a little taller, as if his shoulders were less weighed by the concerns of work. How sad that so many people put up with ugliness and infelicities in their household arrangements! Mrs. Kenner had put much effort into the house: going to countless sales, embroidering for hours, enduring the skepticism of the housepainters as she described the colors she wanted. But, the house was worth the effort, for her family was happy in it. In her bedtime prayers, Mrs. Kenner always included a word of thanks for their home.

Artistic householders in America worked for beauty because they knew beauty was a powerful influence. The greatest achievement of the Aesthetic movement in America was the home, especially the middle class home. The era produced marvelous objects that survive to testify to the era: wonderful cabinets and china plates, silver teapots and even fragile silks. Queen Anne and Shingle Style houses still dot our landscape, but most are much altered. Sadly, the house interiors survive mainly only in pictures: the black-and-white engravings from household art books, the rare chromolithograph supplement from magazines, a few oil paintings and many, many photographs. Word pictures, too, from novels and nonfiction writings, document the interiors. These survivors are poignant testimony to the effort that Americans of all classes put into making their homes beautiful.

The Aesthetic movement in Europe and Britain looked different. There, the movement filtered down from esthetes, who pursued new forms of beauty in poetry, prose and painting. The phrase "art for art's sake," so often cited as the motto of the Aesthetic movement, comes from the writings of French writer Theophile Gautier. He formulated the concept of *l'art pour l'art* in the preface to his 1835 novel *Madamoiselle de Maupin*. The title character constructed a love triangle through seduction and cross dressing. The prose was florid, as was Gautier's own private life and as were the lives of the rest of his circle, the Parisian bohemian avant-garde. So, from the first, "art for art's sake" was a watchword for edgy artistry and sexuality. A British literary elite, centered among Oxford professors and students of the 1850s and 1860s, took up the ideas of the French bohemians. Walter Pater, in his study on Renaissance art, urged readers to look at all art avidly. "What we have to do is to be forever curiously testing new opinions and courting impressions, and never acquiescing in a facile orthodoxy . . . to burn always with this hard, gem-like flame, to maintain this ecstasy, is success in life."[28] The Oxford esthetes, who included Algernon Swinburne and the young Oscar Wilde, joined London painters and poets, including Whistler, E. W. Godwin and the Pre-Raphaelites, in a veritable cult of beauty. The operetta *Patience* satirized these esthetes as wholly consumed by fourteenth- and fifteenth-century art, Japanese pottery and sunflowers. But, these artists insisted that they were responsible only to their art—not the larger world. Artists were obligated to cultivate their own aesthetic sensibilities in order to make art that would, in turn, achieve great sensuality. Wilde was the spokesperson for the movement, and he consistently echoed Pater's heartfelt call to adore and embrace life and art.

The achievements of the British and European Aesthetic movement are many and impressive. They are centered in literature and poetry, drama and the visual arts. But Americans were deeply suspicious of the sensationalist aspects of the movement. Rejecting the standard bourgeois worldview, using prose with barely veiled sensual connotations, the strange and severe images of Whistler, the florid poetry of Pater—Americans believed that all of these acts at least flouted conventions, if they did not amount to outright immorality. Americans were not surprised when, in 1895,

Wilde was convicted of "gross indecency" for his conduct in a love affair with Lord Alfred Douglas. "Art for art's sake," the European Aesthetic movement, had become decadent.

The Aesthetic movement played out quite differently in America. Americans, especially the Transcendentalist writers and the Hudson River School painters, formulated their own concept of a "natural theology"—which found God in Nature, especially in the seemingly divinely ordained New World landscapes. Their ideas were congruent with the writings of John Ruskin, the English art critic who championed Pre-Raphaelite art and Gothic architecture, especially its pious, didactic aspects. When Ruskin linked Religion to Nature and to Art, the ideas rang true in America. He legitimized aesthetic issues and made them palatable to a Christian audience. So, aesthetic theory in America, more than in Britain, had an underpinning in the landscape and in theology.

But, while British esthetes were writing refined poetry and painting radical canvases, Americans were torn apart by the Civil War. In the aftermath, the country's institutions were shattered or eroding. Would the young political system stand? In the face of such destruction, what authority did our nation's clerics have? The new theory of evolution challenged the specialness of human beings and questioned whether we were God's chosen people. A multiplicity of Protestantisms sprang up. Periodic financial panics wrenched the country. Immigration strained the system of labor. For the first time, the country experience widespread strikes; many included brutal violence. The cities housed a very visible and very populated underclass.

Against these tensions, there was the refuge of the American home, especially the American suburban home. The suburban home of the artistic era was a new place. It was neither urban (where homes were cells within an organic unit) nor rural (where homes were the base of business operations); it existed for itself. In the new economy of the post–Civil War period, most Americans clung to the idea that capitalism was fair, right and eventually would be a social leavener. Americans embraced the right of the wealthy, especially the self-made man, to display wealth in the home and refuge. Above all, Progressivism permeated American thinking. Americans reconciled the theories of Darwinian evolution with their innate belief that human character could be perfected. The result was a progressive Protestantism based in homes throughout America. Altogether, this was a cultural mindset, which accommodated the modern world and a moral life, and that found a home in the home.

-- --
[28] Pater, *The Renaissance*, 236–237.

NATIONALISM AND HOMEMAKING

As a society, Americans saw homemaking as a progressive, righteous and particularly American solution to the conflicts of the modern world. Almon Varney, editor of *Our Homes and Their Adornments*, a thoroughgoing guide to planning, building and using a house, dedicated the book to the "Home-Loving and Home-Building People of America." The proliferation of single-family homes was only natural for a people who prized independence and self-reliance. In explaining the remarkable rise of interest in home design, Candace Wheeler noted, "The instinct of self-expression is much stronger in us than in other races."[29] Furthermore, it was only by following this instinct that Americans could build their national character. In an essay, "The Development of American Homes," the art and architectural writer Mariana Griswold Van Rennselaer described this phenomenon. She felt that the character of a people was reflected in its architecture, and because America was focused on the individual (not any municipal authority) we should not be surprised to find that the home is the expression of Americanness. "To see where the American people stand in the matter of taste, to see how far it has got on the road of aesthetic progress, and whither this road is likely to lead, we must look at its homes and especially at their interiors."[30] It was a seeming contradiction: self-expression naturally took varied forms, yet these forms expressed the collective character of the future of our nation. The contradiction was resolved as Americans built diverse homes that formed unified, progressive neighborhoods, towns and cities.

Homes helped build the nation because they were such a potent force binding the family together. The mid-nineteenth-century cult of domesticity had elevated homemaking beyond a set of chores; it was a holy calling. The family was the congregation that populated this

Dual portrait of an unidentified man and woman, ca 1890s. In this dual portrait of a couple, the woman is superimposed upon her sphere, the home, and the man (presumably her husband) is seen in his sphere, the outside world. Together the two made their home.

-- --
[29] Wheeler, *Principles of Home Decoration*, 8.
[30] Van Rensselaer, "The Development of American Homes," in Wheeler, ed., *Household Art*, 37.

domestic religion, bound together by ties of mutual affection nurtured in the home. The home had to be a healthy nursery for the family, and pleasant surroundings were a necessary condition of such a home. In fact, Clarence Cook argued that aesthetically superior surroundings were vital to raising a good family:

> I look upon this living-room as an important agent in the education of life; it will make a great difference to the children who grow up in it, and to all whose experience is associated with it, whether it be a beautiful and cheerful room, or a homely and bare one, or a merely formal and conventional one. . . . It is no trifling matter, whether we hang poor pictures on our walls or good ones, whether we select a fine cast or a second-rate one. We might almost say it makes no difference whether the people we live with are first-rate or second-rate.[31]

Good decor was a soft but strong forge in shaping people who shaped the nation: "The art of furnishing comprehends much more than the knack of putting pictures and tables and chairs into suitable co-relation; it comprehends a large part of the art of making home attractive, and of shaping the family with the gentle manners that make life easier to one and pleasanter to all; and it would seem as if the people who came out of pleasant homes would have their sympathies and humanities so cultivated by the influence of their surroundings that they would be more earnest to make pleasant homes possible for all."[32]

Beautiful homes produce harmonious families and charitable citizens who could spread the goodwill wrought of domesticity.

THE MINISTRY OF WOMEN

But who was to do this good work of making homes beautiful? Women, of course. There were differing opinions on the value of this work. Some felt that homemaking was the spiritual calling of women. George Weaver, a minister and author of *The Heart of the World*, an 1883 book on the value of home, put it precisely: "The woman is the priestess of home. . . . Her talents and tastes have given her a natural ordination to this holy office."[33] Note that this was followed immediately by a chapter titled "The Equality of Man and Woman." Jacob von Falke, a writer on art and history and author of *Art in the House*, included a chapter titled "Woman's Aesthetic Mission." This was, of course, homemaking (not the creation of great works of art), and although homemaking was inherently of small compass, it was still important. Von Falke believed that the home was the domain where the beautiful and the useful were united, and all art, however utilitarian, "refines the manner, diverts our thoughts from low and vulgar things, consoles us for the many troubles and discomforts of material existence, and raises us above them into a higher spiritual sphere: it

---

[31] Cook, *The House Beautiful*, 49.
[32] Spofford, *Art Decoration Applied to Furniture*, 232.
[33] Weaver, *The Heart of the World*, 36.

humanizes us, and idealizes our life."[34] But, Candace Wheeler more cynically noted, "In the great race for wealth which characterizes our time, it is demanded that women shall make it effective by so using it as to distinguish the family; and nothing distinguishes it so much as the superiority of the home."[35] She felt that the woman of moderate means who was a successful home decorator was even more talented than one who was wealthy. Although some thought women's role was noble, while others were less sure, consensus reigned: women, not men, were the homemakers.

Happily, women had a special affinity for beauty, which would serve them well in the mission of homemaking. "It has been said with truth that taste, or, in other words, the sense of beauty, that is, the faculty of distinguishing the beautiful from the ugly, is intuitive, and it is customary to attribute it more especially to the female sex."[36] Because of her inherent capacity for taste, and her role as homemaker, American women very often excelled in home decorating. This seemed magical to Candace Wheeler since few women had practical training in interior design: "It is as much of a marvel when a woman without training or experience creates a good interior *as a whole*, as if an amateur in music should compose an opera."[37] Fortunately, American women were "a teachable and a studious people, with a faculty of turning 'general information' to account; and general information upon art matters has had much to do with our good interiors."[38] As we have seen, women embraced design education, going to art school, reading household art books and magazines and shopping studiously.

Americans made a crucial mental leap: beautiful surroundings, in and of themselves, elevated the moral soul, therefore making the surroundings beautiful was a moral act. That noble act was the mission of women, and it was their joy. "What pleasure there may in slowly bringing to perfection a little home which shall show at every turn the thought and care, the real affection, that have been bestowed upon it!"[39] So claimed Maria Oakey Dewing; Mrs. Kenner certainly agreed.

Ironically, it was Oscar Wilde, the ultimate British esthete, who provided a crucial prod to this process with his 1882 tour. His lectures on the decorative arts and interior design cited the products of design reformers like William Morris and E. W. Godwin. And, because he pitched his speeches to women, he shifted the power balance in America in matters artistic from male British esthetes to women homemakers. He acknowledged women not only as homemakers but as tastemakers. He urged American women to reform their worlds. We have seen how American women took up this challenge and what they achieved in homes all over the country. Their victories added up to a national triumph: beauty, home and virtue linked under the authority of women.

In the artistic era, Americans shaped their homes and their homes shaped Americans. Our modern civilization was built on this reciprocal influence. Homemakers could formulate furnishings to reflect a conception of beauty, trusting in beauty to form the soul of the inhabitants. "It is art that helps to beautify life through the multiplicity of small, lovely, and charming objects with which, in our ceaseless yearning for beauty . . . we are continually striving to surround ourselves; it is art which decorates our walls and our domestic utensils, brings our whole dwelling into harmony, and fills it with an atmosphere of beauty and an impression of comfort charming alike to the eye and the heart."[40] The artistic home was beautiful, and the bulwark of that beauty was virtue.

facing: Trade card for E. P. Waite & Co., Crayon Portrait Artists, ca 1880s. E. P. Waite's trade card shows an utterly idealized image of harmonious life in an artistic household. Waite conducted a mail-order business making "crayon portraits." He probably began with a photographic print supplied by the customer and then enlarged it and enhanced it with pastel, charcoal, pencil and/or paint. Judging from his trade card, he was able to supply charming, if flattering, portraits of his subjects.

---

[34] Falke, *Art in the House,* 316.
[35] Wheeler, *Principles of Home Decoration,* 11.
[36] Falke, *Art in the House,* 318.
[37] Wheeler, *Principles of Home Decoration,* 13.
[38] Ibid., 10.
[39] Dewing, *Beauty in the Household,* 13.
[40] Falke, *Art in the House,* 314–15.

THE ARTFUL HOME TODAY

Today, whether or not women's highest calling is mother-hood and homemaking is an issue dividing many cultures. I don't pretend to answer that question with this book—feminists and conservatives will both find ammunition in its pages. Nor do I mean to suggest that a beautiful home is a necessary condition for nurturing morals. I leave the study of which environments best induce character and conscience to ministers and anthropologists. But, I do hope to have per-suaded the reader that in America in the late nineteenth century the culture was not divided: women homemakers were the honored norm and men earned respect along with wages at their jobs outside the home. Women might be physically weaker than men, even intellectually weaker (many

debated this last point), but their capacity for unselfish love was greater and their moral compass was truer. Making a beautiful home was a noble calling because it made happy families and responsible citizens.

In twenty-first-century America, the home front is more complex, or at least seems so without the benefit of hindsight. The two-parent household is increasingly uncommon, and most women work outside of the home. Women do not have a lock on morality; men are supposed to be full partners in homemaking. The influence of a pro-gressive Eastern and Protestant white Anglo-Saxon elite on political, religious and cultural matters is no longer unques-tioned. Portions of our culture are fiercely secular, while other portions are fiercely religious; moderates are either outnumbered or voiceless. But most men and women muddle along, celebrating their options, even as they struggle to earn a living and raise a family.

Along the path to this multicultural, multi-optioned society, artistic homemaking has fallen by the wayside. Everyone knows the importance of four well-insulated walls and a roof that does not leak. Everyone understands the value of systems that work, whether it is a strong shower or a good kitchen floor plan. Everyone wants a comfortable home, whether that means a plush sofa or a Jacuzzi or both. But few seem to realize that beauty plays a vastly important role in making a happy home. Security, efficiency and comfort are better understood in twenty-first-century America than beauty, yet we feel the need for all of these. In our bones, we feel that beauty is an influence for the good, but we don't know how to act upon that feeling. We see extreme and bizarre expressions of the belief that our home surroundings influence us: an occult belief in feng shui, obscene budgets for decorators, panacea purchases of McMansions. It doesn't help that we get little formal training in art at school. Instead, the most pervasive visual images in our culture, by far, come from advertising. An unfortunate byproduct of too little art education and too much TV is that our ideas of beautiful homes are shaped by the companies with the largest advertising budgets and the most sensationalist takes on home decor. So, our role models for beautiful homes come from ads for giant flat screen TVs in slick apartments or from *Lifestyles of the Rich and Famous*. The prior generation's total adherence to a minimalist aesthetic, which still dominates many design magazines, also closes options. There are hopeful signs: entire TV channels devoted to home-decorating advice (unfortunately dominated by advertising); millions spent on home renovations annually; and legions of home-crafters making everything from front-door knockers to attic curtains.

To embrace homemaking (not just living in a home), we need to recognize beauty and cultivate our own taste. If we understood more about basic aesthetic concepts, we'd be better off. We need to understand why certain forms, lines, textures and colors are pleasing and how to combine them. We need to trust our yearning for ornamentalism and lush surfaces. Yes, each homemaker needs to know his or her specific needs for security, comfort and efficiency and how to fulfill those on a budget. But, each homemaker also needs to recognize what she or he finds aesthetically pleasing. We need to realize that there are many roads to beauty and whatever provides the most pleasure and utility is right for us. This was the trail that the artistic homeowner blazed; we have only to follow the path.

NOTES ON SOURCES

Several sources document and describe Aesthetic movement architecture. For a photographic survey of the architecture of upper-class country homes, see Lewis, *American Country Houses of the Gilded Age*. The excellent color illustrations in Moss and Winkler, *Victorian Exterior Decoration*, explain how color contributed to the aesthetic effect of architecture. The discussions of exterior color can be extrapolated to interiors of the era. Two books provide a good analysis of the cultural history of American homes, with an emphasis on exterior architecture: Handlin, *The American Home*, and Clark, *The American Family Home*. For a look at how homeowners used pattern books to customize the "National Style" of Aesthetic movement architecture, see Reiff, *Houses from Books*.

Aesthetic movement interiors are documented in two photographic sources. All the photographs from Sheldon's survey of deluxe interiors, but unfortunately none of its text, are reprinted in Lewis, Turner and McQuillin, *The Opulent Interiors of the Gilded Age*. A marvelous photographic survey of late-nineteenth-century interiors, from the most deluxe to the most pedestrian, is provided in Seale, *The Tasteful Interlude*. A pictorial and textual survey of aesthetic interiors can be found in a chapter of Mayhew and Myers, *A Documentary History of American Interiors*. The basic components of Aesthetic movement interiors (and

non-Aesthetic interiors) are enumerated in Moss and Winkler, *Victorian Exterior Decoration*. For an essay surveying Aesthetic movement interiors, see Johnson, "The Artful Interior," *In Pursuit of Beauty: Americans and the Aesthetic Movement*. Another essay describes the stylistic changes in high-end interior design by professionals: Gray, "Tiffany's Contemporaries," in Johnson, *Louis Comfort Tiffany*.

A few sources deal with particular aspects of the interior. Carbone, *At Home with Art*, shows American interiors in which fine art figures prominently. This catalog also includes a short but excellent essay by Stayton on the interior as it was depicted in novels. For a look at British aesthetic interiors, see Gere and Hoskins, *The House Beautiful*.

The modern luxury housing industry and the probable development of American suburbs is described in "Chasing Ground," an article in the *New York Times Magazine* section, by Gertner. The life story of an existing luxury home is told by Uchitelle, in "At 150 Edgars Lane," another *New York Times* article.

The very best sources for the Aesthetic interior are the primary sources cited in the footnotes; all can be found in the bibliography. These wonderful books document both what interiors looked like and what the authors *wished* they looked like.

Bibliography

This bibliography cites every source in the footnotes and Notes on Sources sections, plus other items that may be of interest to the general reader.

"The Aesthetic Craze." *Buffalo Courier*, February 13, 1882, 1.

Arms, George, and Christopher K. Lohmann, eds., *W. D. Howells: Selected Letters*. 2 vols. Boston: Twayne, 1979.

"Art, Music and Drama." *Appleton's Journal* 10, no. 227 (July 12, 1873): 123.

Barnes, Thurlow Weed, ed. *Catalog of Albany's Bicentennial Loan Exhibition*. Albany, NY, 1886.

Beck, Martha. "What Your House Says About You." *O at Home*, Fall 2004, 56, 58.

Bendix, Deanna Marohn. *Diabolical Designs: Paintings, Interiors, and Exhibitions of James McNeill Whistler*. Washington: Smithsonian Institution Press, 1995.

Blackburn, R. Barry. ed. *Art, Society, and Accomplishments: A Treasury of Artistic Homes, Social Life and Culture*. Chicago: The Blackburn Company, 1891.

Blanchard, Mary Warner. "Boundaries of the Victorian Body: Aesthetic Fashion in Gilded Age America." *The American Historical Review*, no. 100 (February 1995): 21–50.

Blanchard, Mary Warner. *Oscar Wilde's America: Counter Culture in the Gilded Age*. New Haven: Yale University Press, 1998.

Boris, Eileen. *Art and Labor: Ruskin, Morris and the Craftsman Ideal in America*. Philadelphia: Temple University Press, 1986.

Boston Society of Decorative Art, *Annual Report*. Boston: Society of Decorative Art, 1880.

Boyer, M. Christine. *Manhattan Manners: Architecture and Style, 1850–1900*. NY: Rizzoli International Publications, 1985.

Brandimarte, Cynthia A. "Japanese Novelty Stores." *Winterthur Portfolio* 26, no. 1 (Spring 1991): 1–25.

Briggs, Asa. *Victorian Things*. Chicago: University of Chicago Press, 1980.

Bronner, Simon, ed. *Consuming Visions: Accumulation and Display of Goods in America, 1880–1920*. Winterthur and NY: W. W. Norton & Company and the Henry Francis du Pont Winterthur Museum, 1989.

Brownell, William C. "The Art-Schools of New York." *Scribner's Monthly* 16, no. 6 (October, 1878): 761–81.

Burns, Sarah. *Inventing the Modern Artist: Art and Culture in Gilded Age America*. New Haven and London: Yale University Press, 1996.

Calloway, Stephen. *Divinely Decadent*. London: Mitchell Beazley, 2001.

Carbone, Theresa. *At Home with Art: Paintings in American Interiors, 1780–1920*. Katonah, NY: Katonah Museum of Art, 1995.

Castillo, Encarna. *MXM: Maximalist Interiors*. NY: HarperCollins, 2003.

Church, Ella Rodman. *How to Furnish a Home*. NY: D. Appleton and Company, 1881.

Clark, Clifford Edward Jr., *The American Family Home, 1800–1960*. Chapel Hill: The University of North Carolina Press, 1986.

"Concerning Furniture." *Scribner's Monthly* 11 (November 1875–April 1876), suppl. "Scribner's Miscellany," 9.

Cook, Clarence. "Culture and Progress: Cottier and Company." *Scribner's Monthly* 8, August 1874, 500–1.

Cook, Clarence. *The House Beautiful: Essay on Beds and Tables, Stools and Candlesticks*. NY: Charles Scriber's Sons, 1881.

"Costly Tints in Glass." *Boston Herald*, nd, Doc 20:7, Corning Museum of Glass Library.

Cuito, Aurora, et al. *Maximalism from Minimalism*. Edited by Paco Asensio. NY: HarperCollins, 2002.

D'Ambrosio, Anna Tobin. *A Brass Menagerie: Metalwork of the Aesthetic Movement*. Utica: The Munson Williams Proctor Arts Institute, 2005.

Detroit Institute of Arts. *The Quest for Unity: American Art between World's Fairs, 1876–1893*. Detroit: Detroit Institute of Arts, 1983.

Dewing, Mrs. T. W. [Maria Richards Oakey]. *Beauty in the Household*. NY: Harper & Brothers, 1882.

Dewson, Edward. "Screens and Their Uses." *Decorator and Furnisher* 2, no. 1 (April 1883): 14–15.

Donnelly, Max. "Cottier and Company, Art Furniture Makers." *Antiques Magazine*. June 2001, 916–25.

Eastlake, Charles L. *Hints on Household Taste: The Classic Handbook of Victorian Interior Decoration*. NY: Dover Publications, Inc., 1969.

Elliott, Charles Wyllys. *The Book of American Interiors*. Boston: James R. Osgood and Company, 1876.

Ellmann, Richard. *Oscar Wilde*. NY: Random House, 1988.

"Exceedingly Pretty Curtains." *Decorator and Furnisher* 2, no. 3 (June 1883): 94.

Falke, Jacob von. *Art in the House: Historical, Critical, and Aesthetical Studies on the Decoration and Furnishing of the Dwelling*. Edited and translated by Charles C. Perkins. Boston: L. Prang and Company, 1879.

Fuller, Albert W. *Artistic Houses in City and Country*. Boston: James R. Osgood and Company, 1882.

Gallagher, Winifred. *House Thinking: A Room-by-Room Look at How We Live*. NY: HarperCollins, 2006.

Garvey, Ellen Gruber. *The Adman in the Parlor: Magazines and the Gendering of Consumer Culture, 1880s to 1910s*. NY and Oxford: Oxford University Press, 1996.

Gere, Charlotte, and Lesley Hoskins. *The House Beautiful: Oscar Wilde and the Aesthetic Interior*. London: Lund Humphries and the Geffrye Museum, 2000.

Gertner, Jon. "Chasing Ground." *The New York Times Magazine*. October 16, 2005, 46–53, 68, 81–82.

Gibson, Louis H. "Architecture and the People." *New England Magazine* 18, March 1898, 21–25.

Gilbert, W. S., and Arthur Sullivan. *The Complete Plays of Gilbert and Sullivan*. NY: W. W. Norton & Company, 1976.

[Godkin, Edward Lawrence]. "Chromo-Civilization." *The Nation* 19, no. 482 (September 24, 1874): 201–2.

Godwin, E. W. "My Chambers and What I Did to Them, Chapter 1: A. D. 1867." *Architect*. July 1, 1876, 4–5, 187.

Goodman, Wendy. "The New Eccentrics." *New York Magazine*, April 11, 2005, 45–74.

Gordon, Beverly. *Bazaars and Fair Ladies: The History of the American Fundraising Fair*. Knoxville, TN: University of Tennessee Press, 1998.

Gordon, Beverly. "Woman's Domestic Body: The Conceptual Conflation of Women and Interiors in the Industrial Age." *Winterthur Portfolio* 31, no. 4 (Winter 1996): 281–301.

Green, Harvey. *The Light of the Home: An Intimate View of the Lives of Women in Victorian America*. NY: Pantheon Books, 1983.

Greir, Katherine. *Culture and Comfort: People, Parlors, and Upholstery, 1850–1930*. Rochester, NY: The Strong Museum, 1988.

Handlin, David. *The American Home: Architecture and Society, 1815–1915*. Boston: Little, Brown and Company, 1979.

Harper's New Monthly Magazine 67 (July–December 1883).

Harrison, Constance Cary. *Woman's Handiwork in Modern Homes*. NY: Charles Scribner's Sons, 1881.

Haweis, [Mary Eliza Joy]. *The Art of Dress*. London: Chatto and Winders, 1879.

Hewitt, Emma Churchman. *Queen of Home*. Philadelphia: International Publishing Company, 1889.

Hirschfeld, Charles. "America on Exhibition: The New York Crystal Palace." *American Quarterly* 9, no. 2, pt. 1 (Summer 1957): 101–116.

Hosley, William. *The Japan Idea: Art and Life in Victorian America*. Hartford, CT: Wadsworth Atheneum, 1990.

Household Conveniences: Being the Experiences of Many Practical Writers. NY: Orange and Judd, 1884.

Howe, Jennifer L., ed. *Cincinnati Art-Carved Furniture and Interiors*. Athens, OH: Cincinnati Art Museum and Ohio University Press, 2003.

Howe, Katherine, et al. *Herter Brothers: Furniture and Interiors for a Gilded Age*. NY: Harry N. Abrams, Inc. and the Museum of Fine Arts, Houston, 1994.

Howells, William Dean. *The Coast of Bohemia*. NY: Harper & Brothers Publishers, 1893.

Jarves, James Jackson. "The Pursuit of Bric-à-Brac." *Italian Rambles: Studies of Life and Manners in New and Old Italy*. NY: G. P. Putnam's Sons, 1885.

Jay, Robert. *The Trade Card in Nineteenth-Century America*. Columbia: University of Missouri Press, 1987.

Johnson, Marilynn A., et. al. *Louis Comfort Tiffany: Artist for the Ages*. London and NY: Scala Publishers and Exhibitions International, 2005.

Karlson, Norman. *American Art Tile, 1876–1941*. NY: Rizzoli, 1998.

Kinchin, Juliet, and Paul Stirton. "Is Mr. Ruskin Living Too Long?" *Selected Writings of E. W. Godwin on Victorian Architecture and Design*. Oxford: White Cockade Publishing, 2005.

Kurtz, Charles M. "Women in Art." *New York Star*, October 6, 1889, 10.

Lambourne, Lionel. *The Aesthetic Movement*. Boston: Phaidon Press, 1996.

Leach, William R. *Land of Desire: Merchants, Power and the Rise of a New American Culture*. NY: Random House, Inc., 1993.

Lears, T. J., Jackson. *No Place of Grace: Antimodernism and the Transformation of American Culture, 1880–1920*. NY: Pantheon Books, 1981.

Lewis, Arnold. *American Country Houses of the Gilded Age (Sheldon's "Artistic Country Seats")*. NY: Dover Publications, 1982.

Lewis, Arnold, James Turner and Steven McQuillin. *The Opulent Interiors of the Gilded Age: All 203 Photographs from "Artistic Houses."* NY: Dover Publications, 1987.

Lynes, Russell. *The Tastemakers: The Shaping of American Popular Taste*. NY: Dover Publications, Inc., 1980.

Lynn, Catherine. *Wallpaper in America: From the Seventeenth Century to World War I*. NY: Barra Foundation, Cooper-Hewitt Museum, W. W. Norton & Company, 1980.

Macdonald, Stuart. *The History and Philosophy of Art Education*. London: University of London Press, Ltd, 1970.

Mayer, Roberta, and Carolyn Lane. "Disassociating the 'Associated Artists': The Early Business Ventures of Louis C. Tiffany, Candace Wheeler and Lockwood de Forest." *Studies in the Decorative Arts* 8, no. 2 (Spring–Summer 2001): 2–38.

Mayhew, Edgar de Noailles, and Minor Myers Jr. *A Documentary History of American Interiors from the Colonial Era to 1915*. NY: Charles Scribner's Sons, 1980.

McCarthy, Kathleen, D. *Women's Culture: American Philanthropy and Art, 1830–1930*. Chicago: University of Chicago Press, 1991.

McClaugherty, Martha Crabill. "Household Art: Creating the Artistic Home, 1868–1893." *Winterthur Portfolio* 18, no. 1 (Spring 1983): 1–26.

Metropolitan Museum of Art. *In Pursuit of Beauty: Americans and the Aesthetic Movement*. NY: Metropolitan Museum of Art, 1987.

Miller, Joaquin. "The Great Centennial Fair and Its Future." *Independent*, July 13, 1876, 1–2.

"Morality of Home Decoration." *The Manufacturer and Builder* 14, no. 2 (February 1882): 41.

Moss, Roger W., and Gail Casey Winkler. *Victorian Exterior Decoration: How to Paint Your Nineteenth-Century American House Historically*. NY: Henry Holt and Company, 1987.

"Mr. Wilde and his Gospel." *Critic* 2, January 14, 1882, 14.

O'Brien, Kevin. *Oscar Wilde in Canada: An Apostle for the Arts*. Toronto: Personal Library, 1982.

O'Brien, Maureen C. *In Support of Liberty: European Paintings at the 1883 Pedestal Fund Art Loan Exhibition*. Southampton, NY: The Parrish Art Museum, 1986.

"Oscar Wilde. Arrival of Apostle of Aestheticism in America, His Philosophy, His Poetry and His Intentions." *New York Herald*, January 3, 1882, sec. 6:4.

"Oscar Wilde, the Esthete." *Brooklyn Daily Eagle*, January 4, 1882, 2.

"Oscar Wilde's Arrival. The Apostle of the Intense Coming on a Mission to Frivolous America." *New York World*, January 3, 1882, sec. 1:4.

Palliser, George, and Charles Pallister. *Pallister New Cottage Homes and Details*. NY: Palliser, Palliser & Co., 1887.

Pater, Walter Horatio. *The Renaissance: Studies in Art and Poetry*. London: MacMillan and Company, 1877.

Peck, Amelia, and Carol Irish. *Candace Wheeler: The Art and Enterprise of American Design, 1875–1900*. NY: Metropolitan Museum of Art and Yale University Press, 2001.

Peirce, Donald. *Art and Enterprise: American Decorative Art, 1825–1917: The Virginia Carroll Crawford Collection*. Atlanta: High Museum of Art, 1999.

Pickering, Thomas R. *Paris Universal Exposition 1878: Official Catalog of the United States Exhibitors*, London, 1878.

Pisano, Ronald, Mary Anne Apicella and Linda Henefield Skalet. *The Tile Club and the Aesthetic Movement in America*. NY: Harry N. Abrams and the Museums at Stony Brook, 1999.

Post, Robert C., ed. *1876: A Centennial Exhibition*. Washington, DC: Smithsonian Institute, 1976.

Prieto, Laura. *At Home in the Studio: The Professionalization of Women Artists in America*. Cambridge, MA: Harvard University Press, 2001.

Reiff, Daniel D. *Houses from Books: Treatises, Pattern Books, and Catalogs in American Architecture, 1733–1950; A History and Guide*. University Park, PA: Pennsylvania State University Press, 2000.

Rohrlich, Marianne. "More Shows Less the Door." *New York Times*, September 30, 2004, sec. F1, 6.

Roof, Katharine Metcalf. *The Life and Art of William Merritt Chase*. NY: Charles Scribner's Sons, 1917.

Ruskin, John. *The Works of John Ruskin*. 39 vols. Edited by E. T. Cook and Alexander Wedderburn. London: George Allen, 1903–12.

Ruutz-Rees, Janet. *Home Decoration: Art Needle-Work and Embroidery; Painting on Silk, Satin, and Velvet; Panel-Painting; and Wood-Carving*. NY: D. Appleton and Company, 1882.

Rydell, Robert. *All the World's a Fair: Visions of Empire at American International Exhibitions, 1876–1916*. Chicago and London: The University of Chicago Press, 1984.

Schlereth, Thomas J., *Victorian America: Transformations in Everyday Life, 1876–1915*. NY: Harper Collins, 1991.

Scully, Vincent. *The Shingle Style and the Stick Style: Architectural Theory & Design from Downing to the Origins of Wright*. Revised ed. New Haven and London: Yale University Press, 1971.

Seale, William. *The Tasteful Interlude: American Interiors through the Camera's Eye, 1860–1917*. 2nd ed. Nashville, TN: American Association for State and Local History, 1981.

Sherwood, Mary Elizabeth Wilson. *Home Amusements*. NY: D. Appleton & Co., 1881.

Smith, J. Moyr. *Ornamental Interiors, Ancient and Modern*. London: Crosby Lockwood and Co., 1887.

Spenlow, Richard. "Decorating and Furnishing." *New York Times*, October 9, 1887, 5.

Spofford, Harriet Prescott. *Art Decoration Applied to Furniture*. NY: Harper & Brothers, 1877.

Steele, Frances Mary, and Elizabeth Livingston Steele Adams. *Beauty of Form and Grace of Vesture*. NY: Dodd, Meade & Company, 1892.

Stern, Robert A. M, Thomas Mellins, and David Fishman. *New York 1880: Architecture and Urbanism in the Gilded Age*. NY: The Monacelli Press, 1999.

Stillinger, Elizabeth. *The Antiquers*. NY: Alfred A. Knopf, 1980.

Swinth, Kirsten. *Painting Professionals: Women Artists and the Development of Modern American Art, 1870–1930*. Chapel Hill, NC: University of North Carolina Press, 2001.

"Ten Minutes with a Poet. A Reporter Greets Oscar Wilde on His Arrival." *New York Times*, January 3, 1882, sec. 5:6.

Trachtenberg, Alan. *The Incorporation of America: Culture and Society in the Gilded Age*. NY: Hill and Wang, 1982.

Uchitelle, Louis. "At 150 Edgars Lane, Changing the Idea of Home." *New York Times*. January 2, 2006, A1, A10.

Varney, Almon C. *Our Homes and Their Adornments*. Detroit: J. C. Chilton & Co., 1883.

Vaux, Calvert. *Villas and Cottages: A Series of Designs Prepared for Execution in the United States*. NY: Harper and Brothers, 1864.

Venable, Charles L. *Silver in America, 1840–1940: A Century of Splendor*. Dallas, TX: Dallas Museum of Art and Harry N. Abrams, Inc., 1994.

W., L. "How We Spend Our Money." *Lippincott's Monthly* 25, January 1880, 122.

Weaver, G[eorge] S[umner]. *The Heart of the World: Home and Its Wide Work*, Baltimore, MD: Hill & Harvey, 1883.

Weber, Bruce, and Sarah Kate Gillespie. *Chase Inside and Out: The Aesthetic Interiors of William Merritt Chase*. NY: Berry Hill Galleries, Inc., 2004.

Wharton, Edith. *The Age of Innocence*. NY: Charles Scribner's Sons, 1970.

Wheeler, Candace, ed. *Household Art*. NY: Harper's, 1893.

Wheeler, Candace. *Principles of Home Decoration with Practical Examples*. NY: Doubleday, Page & Company, 1903.

Wheeler, Candace. *Yesterdays in a Busy Life*. London and NY: Harper & Brothers, 1918.

White, Samuel G. *The Houses of McKim, Mead and White*. NY: Rizzoli and the Museums at Stony Brook, 1998.

Whiteway, Michael, ed. *The Shock of the Old: Christopher Dresser's Design Revolution*. London and NY: V&A Publications and Cooper-Hewitt Design National Design Museum, 2004.

Winkler, Gail Caskey, and Roger Moss. *Victorian Interior Decoration: American Interiors, 1830–1900*. NY: Henry Hold and Company, 1986.

Yarnall, James. *Newport Through Its Architecture*. Hanover, London and Newport: University Press of New England and Salve Regina University Press, 2005.

"The Yearn of the Romantic." *Century Magazine* 23, April 1882, 957–59.

Yount, Silvia. " 'Give the People What They Want': The American Aesthetic Movement, Art Worlds, and Consumer Culture, 1876–1890." PhD diss., University of Pennsylvania, 1995.

Zukowski, Karen. "Creating Art and Artists: Late Nineteenth-Century American Artists' Studios." PhD diss., City University of New York, 1999.

Resources

In this resource section, you will find a highly biased, highly selective list of access points to the Aesthetic movement in America and modern artful domestic furnishings.

CONFERENCES AND EXPOSITIONS

Brimfield Antiques Fair
Aesthetic movement objects are found throughout the fair.
www.brimfield.com

Salve Regina Conference on Cultural and Historic Preservation
A two-and-a-half-day conference on design and cultural issues that often focuses on the late nineteenth century.
www.salve.edu/heritage/annualconferences

Sculpture, Objects and Functional Art Exposition
Better known as SOFA, this vast show gathers the best of what used to known as "craft," blurring the lines between the fine and decorative arts.
www.sofaexpo.com

The Traditional Building Exhibition and Conference
National trade show and conference (formerly known as the Restoration & Renovation Show) for old-house owners, architects, contractors, developers, building owners and craftsmen who work in historic restoration, renovation, and traditionally inspired new design and construction.
www.traditionalbuildingshow.com

Victorian Society Summer Schools
The Victorian Society in America administers summer schools, consisting of lectures and fieldtrips that focus on the arts and culture.
www.victoriansociety.org

MUSEUMS AND HISTORIC HOUSES

Most of the museums listed have significant collections of Aesthetic movement objects on view in their permanent exhibition galleries; a few even have period rooms in the style. The historic houses listed feature Aesthetic movement architecture or interior furnishings; many have both. Contact information is given, including the organizations that operate the historic houses listed. It is always wise to check hours of operation before planning a visit. Most of the historic houses can only be seen on a guided tour, and a few are open only by appointment.

CALIFORNIA
Cohen-Bray House
1440–29th Ave.
Oakland, CA 94601
510-536-1703
www.cohen-brayhouse.info
vpcopres@att.net
Victorian Preservation Center of Oakland

Haas-Lilienthal House
2007 Franklin St.
San Francisco, CA 94109
415-441-3000
www.sfheritage.org
San Francisco Architectural Heritage

Villa Montezuma
1925 K St.
San Diego, CA 92102
619-239-2211
sandiegohistory.org
San Diego Historical Society

COLORADO
Dexter Cabin
912 Harrison Ave.
Leadville, CO 84061
719-486-0487
www.coloradohistory.org
Colorado Historical Society

CONNECTICUT
Lockwood-Mathews Mansion
295 West Ave.
Norwalk, CT 06850
203-838-9799
www.lockwoodmathews
mansion.org

Mark Twain House
351 Farmington Ave.
Hartford, CT 06105
860-247-0998
www.marktwainhouse.org

Wadsworth Athenaeum Museum of Art
600 Main St.
Hartford, CT 06103
860-278-2670
www.wadsworthatheneum.org

GEORGIA
High Museum of Art, Virginia Carroll Crawford Collection
1280 Peachtree St., NE
Atlanta, GA 30309
404-773-4400
www.high.org
highmuseum@woodruffcenter.org

ILLINOIS
The Art Institute of Chicago
111 S. Michigan Ave.
Chicago, IL 60603
312-443-3600
www.artic.edu

Glessner House
1800 S. Prairie Ave.
Chicago, IL 60616
312-326-1480
www.glessnerhouse.org

INDIANA
Zimmerman Farmhouse, Conner Prairie
13400 Allisonville Rd.
Fishers, IN 46038
317-776-6006
www.connerprairie.org

MASSACHUSETTS
Chesterwood
4 Williamsville Rd.
Stockbridge, MA 01262
413-298-3579
chesterwood@nthp.org
National Trust for Historic Preservation

Gibson House
137 Beacon St.
Boston, MA 02116
617-267-6338
www.thegibsonhouse.org
info@thegibsonhouse.org

Naumkeag
5 Prospect Hill Rd.
Stockbridge, MA 01262
413-298-3239
www.thetrustees.org
westregion@ttor.org
Trustees of Reservations

Trinity Church
206 Clarendon St.
Boston, MA 02116
617-536-0944
www.trinityboston.org

MINNESOTA
James J. Hill House
240 Summit Ave.
Saint Paul, MN 55102
651-297-2555
www.mnhs.org/places/sites/jjhh
Minnesota Historical Society

NEW HAMPSHIRE
Saint-Gaudens National Historic Site
139 Saint-Gaudens Rd.
Cornish, NH 03745
603-675-2175
www.nps.gov/saga
gregory_c_schwarz@nps.gov
National Park Service

NEW JERSEY
Cape May and the Emlen Physick House
Emlen Physick Estate
1048 Washington St.
Cape May, NJ 08204
609-884-5404
www.capemaymac.org
Mid-Atlantic Center for the Arts

Newark Museum of Art, Ballantine House
49 Washington St.
Newark, NJ 07102
973-596-6550
www.newarkmuseum.org/pages/collections/balhse.htm

NEW YORK CITY
Brooklyn Museum of Art
200 Eastern Pkwy.
Brooklyn, NY 11238
718-638-5000
www.brooklynmuseum.org

Metropolitan Museum of Art, American Wing
1000 Fifth Ave.
NY, NY 10028
212-535-7710
www.metmuseum.org

Museum of the City of New York
1220 Fifth Ave.
NY, NY 10029
212-534-1672
www.mcny.org
info@mcny.org

National Arts Club
15 Gramercy Park South
NY, NY 10003
212-475-3424
www.nationalartsclub.org

New-York Historical Society
170 Central Park West
NY, NY 10024
212-873-3400
www.nyhistory.org

Seventh Regiment Armory
643 Park Ave.
NY, NY 10021
seventhregimentarmory.com

NEW YORK STATE
Hudson River Museum of Art
511 Warburton Ave.
914-963-4550
Yonkers, NY 10701
www.hrm.org

Margaret Woodbury Strong Museum
1 Manhattan Square
Rochester, NY 14607
585-263-2700
www.strongmuseum.org

Munson-Williams-Proctor Arts Institute
310 Genesee St.
Utica, NY 13502
315-797-0000
www.mwpai.org/museum/

Olana State Historic Site
5720 State Rt. 9G
Hudson, NY 12534
518-828-0135
www.olana.org
New York State Office of Parks, Recreation and Historic Preservation

Sagamore Hill National Historic Site
20 Sagamore Hill Rd.
Oyster Bay, NY 11771
516-922-4788
www.nps.gov/sahi/
National Park Service

Wilderstein
330 Morton Rd.
Rhinebeck, NY 12572
845-876-4818
www.wilderstein.org

OHIO
Cincinnati Art Museum
953 Eden Park Dr.
Cincinnati, OH 45202
513-721-ARTS
www.cincinnatiartmuseum.org
information@cincyart.org

RHODE ISLAND
Isaac Bell House, Chateau-sur-Mer and Kingscote
All are on Bellevue Ave.
Newport, RI 02840
Admission is through the Preservation Society of Newport County
401-847-1000
www.newportmansions.org
info@newportmansions.org

Newport Casino
194 Bellevue Ave.
Newport, RI 02840
401-849-3990
www.tennisfame.org
newport@tennisfame.com

VERMONT
Wilson Castle
West Proctor Rd.
Proctor, VT 05765
802-773-3284

VIRGINIA
Maymont
2201 Shields Lake Dr.
Richmond, VA 23220
804-358-7166
www.maymont.org
info@maymont.org

WISCONSIN
Villa Louis
521 N. Villa Louis Rd.
Prairie du Chien, WI 53821
608-326-2721
www.wisconsinhistory.org
villalouis@whs.wisc.edu
Wisconsin Historical Society

ON THE WEB

Amazing things can be found on the Web. This list is heavy on commercial sites, like the Internet itself. These sites, however, present historical matters accurately and have good search engines.

Apartment Therapy
www.apartmenttherapy.com

Architecture.About
architecture.about.com

Brocante
www.brocantehome.com

Design Sponge
designsponge.blogspot.com

eBay
www.ebay.com

Fashion-Era
www.fashion-era.com

Old House Web
www.oldhouseweb.com

The Renovator's Supply
www.rensup.com

Ruby Lane
www.rubylane.com

Victorian Station
www.victorianstation.com

Victorian Web
www.victorianweb.org

ORGANIZATIONS
American Association for State and Local History
Links amateur historians to historical resources, especially local museums and historical societies.
www.aaslh.org

National Trust for Historic Preservation
The main public force for historic preservation in the United States.
www.nationaltrust.org

Oscar Wilde Society of America
An academic and literary society that promotes the study, understanding and dissemination of research about Oscar Wilde and his times from the American perspective, especially his 1882 tour of America.
www.owsoa.org

Victorian Society in America
Committed to the protection, understanding, education and enjoyment of America's nineteenth-century heritage.
www.victoriansociety.org

William Morris Society
Founded in London in 1955, with branches in Canada and the United States, the society aims to make the life and work of Morris and his associates better known.
www.morrissociety.org

SPECIALIZED MERCHANDISERS AND SERVICE PROVIDERS

Following is a list of manufacturers and retailers with a brick-and-mortar presence. The vendors listed sell reproduction, adaptation and antique items directly to the public.

ABC Carpet and Home
A modern souk of artful household furnishings, most showing a delightfully over-the-top sensibility. The imports from the Middle and Far East are especially wonderful.

888 Broadway
NY, NY 10003
212-473-3000
www.abchome.com

Associated Artists, LLC
Headed by David Parker, the firm sells fine Aesthetic movement furnishings and supplies architectural services for restoration-oriented clients.

170 Pequot Ave.
Southport, CT 06890
203-255-2281
www.associatedartists.net

Blue Spiral
Modern crafts from the southeastern United States.

38 Biltmore Ave.
Ashville, NC 28801
800-291-2513
www.bluepsiral1.com

Bradbury and Bradbury
Wallpapers adapted from famous Aesthetic movement designers, like Christian Herter and Christopher Dresser, as well as anonymous designers.

PO Box 155
Benicia, CA 94510
707-746-1900
www.bradbury.com

Country Dining Room Antiques
Tableware, including long sets of transferware.

178 Main St.
Great Barrington, MA 01230
413-528-5050
www.countrydiningroomantiq.com

Elise Abrams
Tableware, especially English formal.

11 Stockbridge Rd., Rt. 7
Great Barrington, MA 01230
413-528-3201
www.eliseabrams.com

Garth Clark Gallery
The leading gallery of modern ceramics.

24 W. 57 St., Ste. 305
NY, NY 10019
212-246-2205
www.garthclark.com

J. R. Burrows and Company
Rugs, wallpaper, lace curtains and furnishing fabrics, made with much the same materials and processes as they were in the late nineteenth century.

PO Box 522
Rockland, MA 02370
800-347-1795
www.burrows.com

Lauren Stanley
Aesthetic movement silver.

300 E. 51st St.
NY, NY 10022
212-888-6732
www.laurenstanley.com

Leo Kaplan Modern
Glass, furniture, jewelry and other modern crafts.

41 E. 57 St.
NY, NY 10022
212-872-1616
www.lkmodern.com

Post Road Gallery
A selection of Aesthetic movement furniture and decorative arts is usually on hand.

2128 Boston Post Rd.
Larchmont, NY 10538
914-834-7568
www.postroadgallery.com

Reproduction Fabrics
A source of cotton reproduction fabrics, organized by time period, including the Aesthetic movement era. Many fabrics are based on "documents" (i.e., dated period fabrics).

25 N. Willson Ave., Ste. A
Bozeman, MT 59715
406-586-1775
www.reproductionfabrics.com

Secondhand Rose
Dealer in antique wallpaper, fabrics and other architectural finishes.

138 Duane St.
NY, NY 10013
212-393-9002
www.secondhandrose.com

William Traver Gallery and Vetri
William Traver and its younger, edgier sister gallery Vetri carry modern crafts, especially glass.

110 Union St., Ste. 200
Seattle, WA 98101
206-587-6501
www.travergallery.com

William Turner
Antiques in all media, especially Aesthetic movement.

Turner Antiques
40 W. 25th St, #5
NY, NY 10010
212-645-1058
www.nyshowplace.com/galleries/005.htm

Wexler Gallery
A leading gallery selling modern craft.

201 N. 3rd St.
Philadelphia, PA 19106
215-923-7030
www.wexlergallery.com

Index